EARTHMOVING

EARTHMOVING

EXTRACTIVISM, WAR, AND VISUALITY IN NORTHERN KURDISTAN

Eray Çaylı

University of Texas Press *Austin*

Printed in the United States of America
First edition, 2025

♾ The paper used in this book meets the minimum requirements of ANSI/NISO Z39.48-1992 (R1997) (Permanence of Paper).

Library of Congress Cataloging-in-Publication Data

Names: Çaylı, Eray, author.
Title: Earthmoving : extractivism, war, and visuality in Northern Kurdistan / Eray Çaylı.
Description: First edition. | Austin : University of Texas Press, 2025. | Includes bibliographical references and index.
Identifiers: LCCN 2024060702 (print) | LCCN 2024060703 (ebook)
ISBN 978-1-4773-3277-1 (hardcover)
ISBN 978-1-4773-3278-8 (pdf)
ISBN 978-1-4773-3279-5 (epub)
Subjects: LCSH: Environmental degradation—Turkey. | Natural resources—Turkey. | Mineral industries—Political aspects—Turkey. | Quarries and quarrying—Turkey. | Dams—Environmental aspects—Turkey. | Economic development—Environmental aspects—Turkey. | Kurds—Turkey—Environmental conditions. | Kurds—Turkey—Economic conditions. | Kurds—Turkey—Politics and government. | Human ecology—Turkey. | Environmental justice—Turkey. | Racism—Economic aspects—Turkey. | Visual communication—Political aspects. | Decolonization in art. | Human ecology in art.
Classification: LCC HD9506.T92 C39 2025 print) | LCC HD9506.T92 (ebook)
LC record available at https://lccn.loc.gov/2024060702
LC ebook record available at https://lccn.loc.gov/2024060703

doi:10.7560/332771

CONTENTS

ILLUSTRATIONS

ABBREVIATIONS

AKP	Adalet ve Kalkınma Partisi (Justice and Development Party)
BAÇOY-KOOP	Basma, Çoğaltma, Yayma Kooperatifi (Print, Copy, Distribution Cooperative)
CHP	Cumhuriyet Halk Partisi (Republican People's Party)
DSİ	Devlet Su İşleri Genel Müdürlüğü (State Hydraulic Works' General Directorate)
EU	European Union
HDP	Halkların Demokratik Partisi (Peoples' Democratic Party)
ISIS	Islamic State of Iraq and Syria
MHP	Milliyetçi Hareket Partisi (Nationalist Movement Party)
PKK	Partiya Karkerên Kurdistan (Kurdistan Workers' Party)
TİKKO	Türkiye İşçi ve Köylü Kurtuluş Ordusu (Workers' and Peasants' Liberation Army of Turkey)
TMMOB	Türk Mühendis ve Mimar Odaları Birliği (Union of Chambers of Turkish Engineers and Architects)
TRT	Türkiye Radyo Televizyon Kurumu (Turkish Radio and Television Corporation)

GLOSSARY

The non-English words and phrases are presented here according to English alphabetical order. Arabic transliteration follows the *International Journal of Middle East Studies* Transliteration Chart for Arabic, Persian, Ottoman, and Modern Turkish. A = Arabic, AT = Arabic transliteration, F = French, Gr = Greek, K = Kurmanji (the most widely spoken Kurdish dialect in Turkey), T = modern Turkish.

ánthrōpos (Gr)	humanity
aşk (T)	passionate love
ax (K)	curse, bad spell; mournful exclamation; country; soil
axîn kişandin (K)	to pull, move from one place to another, weigh or carry *ax*; to sigh mournfully
burdayım (T)	I'm here
büyü (T)	bad spell
hafriyat (T)	collective noun referring to what is dug up from the earth; the stuff of earthmoving
hafriyatçılık (T)	the practice of dealing in *hafriyat*; earthmoving
içten (T)	from inside
inlerine gireceğiz (T)	we will penetrate their nests
intimus (T)	inmost
kayyım (T)	centrally appointed mayors replacing democratically elected ones; literally, that which poises over; watchperson
mise en abyme (F)	an image within an image
sahne (T)	stage, scene
ṣamīm (AT); صميم (A)	inmost
samimi (T)	intimate
sevda (T)	a patriot's feeling for their country or mother
sokağa çıkma yasağı (T)	ban on going out on the street
Sur'dayım (T)	I'm in Sur (Amed's historic city center)
taş atan çocuklar (T)	rock-throwing children

AUTHOR'S NOTE

ON PLACE-NAMES

Much of this book revolves around Amed, Turkey's largest predominantly Kurdish city (officially Diyarbakır in Turkish). For many Kurds living in the region and elsewhere, Amed is the unrecognized capital of northern Kurdistan, or the Kurdish capital of Turkey. The city has been known by various names throughout its history; those directly relevant to this book's focus on extractivism are discussed below.

Since the early 2000s, the name *Amed* has gained prominence especially among sympathizers of the pro-Kurdish democratic political movement, which has grown in popularity both regionally and internationally. Acknowledging that any act of naming is decisively political, I use the name Amed in this book except when referring to official institutions (e.g., the Diyarbakır Metropolitan Municipality). This decision is not ethnically motivated; it is not intended to reproduce the violent erasure of the multiple peoples who have inhabited this city and who have named it in their respective languages, one particularly significant example being the Armenian name Tigranakert, after Tigranes the Great, the King of Armenia between 140 and 55 BC. If anything, before nation-states appeared in the region, language and ethnicity mapped onto one another in far less straightforward ways than is now commonly assumed. For example, the linguistic Kurdishness of the name Amed remains disputed.[1] A significant portion of the region's erstwhile Armenian population spoke Kurdish as a first language before they were killed or deported en masse during the Armenian genocide.[2]

I call the city Amed and prefer to use the Kurdish names of other towns in the region so as to situate my work politically.[3] This preference for Amed mirrors the motivations that Zeynep Kaya has articulated regarding her use of the term *Kurdistan*, which I also employ in this book. Using the term

> does not imply that the region was historically defined as Kurdistan, or its inhabitants were all Kurdish, or the area had clearly demarcated borders / or its extent was clear. The concept of Kurdistan does not refer to ahistorical and ontologically permanent locations

> or territories but to the geographical context upon which social, economic and political interactions take place and in return, to a territory or geography shaped by these interactions.[4]

Kurdistan literally means "land of the Kurds," whose homeland and largest populations today fall within the nation-states of Turkey, Iraq, Iran, and Syria (alongside sizable diasporas in Germany, France, Sweden, Belgium, the Netherlands, and Russia). The borders that separate these four nation-states while also denying the Kurds themselves a nation-state largely date from the aftermath of World War I.[5] It was then that Britain and France defeated the Ottoman Empire to take what is now Iraq and Syria and created these two nation-states as we know them today. Meanwhile the Turkish national campaign succeeded in holding onto the lands that are now within Turkey and founding a Turkish supremacist republic here (to this day, Turkey's constitution says all citizens of the republic are Turks). In the 1930s, the nascent republic implemented spatial policies that their proponents rationalized in unmistakably colonial terms (e.g., as a civilizing mission and a racial reordering through assimilation, conversion, or both), including forced resettlement of Turkish-speaking non-Anatolian populations into Kurdistan, displacement of Kurdistani communities to western Turkey, and construction of assimilatory settlements.[6] In 1941, the Turkish state recruited German geographer Herbert Louis to create Turkey's seven geographical regions, which remain in official use.[7] The new regionalization invented Southeastern Anatolia and Eastern Anatolia (historically "Anatolia" had almost never referred to lands east of the Euphrates), overriding sociopolitically and historically grounded regional markers such as northern Kurdistan, western Armenia, and upper Mesopotamia. Kurdish was banned in Turkey for decades and, while the ban was removed in the 1990s, neither the language nor the Kurds have been given any official status, as evident in the Turkish state's persistent refusal to provide or fund Kurdish tuition. Since the 1990s, the pro-Kurdish political movement has formed parliamentary parties demanding change on these issues alongside becoming the only major institutional political force in Turkey to demand official reckoning with the episodes of violence that founded the Turkish state, such as the Armenian and Assyrian-Syriac genocides of 1915–1916.[8]

The focus of this book, then, is a country where colonial borders morphed into racial nation-state policies denying the social, cultural, and political status that Kurdish-led struggles for recognition have demanded. Specifically, the book focuses on northern Kurdistan, which today falls within the borders of the Turkish nation-state and within its official regions of Southeastern Anatolia and Eastern Anatolia. Southern Kurdistan is in northern Iraq and home to the entity closest to an internationally recognized Kurdish state, as it is governed by the Kurdistan Regional Government. Western Kurdistan is in northern Syria, where a de facto autonomous administration led by members of the Kurdish liberation movement has emerged during the Syrian civil war and continues to seek international recognition. Finally, eastern Kurdistan is in western Iran, where there has long been an official province called Kurdistan but where Kurdish social and political rights remain denied. In short, while social, cultural, and political unrecognition continues to affect all four parts of Kurdistan in different ways, northern Kurdistan is where statuslessness is most palpable. It is denied even the status that Iran has granted to the geographical name Kurdistan, not to mention the autonomies of the Kurdish-run administrations located in southern and western Kurdistan today.[9]

ON THE WAR'S TIMELINE

A similar politics permeates the names that I use in this book to talk about the violence that northern Kurdistan has seen over the last four decades. While I alternate between the terms *armed conflict*, *fighting*, and *counterinsurgency* (among others) in speaking of individual episodes, I use the term *war* to refer to the totality of these events. This use echoes the way the pro-Kurdish democratic movement refers to the same totality as *savaş*, the Turkish-language word that translates as "war" and simultaneously, in this context, references a sociopolitical paradigm or "continuum" where violence is the predominant mode through which Turkish politics relevant to the Kurds is enacted, whether overtly violent events take place or not.[10] The following chronological summary of the "war" in the sense described here intends to help readers contextualize its most recent decade (2010–2020), which witnessed the developments discussed in this book.

On September 12, 1980, a violent coup d'état took place that instituted neoliberalism in Turkey with the support of major Western powers, including the US and the UK. The junta government banned all left-wing groups in Turkey, including the PKK (Partiya Karkerên Kurdistan, the Kurdistan Workers' Party), founded in 1978 contemporaneously with numerous other leftist parties. While activists and politicians from across the leftist spectrum were imprisoned and tortured at this time, torture took a particularly violent and racist character in the Kurdish case when a section of Diyarbakır Prison No. 5, located in Amed, was turned into a military prison for

Turkifying the Kurds. The PKK responded by moving some of its members abroad and setting up armed insurgency camps in northern Iraq and Syria.

In August 1984, the PKK mounted its first guerrilla attack within Turkey's borders. In 1985, Turkish authorities launched a comprehensive counterinsurgency campaign with diverse components, ranging from recruitment of Kurdish villagers as "village guards" to declaration of a Kurdistan-wide state of emergency in 1987. As the junta gave way to parliamentary democracy in the late 1980s, Kurdish politics began to regroup among civilians and achieve popular political mobilization, only to be met with a new round of repression and mass detentions enabled by the region-wide state of emergency, which remained in force until 2002.

In the 1990s, extrajudicial killings by paramilitaries and destruction of villages became frequent occurrences in the region. In 1999, as part of a US-assisted operation, the Turkish secret service captured the PKK's leader, Abdullah Öcalan, in Nairobi outside the Embassy of Greece, where he was looking to secure refuge. Öcalan's call for a ceasefire from his prison cell prompted the PKK to change tack and launch a "democratic republic" project in 2000, significantly reducing the intensity of armed conflict, even as sporadic attacks continued. The Kurdish liberation movement reoriented away from traditional Marxist Leninism and the pursuit of a nation-state, toward democratic autonomy and confederalism driven by ecological consciousness and gender equality.[11]

The 2000s were marked by the rise of the AKP (Adalet ve Kalkınma Partisi, the Justice and Development Party) to power in 2002 and its promises of democratization and enhancement of minority rights as part of Turkey's EU membership bid. These promises manifested in de facto peace talks with the PKK alongside cultural reform packages addressed to Kurds (among other historically disenfranchised communities). Meanwhile, pro-Kurdish parties gained the right to stand for election and began to win municipalities, finding an opportunity to put principles of confederalism into practice as municipalism, especially through policies oriented toward women, multilingual public services, environmental welfare, and improved infrastructure. Such developments increased the pro-Kurdish political movement's expectations regarding full-fledged peace. These expectations remained unfulfilled by the turn of the decade, and the informal peace talks came to an end, leading to a new cycle of guerrilla attacks and military responses as well as arrests and lawsuits targeting Kurdish activists, journalists, and politicians.

In 2013, a new process promising peace was launched in spectacular fashion, with a public gathering held on the Kurdish holiday of Newroz that was attended by tens of thousands in Amed. A letter from Öcalan instructing the PKK to move all its forces out of Turkey was read out during the event and broadcast to millions on mainstream Turkish TV channels. The government acknowledged the letter and responded favorably, releasing a number of Kurdish political convicts, creating committees composed of mainstream writers and artists who were to communicate the de facto peace process to the general public, and enabling a ceasefire that lasted twenty-seven months. But by 2014, the process had begun to wane. The Syrian war increasingly engulfed Syria's predominantly Kurdish north, known as Rojava (the Kurdish word for "west" to denote western Kurdistan), especially through attacks by ISIS. Kurdish guerrillas based in Rojava met the war not only with guns but also by putting self-governance into practice, whereas the Turkish state increasingly sided with the Islamist (and mainly Sunni) factions taking part in the Syrian war.[12] When ISIS laid siege to the Syrian Kurdish town of Kobanê and threatened its destruction, Turkish president Recep Tayyip Erdoğan appeared to welcome its potential fall, and the conflict spilled over the border, with street clashes taking place in Amed and nearby towns.[13] April 2015 saw the peace talks stall. That summer, the AKP government walked away from them entirely when the general election of June 7 revealed that the electorate credited steps toward peace not to the AKP, who had lost sixty-nine seats, but to the pro-Kurdish HDP (Halkların Demokratik Partisi, the Peoples' Democratic Party), who had gained forty-five seats to become Turkey's third-largest party.

After a summer marked by an Erdoğan administration unwilling to accept electoral defeat and several declarations of democratic autonomy by "people's assemblies" in towns across northern Kurdistan (inspired by the then-burgeoning de facto Autonomous Administration of North and East Syria in Rojava), fall 2015 witnessed the flare-up of all-out war in the region. The state's counterinsurgency campaign used wartime emergency powers to declare curfews in urban centers, raze to the ground sites where fighting took place, oust democratically elected mayors and replace them with centrally appointed bureaucrats, and expel thousands of municipal workers and public officers deemed to be PKK sympathizers. These powers reached new heights in the aftermath of the July 2016 failed coup attempt. The Erdoğan administration placed primary blame for the coup attempt on the Gülen movement (led by the Turkish Islamic cleric Fethullah Gülen), with which the AKP had formed an unofficial coalition for most of its fourteen-year rule but which the authorities now deemed a terrorist organization. The administration responded by declaring a countrywide state of emergency and seeking to prosecute anyone and everyone it deemed a terrorist sympathizer (i.e., not just those it associated with the Gülen movement), resulting in the imprisonment of hundreds of Kurdish and pro-Kurdish politicians, journalists, academics, and activists. While the state of emergency was lifted in July 2018, several of the measures then implemented against the Kurds remain in force at the time of writing, including the imprisonment of activists and politicians involved in the pro-Kurdish political movement and the confiscation of municipalities.[14]

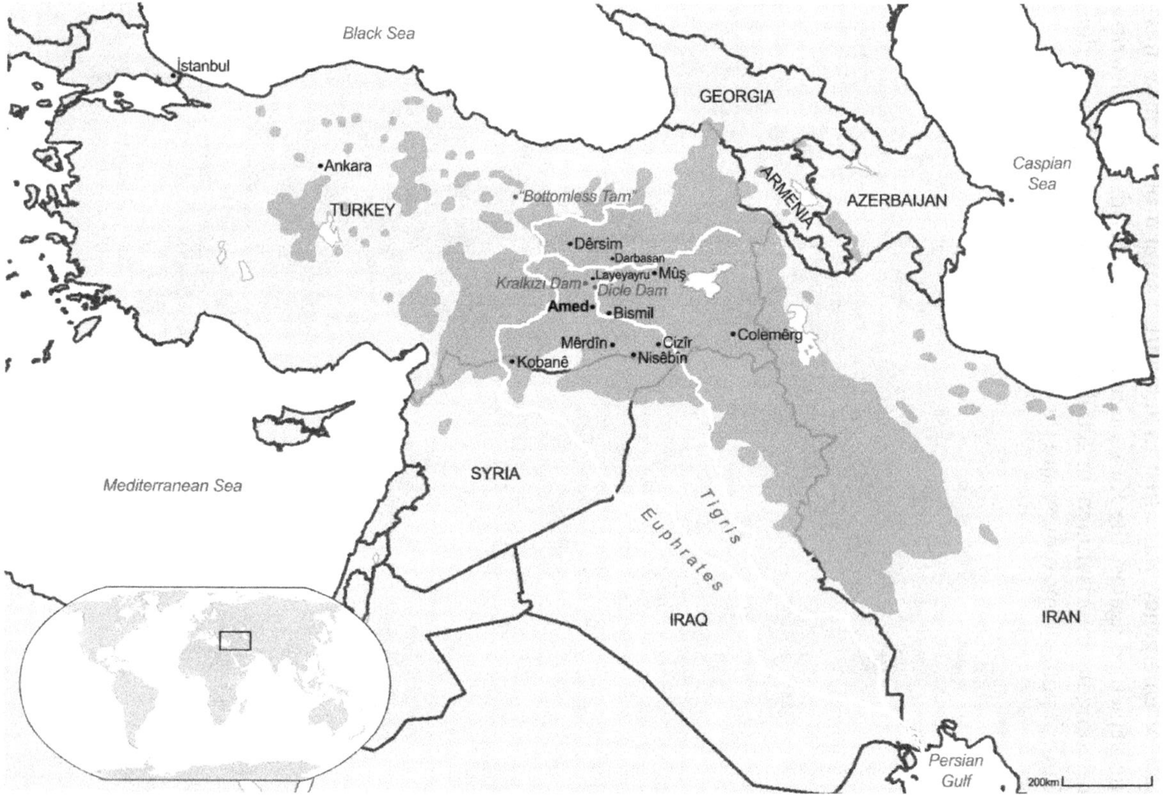

Kurdistan (Jordan Engel, *Decolonial Atlas*, https://decolonialatlas.wordpress.com/; revised to pinpoint the sites discussed in this book).

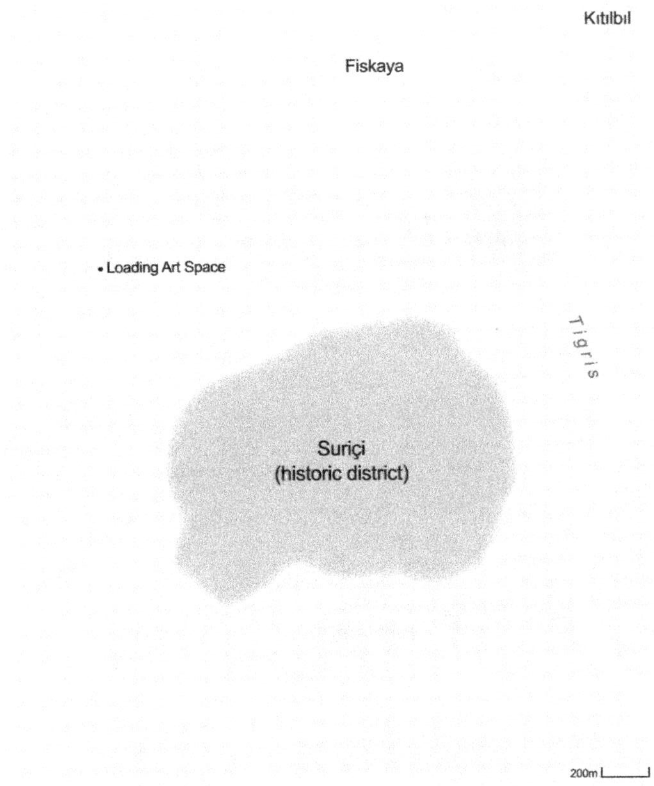

Central Amed.

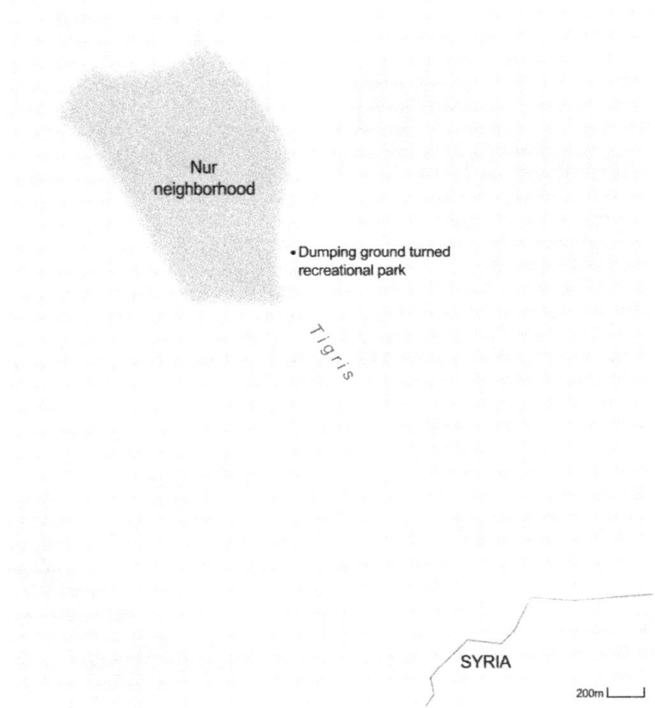

Central Cizîr.

EARTHMOVING

MOVEMENT OF AND THROUGH EARTH, OR EXTRACTIVISM AND ITS AESTHETICS

July 2019, Fiskaya neighborhood: I am with Berivan, looking out over the Tigris River from the rooftop of her family's home in what is one of central Amed's few riverside neighborhoods. Having spent the afternoon with her dad in the family's allotment by the river, Berivan and I are now finalizing our plans for the free-of-charge public workshop we will lead for an independent, artist-run space in the city. A horticulturalist by training, she is one of the several Amed-based collaborators with whom I have spent the better part of this year volunteering to coordinate ecology-themed informal academy programs upon the invitation of artistic and architectural communities in the city. Across the river from us is an industrial fishpond that originated in a sand quarry. Berivan says she still vividly remembers the earthmovers—called *hafriyat* trucks in Turkish, the language of our conversation—working day and night in the mid-2000s to move the sand quarried here to building sites across Amed in those early days of the city's construction boom. The quarry was possible to dig because in 1990 this stretch of the Tigris was exempted from legal protection against physical interventions—a status granted to all other major rivers in Turkey. When the sand quarry ran its course, its operators extracted water from the Tigris to fill the sandpit and created the industrial fishpond. I know of the sandpit-turned-fishpond because of a major embankment project that the Turkish state's Hydraulic Works department DSİ (Devlet Su İşleri) recently completed here (figure 0.1). Press reports from the project launch singled out "senseless water use and sand extraction" as the chief cause of riparian damage that prompted the authorities to step in and, in the DSİ regional director's words, "clean the river's dirty appearance," "create a pleasurable view," and "reveal the river's beauty at a higher resolution."[1]

As afternoon turns into evening, Berivan's dad joins us on the rooftop. He is exhausted from several hours of work in the allotment, but also gratified. He has been spending more time in the allotment since the central government summarily dismissed him from his municipal job a few years ago, when it replaced democratically elected Kurdish mayors with centrally appointed ones called *kayyım* (literally, "watchperson") as part of its violent counterinsurgency campaign.[2] "Few people know the history of these parts better than my dad," says Berivan. He points to the lands just downstream from the industrial fishpond. Named Kıtılbıl, the area is home to the campus of Amed's only university, which the Turkish state founded here in the 1970s. According to him, the name comes from *xirtebil*: *xirte*, a Kurdish word that refers to incised or severed body parts, suffixed with *-bil*, meaning "place." The area acquired this name only in the early to mid-twentieth century, he says; before then it was an Armenian village, home to a people that genocide severed from the land during the decades that witnessed the transition from the Ottoman Empire to the Republic of Turkey. "Whatever we're experiencing now is what they experienced then," he aphorizes. The cross-historical connection he makes has recently had a direct manifestation here. Kıtılbıl, Berivan's dad reminds us, is where DSİ's earthmovers dumped the war rubble they removed from Amed's historic center, where the Turkish state recently carried out its violent counterinsurgency campaign.[3]

HOW DOES THE ENVIRONMENTAL AND racial violence that has marked capitalism and colonialism since their interlinked origins in the fifteenth century continue to proliferate today in a world where ecological and humanitarian sensibilities are unprecedentedly widespread? This book argues that the answer lies in the increasing interdependence between the

FIGURE 0.1. DSİ's regional director launching the Tigris embankment project to the press, in situ with design drawings on easels (reproduced by permission of the photographer, Ahmet Ün).

violence and the sensibilities in question. The context-specific notion of hafriyat—the stuff of earthmoving—conveys this interdependence best. Hafriyat is stuff extracted from the earth and transported by earthmovers serving the political and business interests that the Turkish state endorses. The environmental violence at work here is an earthmoving force: a force that not only geologically moves what it extracts from the earth but also seeks to dominate the ways in which its devastating consequences leave their witnesses sentimentally moved. *Hafriyatçılık* is what I have come to call this dual force, in the official language of the nation-state where I first noticed it.[4] The Turkish suffix *-çı* denotes professions, and *-lık* refers to groups of ideas, things, or practices (similarly to the English-language suffix *-ery* or *-ry*). Rendering *hafriyatçılık* as "earthmoving" denotes the dual workings of an environmentally and racially violent movement that both moves earth itself and moves the senses through earth—a movement that is sensorial as well as geological.

Earthmoving is a cousin of what scholars writing in the European languages have come to call "extractivism." I contribute to this scholarship first by theorizing extractivism as inclusive of but not limited to extraction: the drawing out and exploitation of the lifeblood and wealth of peoples and the environments they live in and with. Extraction moves parts of the earth from one place to another. Extractivism also includes making sense of this movement by making it available to the senses. Its political workings include not only extractive industries' overtly harmful consequences for the communities and regions they unevenly effect but also how harm is made sensible or available to the senses and how this sensibility is produced, managed, and acted upon both materially and symbolically. Today, many representatives of state and capital interests can no longer evade the question of the harm that they and their predecessors have caused through extractive industries. Far from it. As seen in the opening vignette, they make sense of this harm by making it available to the senses in their own way. The state department that oversees extractive dams and irrigation canals legitimizes its new embankment project as a way of repairing the damage caused by water overuse and sand extraction—problems triggered by its own infrastructures. Its regional director speaks in a primarily visual register—by referring to dirty appearances, pleasurable views, and beauty revelation at a higher resolution—not to mention the visually charged and colonially inspired (i.e., Kurdistan-specific) instrument of the kayyım, or watchperson, under whose watch the extractivist harm-repair cycle intensified. In the context discussed in this book, and in many other contemporary cultural contexts afflicted by extractivism, extractivist sensemaking operates in a primarily visual register. My critical analysis therefore focuses extractivism on images of the environments—both built and natural—in which and on which it inflicts its violence and harm.

The past two decades have seen a growing body of decolonial scholarship on extractive industries such as mining, hydropower, speculative construction, and corporate agriculture. This scholarship is decolonial in that it has shown how such industries have historically been formed by and formative of not only capitalism but also coloniality and imperialism—and their long-standing racialization of peoples and territories. The racialization in question has operated especially by reducing the worth of the territories and the peoples it targets to the quantifiably measurable and marketable value of the resources and labor extractable from them.[5] As such, the violence involved in this racialization has from the outset had a symbolic and epistemic as well as a corporeal and systemic character. Coal-driven British colonialism in the early nineteenth century, a milestone in the history of the fossil economy, attracted investors through representations of colonized lands and peoples as an extractable resource, thereby "affix[ing] . . . race to space."[6] The slavery-based plantation economy, which drove colonialism in the Americas by extracting land and labor from the enslaved and the colonized, hinged on a "grim calculus of cheap labor-power and acceptable deaths" that turned the continent into one of "capital's laboratories of modernity" and "proletarianization."[7] These calculations and representations helped quantify and marketize colonized and enslaved peoples, and the places they inhabited, as "things."[8] They instituted a symbolic and epistemic paradigm based on a racialized logic of quantifiability and marketability.

Scholars have engaged critically with extractivism also as an ongoing problem. They have highlighted its physically destructive effects on the racialized, and failed promises to the "developing" nation-states that have embraced it: elevation out of poverty into prosperity and respect on the world stage.[9] This critical analytical tendency has often followed from an empirical preference for sites of overt ecological import (e.g., the mine, the dam, the logged old-growth forest, the plantation, and the oil well) and a contextual preference for regions of direct European colonialism and postcolonial nation-states founded in its wake (e.g., those in Africa, Australasia, South Asia, and the Americas).[10] Meanwhile, extractivism's novel workings that mean it is no longer confined to these sites and regions have tended to slip under the radar. Most importantly, extractivism's socially and spatially uneven harm and benefit have been rendered amply visible, but the fact that this visibility is now the subject of unprecedentedly widespread ecological and humanitarian sensibilities has largely remained unaddressed. The question, then, becomes how the visibility of extractivism's harm is produced, managed, and acted upon, not least by the very forces that benefit from or are cognate with it—how it is made sense of by being made available to the senses.

Even as this question remains inadequately addressed in current scholarship, it is only a starting point for me. In this book I begin by using the analytic of *extractivist aesthetics* to problematize extractivism's affirmative workings, which materially and spatially combine with its overtly violent and better-explored operations as a negational force. If extractivism's overt violence involves negating racialized lives and agencies, its affirmative workings repurpose that which escapes this negation. These affirmative workings repurpose extractivism's unconcealable and unprofitable excesses by affirming racialized lives and agencies—by rendering them sensible in the racialized terms of quantifiable measurability—thus obfuscating questions of causality, responsibility, and culpability. They help extractivism *make sense* literally, materially, by *making sense*—by engaging the senses and, through them, sensibilities. How, then, to break with extractivism as such? This question guides the book's ultimate aim: to chart nonextractivist pathways. They already exist among inhabitants of extractivism-afflicted environments, who have their own ways of sensing, making sense of, and being moved by the landscape. The bodily knowledge of the riverbank that Berivan and her dad have long had, coupled with their direct experience of recent kayyım measures, makes for a sensibility that is entirely different from that of the colonial watchperson and the extractivist repairer. The way Berivan and her dad articulate this sensibility from their rooftop complicates ocular determinisms that may associate such a topographically superior viewpoint with oppressive politics. What Berivan and her dad see, look for, and look back on from this viewpoint not only exposes the contradictions of contemporary extractivism but also rehistoricizes it by bringing in communities and histories seemingly different from the family's own, such as Armenians and the genocide that targeted this community.[11] This is a viewpoint whose challenge to extractivism derives from an embodied and self-reflexively relational positionality within the landscape (and its constitutive injustices), as well as its medium specificity: its visuality.

This dual emphasis on positionality and the visual medium is not the outcome of a theoretical preoccupation or an empirical observation for me. It is the very reason this book exists. The process started in late 2018 and has seen me become a close collaborator of Amed's architectural and artistic communities, hence my work with Berivan mentioned in the vignette. What started it was an invitation from the city's professional architects' organization to coordinate a free-of-charge summer school in 2019. Then followed a series of workshops I led for an independent arts space called Loading, lasting until 2021. This was a time when the overtly violent phase of the state's counterinsurgency campaign had just ended, but its social and spatial injustices were continuing to unfold. Previously Kurdish-run municipalities remained confiscated by the central government and their technical and cultural cadres barred from returning to work. To regroup, many turned to professional organizations such as the architects' organization that invited me to coordinate the summer school. Meanwhile, entire neighborhoods were being rebuilt by the state in the name of postwar repair. Our summer school aimed to give young architects, designers, planners, and artists a platform for responding critically to these developments. Our premise, based on a detailed report by our host organization, was that the state-endorsed causality between wartime destruction and postwar reconstruction was baseless. The report had found that much of what the authorities had been doing behind construction site fencing in fact involved destruction.[12] They were razing buildings that had survived the fighting so that they could redesign Amed's historic district for purposes of surveillance and assimilation. The district's historic significance, for which the Kurdish municipality had secured UNESCO World Heritage Site status just months before the counterinsurgency campaign, was now endangered, including buildings listed as heritage under Turkey's own laws. The authorities not only contravened national laws and international obligations but also concocted new legislation to justify their actions.[13] To legitimize expropriation of 80 percent of the historic district, the government amended a disaster preparedness law from 2012, adding "the interruption of public order and security" to what constitutes disaster.[14] For our summer school hosts, these transgressions of legality and causality were not an aberration but rather the cornerstone of a long-standing attitude toward Kurdistan: "This is colonialism without even the status of a colony," some aphorized.[15]

If colonialism has always relied on sensing and making sense of the landscape for its own objectives, in a statusless colony this reliance is a constant work in progress. Lack of stasis means ocular views keep changing. Violence is especially exploratory, the landscape continually altered. Even colonialism's proponents and beneficiaries are often confused about the formally correct way to view this landscape, having to reconsider it at every turn. Where colonialism's manifestation in the landscape continually flickers, playing catch-up with its extractivist movement of and through earth is futile. If this extractivist movement approaches views as content to be incessantly generated for overwhelming the visual field with ever more novel forms and dominating it quantitatively, inhabitants of the extractivist-afflicted landscape depend on an altogether different approach. They use views for moving in and with the landscape—in and with each other's landscapes—rather than for formal innovation or quantitative domination. They use views to recognize and mobilize each view for the embodied position the view comes from—embodied *differentially* in relation to the landscape and its constitutive injustices. They do so to unlock the distinct contribution each view might make to a world beyond extractivism. The importance of moving in and with rather than of and through earth is what my artistic and architectural collaborators have taught me.

EXTRACTIVISM, WAR, AND VISUAL ECOLOGIES IN A STATUSLESS COLONY

Taking seriously my collaborators' references to Kurdistan as a statusless colony, in this book I converse with and contribute to decolonial scholarship on environmental politics and particularly its visually charged strands. The contribution concerns where I look for the colonial and decolonial politics of environmental violence and defiance, and what role I consider visuality—as a field of symbolic and knowledge production—to play in this politics. Existing scholarship of relevance has been indispensable in parsing the dually material—both environmental and corporeal—character of the violence that colonialism and capitalism have historically involved since their interlinked origins in the fifteenth century.[16] Meanwhile, its approach to what makes symbolic and knowledge production significant to this violence today has oscillated between two tendencies. One tendency has been to derive this politics directly from the products of symbolic and knowledge production (e.g., from images, in the case of visual culture), while the other has focused exclusively on genealogies and systemic legacies separated temporally from the overtly violent processes of today: epistemologies, methodologies, and institutional infrastructures.[17] As I detail below, these tendencies come up short in grappling with contemporary extractivism as I understand it through the lens of northern Kurdistan. Here, violence and defiance are the stuff of current and continually dynamic *visual ecologies*—networks of visually constituted environmental relations. Defiant agency neither derives from symbols and knowledges themselves nor confronts violence only as a structural dynamic. It is organized relationally, collectively, and processually through symbolic and knowledge production (rather than following on from the products of this production) and against violence as a corporeal and emplaced phenomenon.

As the past two decades have seen the literatures on environmental politics and political violence grow ever closer, coloniality has come to figure prominently in the scholarship that interweaves them.[18] A latest strand in this scholarship, and one that is especially relevant to my focus on extractivism, has come to be known as "political geology," its premise being the idea that the geological and the political are inextricable from one another.[19] Today this idea resounds in the Anthropocene thesis proposed in 2000 by a group of natural scientists positing humanity as the single most decisive factor shaping the planet's workings and physical makeup, especially in the context of climate change.[20] In the humanities and social sciences, the same idea has inspired contemporaneous methodological turns toward the posthuman and the nonhuman, albeit not always with sufficient critical reflection on the long histories of violence and defiance that have rendered geology political and politics geological.[21] Political geology scholarship offers just such critical reflection by approaching the production and dissemination of scientific knowledge about the earth as a contested political field in its own right and as a racialized one at that.[22] This scholarship has been indispensable in its approach to the racial and colonial politics of geology, not only as a discursively ideological question but also as a material and practical one involving geologists' sensing the earth and making it available to the senses through techniques of visual representation.[23]

My contribution to political geology derives from the ways I approach its visuality as a medium-specific question and the corporeal violence involved in it as a contemporary phenomenon. Visual culture is a field of knowledge production and dissemination where representation and its visuality constitute not simply a question of technique but rather an all-encompassing modality. Visuality does not always necessarily figure in this field as per a causality, where knowledge producers intent on knowing the earth use visual representation as a means for reaching the ends they are after (e.g., mapping or drawing for measurement).[24] Visuality's significance to political geology is often also as an end in itself. Seen through the lens of northern Kurdistan, the violence of racial and colonial geological politics is overt and corporeal rather than being a historical legacy or a methodological and epistemological influence, and it continues to be contested as such. This reorientation of political geology toward visual culture and toward present-day colonialism is rendered particularly timely due to the intensification of newfangled environmentalist and humanitarian sensibilities simultaneously with that of extractivism and with its forays into new cognitive sectors such as the visual cultural sector and specifically the contemporary art world.

Dovetailing with the convergence of the literatures on environmental politics and political violence, visuals of built and natural environments have, over the past decade, taken center stage in activist, artistic, and scholarly efforts to document, represent, and condemn rights violations.[25] These efforts have responded critically to a post-Holocaust epistemic culture that prioritizes victims and survivors as the most authoritative source of knowledge about violence and that celebrates the resulting inevitably fragmented truths as an accurate reflection of the complexity and multiplicity of experiences of suffering.[26] The critical response has been to mobilize visuals of the environments in which violence takes place as a way of producing truths that are materially evidenced and therefore available for all (not just the victims and those already sympathetic to their plight) to see, feel, and agree upon.[27] But more recently, this mobilization has itself become the subject of critique for tending to assume that imaging and looking are self-evidently emancipatory acts, and for divorcing visuality both from the violence that has historically conditioned it and from the political labor required for it to engender progressive social change.[28] I take my cue from this critique in *ecologizing* the politics of visuality. I premise *this politics* not simply on what visuals show but on questions they raise about the formal modalities through which, the political aims with which, the ethical grounds on which, and the publics for which environmental and racial violence is visualized. My understanding of "ecology" is therefore broadly situated within the late twentieth-century scholarly tradition stretching from Gregory Bateson to Félix Guattari. Ecology, in this sense, entails the full range of relations between and among the various constituents that inhabit and make up the universe—including human and nonhuman ones—and the multifarious registers in which these relations take place: natural, social, psychological, cognitive, epistemological, and technological, among others.[29] But my understanding of "ecology" also follows recent postcolonial and decolonial reworkings of this tradition in their rejection of ecology's deep-seated associations with equilibrium and harmony. I attend to the violence and injustice inflicted on some communities for the equilibrium and harmony of others.[30]

The visual ecologies of violence I explore comprise networks of relations formed by and formative of the extractivism-afflicted landscape, including those that challenge this affliction. Understanding violence and agency as per visual ecologies—networks of visually constituted environmental relations—helps avoid the assumption that they are always each other's antitheses. Agency is always necessarily a product of the same visual and environmental relations afflicted by extractivism and is deployable by not only those who challenge its violence but also those who have benefited from it. The sensorial and especially visual modalities, politics, ethics, and publics involved in this relational understanding of environmental violence and agency are most extensively explored in recent geographical scholarship on aesthetics.[31] Influenced largely by Jacques Rancière's understanding of aesthetics, numerous geographers over the past decade and a half have theorized through aesthetics the political significance of "the distribution of the sensible"—the arrangement and continual rearrangement of matter, space, and bodies in ways that can be *collectively* sensed and made sense of.[32] Such theorization is relevant to my purposes for two interrelated reasons. First, it helps to understand that which is "visual" as involving much more than just vision and images; the visual is instead understood here as comprising the material conditions in which particular kinds of vision—or image production and circulation—become possible. Second, situating the visual within the materialities that condition it helps link it to the rest of the senses while also facing up to the prominence it has held over them throughout modernity/coloniality and still does.[33]

There is recent scholarship that has used the lens of aesthetics to expound the ways visual ecologies are ethically and politically entangled in the racialized violence of colonialism. Examples include scholarship that commends visual cultural production for treating climate change in colonies and postcolonies proper like Australia as an environmental legacy of histories of colonial violence.[34] Others include criticisms of artistic and curatorial practice that narrates and represents species extinction—considered here a violence in its own right—by employing categories and hierarchies founded upon histories of colonialism and facilitatory of contemporary racial capitalism.[35] While I follow such examples of scholarship in linking up the politics of ecology and violence, my understanding of the politics of violence differs from theirs. In this scholarship, violence figures mainly as a force that undergoes sweeping and periodized shifts from one register or scale to another. The implication is that colonialism's historical violence inflicted specifically on the colonized has gradually become a structural force that, whether through epistemic and semantic structures or through spatial ones, now envelops much larger constituencies, be they humans or nonhumans. While such shifts of register and scale are undoubtedly worthy of attention, responding to a context where colonialism is in progress disallows me from periodizing them as belonging either to the past or to the present and from generalizing them as having gradually expanded to impact an ever-swelling constituency.

In cautioning against such periodization and generalization, I follow recent visually charged approaches to the Middle East as a contemporary setting where colonial and decolonial politics play out environmentally and corporeally. Particularly influential on my thinking are Munira Khayyat's work on ecologies of resistance and survival in South Lebanon and Salar Mameni's on artistic challenges to the extractivist violence and harm that have affected the Arab–Persian Gulf region. Against conventional understandings of war that reduce it to instances of overt physical and martial hostility, Khayyat approaches it as a modality of life with all its complexities ranging from suffering to defiance and everything in between, and terms this approach "landscape as method."[36] The language she chooses for talking about war's lifeful environments is consistently a visual cultural one. "Coloring war with the brush of life" helps her trace "ordinary arts" of resistance and survival that evidence "the active agency of its dwellers," which she narrates in visually charged terms such as "frames," "pictures," "gazes," "prisms," "light," "darkness," "illumination," and "sight."[37] Here I echo Khayyat's refusal to reduce war's targets to passive victims, and her visually charged approach to the landscape of war as also one of life. But the medium specificity of the processes that have engendered this book distinguishes my approach from hers in two interrelated ways. First, I feel unready to consider landscape as a medium of life without first confronting and addressing its centrality to war and war's visualities, including those that shape some of the kinds of agency found in landscapes such as those that Khayyat and I are writing about.[38] This unreadiness, in turn, means I cannot take agency for granted as categorically liberatory. Second, the fact that practitioners of visual culture in northern Kurdistan and farther afield have themselves responded critically to the precise violent episodes featured in this book prevents me from conceptualizing landscape on my own as a visually charged medium of resistance and survival in the face of war without thinking and working with such landscapes that have already been imagined, portrayed, and created in medium-specific ways.

If Khayyat frames ordinary worlds in visual terms, Mameni does the opposite. He looks for defiant ecologies in artistic responses to fossil fuel industries that have "gutted and polluted. . . . the Arab / Persian Gulf region" with the backing of "mass-scale military force."[39] Mameni coins the word *Terracene* against the term *Anthropocene* to rectify the latter's sweeping reference to humanity as both culprit and victim.[40] *Terracene* emphasizes "the *terror* brought about by specific militarized (settler)colonial industries" and centers "the perspective of *terrans*: the creative multispecies inhabitants of militarized and extractive regions who bear embodied scars of terror and who also propose and practice resilient strategies for living."[41] Mameni's insistence on the medium specificities of visual politics, approach to the Middle East as a contemporary colonialism-afflicted context, and attention to resilience in the face of agency-negating terror all resonate strongly with me.[42] But I hesitate to follow him in associating extractivist aesthetics with overt destruction only and casting artistic practice in diametric opposition to it. My context is one where extractivist aesthetics operates not only by negating but also by engaging environmentalist and humanitarian sensibilities, for the latter are now an undeniable part of mainstream consciousness. Awareness of extractivist aesthetics' diversity in turn helps me approach nonextractivist aesthetics as a diverse range, too. The range is such that overt marginalization and resistance are but one part of it. Besides, I find it difficult to cast contemporary artists from the Middle East straightforwardly as a group that is both marginalized by extractivism and resilient against it. The difficulty has first to do with my understanding of colonialism and racial capitalism as waged not only by Euro-American powers on this part of the world but also intraregionally.[43] Moreover, I approach artists as positioned differentially vis-à-vis extractivism, where the differences concern not only an artist's personal background but also the sector-specific dynamics involved in transforming art itself into an extractivist industry. I keep these positional complexities in focus not for cynicism but rather for offering a grounded account of how anyone concerned about extractivism has something of their own to contribute to the work of challenging it collectively insofar as they are committed to self-reflection and reciprocity.[44]

This idea—that individuals' roles in the collective work of challenging extractivism rest upon reciprocity and sustained self-reflection on the differential positionality of each individual—escapes predominant analytics of agency. By the latter, I mean the modern, colonial, liberal, and racial capitalist analytics of agency modeled on the singular subject with full bodily, mental, and intentional sovereignty. Sovereignty in the modern, liberal, and capitalist mode has been amply critiqued, especially by the literature on biopolitics (i.e., the governance of populations based on definitions of what is lifeful and lifeworthy versus what is not—or "nonlife").[45] But modern-liberal-capitalist sovereignty's influence on the analytics of agency employed by biopolitics' theorists remains insufficiently problematized. An important exception here is Alexander Weheliye, who has retheorized biopolitics as a racial politics of the flesh, against the grain of its prominent theorists' persistent obliviousness to race as a question of embodiment. He cautions against employing the concepts of resistance and agency simply as tools to explain freedom in the face of biopolitics. When "resistance" and "agency" are employed in this manner, "whether through strenuous denials or exalted celebrations of their existence," they lead critique to foreclose, and therefore not to recognize, the myriad liberational possibilities that emerge through the cracks of biopolitics:

> As modes of analyzing and imagining the practices of the oppressed in the face of extreme violence . . . resistance and agency assume full, self-present, and coherent subjects working against something or someone. Which is not to say that agency and resistance are completely irrelevant in this context, just that we might come to a more layered and improvisatory understanding of extreme subjection if we do not decide in advance what forms its disfigurations should take on.[46]

Weheliye's caution is relevant not only to theorizations of biopolitics in general but also to those that are aesthetically oriented in particular, as sensibility or the capacity to sense and make sense has figured prominently in biopolitical governance and its attendant definitions of life versus nonlife.[47] His caution indicates that any effort to recognize the decolonial political agency of aesthetically charged practices is bound to fall short of its own objective insofar as its analytic of agency remains modeled on the individual sovereign subject. The problem persists even when collectives are thought to possess this sort of agency, including those long excluded from modern/colonial notions of humanity (e.g., nonhumans or the dehumanized).[48] In this book I do not only show the pitfalls involved in modeling agency on the individual sovereign subject. I also unpack how agency is the stuff of relational, if conflict-ridden, collective work involving self-reflexive subjectivities that straddle contradictory, implicated, and at times even complicit positionalities and that are neither omnipotent nor powerless.

ENVIRONMENTAL VIOLENCE AND AGENCY IN NORTHERN KURDISTAN

There are context-specific reasons why a book on environmental violence and agency might do well to focus on extractivism as a set of colonially driven and racial capitalist discourses and practices. In northern Kurdistan, the history of these discourses and practices stretches back to the nineteenth century. In the mid-nineteenth century, the Ottomans adopted from European colonial powers of the time a series of national centralization reforms that began to cost Kurdish tribes the relative autonomy they had enjoyed until then.[49] Meanwhile, various European-style nationalisms gained pace among Ottoman subject peoples, culminating in state-led mass violence against Kurdistan's sizable Armenian and Assyrian Syriac populations in the late nineteenth and early twentieth centuries.[50] The most significant cases in point were the Hamidian massacres of 1894–1896 and the deportations and genocides of 1915–1916, with the Ottoman administration enlisting Kurdish tribes in the implementation of both.[51] The violence has had palpable ecological repercussions. Subsistence farming and seasonal pastoralism, which had developed through the centuries between Armenian peasantry and Kurdish pastoralists and landowners, fell into decline.[52] Landownership became consolidated in the hands of a relatively few genocide collaborators, facilitating more recent processes of land use change into monoculture or urban development.[53]

After World War I, Europe's two foremost colonial powers, Britain and France, drew up the borders that still divide Kurdistan between the nation-states of Iraq, Syria, and Turkey.[54] In the latter, cooperation between Turkish leaders and Kurdish chieftains continued into the late 1910s, when many Kurdish tribes joined the military forces regrouped by Mustafa Kemal against the Allied powers occupying what was left of the Ottoman Empire after World War I. In return, Mustafa Kemal promised the Kurds a significant degree of autonomy.[55] But this promise was never fulfilled. Instead, the Republic of Turkey that replaced the Ottoman Empire yet again opted for centralization. It began eliminating some of the same Kurdish groups that had joined the campaign against the Allied powers a few years earlier, and others too: in 1937–1938, Kurdish-Alevi tribes in Dêrsim (located just northwest of Amed) were subjected to a genocidal campaign.[56] What underpinned the campaign's genocidal scale and distinguished it from the early republic's counterinsurgency campaigns was that it was aimed not against insurgents in the strict sense but rather against the people of Dêrsim as a whole so as to subjugate them to a new and stricter taxation and military conscription regime—to extract free labor and wealth from them.[57]

In Amed, the first few decades of the republic saw the city's urban center gradually move outside the basalt fortress walls of the historic core, a move catalyzed by modernist architecture and town planning. This made the historic core accessible to Kurdish rural-to-urban migrants, who began to move there in increasing numbers from the 1950s onward due first to agricultural mechanization and industrialization and then to the onset of war in the countryside (more on this below). The mid-twentieth century witnessed bans on all things Kurdish as well as sporadic uprisings against state oppression. In the late 1970s, the Kurdistan Workers' Party, or PKK, emerged and became the first Kurdish group in decades to consolidate these armed responses. In 1980, a bloody military coup took place in Turkey that instituted neoliberalism in the country and that cracked down violently on all left-wing groups, including the Marxist-Leninist PKK. Since the 1980s, Kurdistan has seen both armed conflict and extractivist enterprise intensify, especially but not exclusively along the Tigris and Euphrates Rivers. In the early 1980s, the junta pursued a violent Turkification policy in Kurdistan through prison torture and a Kurdish language ban.[58] It also pushed through the Southeastern Anatolia Project comprising mega water infrastructures in the upper Tigris and Euphrates.[59] The ostensibly pro-democracy cabinet that succeeded the junta, headed by its deputy prime minister, declared a region-wide state of emergency in 1987 that remained in effect until 2002 and made the 1990s in northern Kurdistan a decade of rural displacement, extrajudicial killings, and forced disappearances.[60] Rural guerrilla warfare was met with the state's scorched-earth counterinsurgency policy of village evacuations that caused large swathes of arable land to fall into disuse.[61] Those who fled the war for cities like Amed became the urban poor, settling into self-built houses or extensions to existing buildings, including the ones previously owned by the non-Muslims. Meanwhile, the lands that these rural-to-urban migrants left behind gradually became subjected to irrigated monoculture aided by the first two major dams built on the Tigris during the 1990s.

If northern Kurdistan and especially the region's sociocultural and political heartland Amed draw the spatial contours of this book, its temporal contours are bookended by the late 2000s and the late 2010s. In the mid-2000s, a semiofficial peace process accompanying the launch of Turkey's EU membership bid decelerated more than two decades of fighting between Turkish state forces and PKK guerrillas. Pro-Kurdish political parties were permitted to enter elections and ended up winning most municipalities across northern Kurdistan. In Amed, Osman Baydemir became the city's first pro-Kurdish mayor and served two terms between 2004 and 2014. In the late 2000s, physical changes caused by the first two dams became observable along the Tigris, triggering a range of responses, including a mayoral project in Amed to restore the stretch of river that the city overlooks. Those same years witnessed the start of a construction boom that effectively doubled Amed's urban area by the late 2010s. Throughout this period, the government attempted to address the Kurdish question by cultural reform and semiofficial peace talks with the PKK, while also commissioning new dams on the Tigris.[62] In the mid- to late 2010s, however, a fresh episode of full-blown war erupted in Kurdish towns and cities, and the pro-Kurdish political movement once again became the subject of a government clampdown. Around this time, the dams' impact began to affect more than the river itself as profound changes to historical precipitation patterns became salient. Downpours caused one of the dams upstream of Amed to burst, and a flood that dominated the city's panorama of the river ensued due to the authorities' failure to replace the faulty floodgate (its spare had been sent away for use in constructing a new dam nearby). The decade ended with recession in the construction sector. The neoliberal promises of peace and prosperity and their material buoys (the construction sector and energy infrastructures such as dams) that had dominated the late 2000s began to collapse with ever more ostentatiousness toward the end of the 2010s, with towns being turned into theaters of war, construction projects stalling, unseasonable downpours occurring more frequently, and infrastructures failing. In this sense, then, northern Kurdistan, which undoubtedly has its particularities otherwise, crystallizes the contemporary neoliberal juncture. This is a historical juncture where racial capitalism, driven by extractivism, is able to sustain itself only by becoming ever more excessively violent (including in its failures), and where the manifestations of this excessiveness are increasingly conspicuous.[63]

The past decade has seen violence and its legacies in Amed and the surrounding region become the subject of a growing scholarship where three approaches relevant to this book are discernible. The first approach characterizes Baydemir's tenure—and that of his Kurdish mayoral contemporaries—as a shift from the paradigm of colonialist violence to one of "decolonization," "anticolonization," and "de-Turkification" and concurrent "Kurdification" of the urban by "activists in office."[64] Spatial manifestations of this paradigm shift are considered to involve socioculturally significant sites such as monuments, public squares, protest venues, and community centers and the "spectacle" value of activities held therein.[65] The second approach, while sharing the first's observation regarding a paradigmatic shift away from violence, identifies neoliberalism rather than decolonization as the new paradigm's defining characteristic. It points to how developmentalist imaginaries around cultural tourism and an unprecedented variety of commercial interests deriving from local, international, and national actors exerted their influence on the city and municipality, engendering a sociopolitical reality no less problematic or complicated than that of the previous era, due to a new bureaucratic and intellectual elite and economically ascending classes.[66] This second approach is refreshing in its consideration of urban transformation less as an expression of existing and mutually conflicting political positions than as the very medium through which to do politics and which therefore involves everyday spaces such as streets, offices, and homes as well as socioculturally significant sites.

The third approach, while mirroring the second's attention to spatiality and class, uses ethnography to challenge its characterization of this context as postviolent. This approach emphasizes violence's permeations into the rapidly urbanizing city—an emphasis that I share. According to Hişyar Özsoy, violence permeated late-2000s Amed through ongoing militant sacrifice in prisons and guerrilla war in the mountains; it remained central to how the city's communities of resistance gauged commitment to the pro-Kurdish cause.[67] For Umut Yıldırım, who is openly critical of previous scholarship, colonialist violence remained ever-present through the material remnants of the 1990s war: "shanty towns," "bullet marks," "dispossession," and high youth unemployment.[68] Based on the experiences of municipal and civil society workers in the mid to late 2000s who upheld "the imaginary of Kurdistan," Yıldırım suggests that these remnants of war in Amed shaped a politics of "dissonance" theorizable only through "affect" rather than "reason, sight and narrative."[69] This is a dissonance that many of the existing analyses overlook, argues Yıldırım; it is reducible neither to emergent class conflict, nor to a monolithic anticolonial movement, nor to militant sacrifice.[70] Its politics hinges neither on speech, nor on conventional forms of organization or mobilization, nor on compliance with the pro-Kurdish movement, but rather on silence, associational relationality, and negativity.[71]

While all three approaches to recent Kurdish politics in Amed and its environs have influenced the way I interweave questions of coloniality, neoliberalism, and embodiment in this book, I also broaden the way each territorializes the spatial workings of violence and defiance in line with a conventional urban–rural divide. Simply put, my impression is that where they consider urban violence or defiance, they understand it to take place in the city proper, and where they discuss that which is environmental, this is implied to involve only the countryside. City-boundedness overlooks not only the fact that perceptions of "the city proper" continuously fluctuate but also that the urban is as much constituted in "landscapes of extraction" as it is in streets, squares, homes, and offices.[72] In this book I consider spaces and materialities at various scales and of diverse kinds that cut across and transcend the urban/rural divide. For example, the spaces I consider include representational ones where militarized visualities legitimize (as acts of neutral humanitarianism) the wholesale reconstruction of neighborhoods. And the materialities include sand and water extracted in the countryside and fed into Amed's construction boom. Approaching the subject in this way contributes to the growing literature on anti-Kurdish racism in contemporary Turkey, including analyses that focus on cities, by considering the earth itself as the medium through which racialized and "entangled processes of settler colonialism, empire, and . . . capitalism" unfold.[73] I unpack how the racialization of Kurdishness in Turkey functions geologically—through materialities extracted from the earth, made to travel across various spatial scales, including spaces of representation. Attending to materialities and images that traverse spaces of multiple kinds and scales also contributes to existing work on the politics of modern-day damming in northern Kurdistan. It frames dams as a question with cultural and urban implications rather than merely as one of international conflict over riparian resources or militarization of the countryside and dispossession of villagers.[74]

Returning to how this attention to materialities and images that cut across and transcend the urban–rural divide speaks to relevant scholarship on Amed and the surrounding region: it reframes Özsoy's linking of the city to prisons or mountains, so that material interventions, assemblages, representations, and flows are understood as central to this link rather than as only ancillary to or symbolic of ideology. It follows neoliberalism-focused analyses in considering neoliberal politics as deriving from the relations between environments of various kinds and scales rather than just from the city proper and its socioculturally significant or evidently scarred elements (e.g., bullet holes and unemployed youth or public squares and community centers). Finally, it avoids limiting colonialist violence's material and spatial politics to urban remnants that generate corporeally sensible dissonances among and between those upholding the pro-Kurdish cause. Instead, theorizing extractivism as an aesthetic force as I do in this book attends to the ways colonialist violence continues to shape the very regime of sensibility and insensibility that constitutes urban culture and politics. This attention, I argue, helps clarify not only the politics of the urban but also that of scholarship on the urban. Unlike the strategy of (merely) rhetorically spotlighting the dissonances between adherents of an anticolonial imaginary, a methodological focus on extractivism's continuing influence on regimes of (in)sensibility prioritizes colonialist racism as the adversary against which to regroup: to reimagine agency beyond the individual sovereign subject and rebuild it as such collectively.

STRUCTURE OF THE BOOK AND ITS MAIN ARGUMENT

Theorizing extractivism through aesthetics helps pluralize its material, spatial, and visual politics and ethics as a spectrum. At one end of this spectrum is what I term *extractivist aesthetics*—the ways in which extractivism makes sense by reducing the significance of the racialized and the colonized (and the environments they inhabit) to the quantifiably measurable and marketable value of an extractable resource. As indicated above, this valuation logic operates not only by negating but also by affirming the life and agency of those targeted by racial capitalism and colonialism, including nonhuman constituents such as rivers. Challenging extractivist aesthetics directly and from a position situated at the opposite end of the spectrum is what I term *antiextractivist aesthetics*. Its politics is preoccupied primarily with dismantling extraction, not with visual cultural production. But my aim is to chart nonextractivist aesthetics in all its diversity, and antiextractivist aesthetics is only one part of it. Nonextractivist aesthetics begins one notch away from extractivist aesthetics and encompasses a diverse set of approaches, including, for example, what I term *counterextractivist aesthetics*, which involves turning extractivism's own techniques against it. I stay with this diversity because I am wary of the injustice of leaving the work of undermining extractivism only to those diametrically opposed to it and entirely unimplicated in it. Professional artists respond to sites of extractivist violence even as they inevitably inhabit an art world that itself is permeated by extractivism. Scholars working within globalized academe (including myself) who write critiques of extractive industries still operate within a structure of knowledge production shaped by the same racialized valuation logics that underpin extractivism. Heroizing artistic and scholarly production as the stuff of full-blown resistance would therefore be grossly misleading. Heroization also obfuscates the situation of communities that must persevere amid the ruins of colonial destruction; their perseverance often requires refraining from heroic acts of resistance. Racial hierarchies cut across these various groups—scholars, artists, communities—and undeniably permeate their relations with one another. Yet it is out of these inevitably stratified and conflicted positionalities and relations that glimpses of nonextractivist sensibility emerge. I chart this emergence through a close discussion of contemporary art and experimental film practices that operate in a visual field overflooded and overstimulated by news segments, embedded war journalism, social media posts, and construction projects.

Earthmoving demonstrates that extraction continued to operate unabated in northern Kurdistan across multiple episodes of all-out war (the mid-2010s) and putative peace (the late 2000s and the early 2010s), throughout pro-Kurdish mayoral tenures (between the mid-2000s and the mid-2010s), and after these municipalities had been usurped by the central government (from the mid-2010s onward). Specifically, it argues that these operations have engendered and have been enabled by extractivism. Extractivism, I argue, enables extraction not only by accelerating its destructiveness but, more fundamentally than that, by shaping the meanings and knowledges produced about the landscape it afflicts. Meanings and knowledges shaped by extractivism adhere to a racial logic of quantifiable measurability and marketability even where they may seem to lay extraction bare or to repair its harm. In northern Kurdistan, extractivist aesthetics has rendered extraction-afflicted landscapes ever more visible—available to the senses and ecological sensibilities—but has done so both by obfuscating violence's authors, beneficiaries, and proponents and by deepening the racialization of those it has disadvantaged. But visuality's centrality to extractivist aesthetics has also rendered the visual a primary arena for grappling with this violence by making the extractivism-afflicted landscape available to the senses otherwise. *Earthmoving* therefore argues that extractivism—its coloniality and its racialization—cannot be understood without attending to the central role that image production and circulation play in making sense of and making available to the senses the landscape it afflicts. The book unpacks this argument using a structure that proceeds near-chronologically to demonstrate the historical changes and continuities that characterize extractivism's operations across periods of apparent calm (chapters 1 and 2) and episodes of overt violence (chapters 3, 4, and 5).

Titled "Extractivist and Antiextractivist Aesthetics," chapter 1 examines, through the interlinked extractive instruments of dams and sand quarries, how the logic of quantifiable measurability characterizing the racialized violence of conventional extraction also permeates the less overtly violent ways certain kinds of life and agency are rendered sensible. Existing scholarship approaches extractivism's racialization of geography as involving the negation, or rendering insensible, of humans and nonhumans to legitimize their reduction to an extractable resource. The rare examples that explore extractivism's affirmative operations do so through sites that are different from those of negation.[75] In this chapter, I not only demonstrate that extractivism operates by affirming or rendering sensible human and nonhuman agency and life in quantifiably measurable terms; I also argue that these affirmations work in material and spatial entanglement with extractivism's negations and become particularly prominent in contexts where extractivist excesses are increasingly unconcealable and unprofitable. Such excesses discussed in the chapter include sandpiles left unused due to recession in the construction sector and flooding triggered by faulty dams and unusual downpours symptomatic of climate change. Visuality is the primary medium used (whether intentionally or not) in repurposing these excesses for affirming life and agency—affirmations that imbue the very sites and communities targeted by extractivism with an omnipotent resilience in the face of it. These affirmations, I argue, obfuscate questions of causality, responsibility, and culpability, losing sight of the fact that extractivism is in fact enabled by ongoing histories of colonialist and nation-statist violence. Affirmations therefore reproduce these histories' racializing and racialized outlook on sites and communities affected by extractivism—this time, not through demonization of colonized peoples and geographies but through their heroization. Activism in the same sites and among the same communities contests extractivism by complicating these affirmations. Rather than dovetail with the heroization of their own local geography and identity, activists highlight extractivism's differential impacts within and beyond this locality by mobilizing qualitatively valuated relationality. Even as these activists are not primarily concerned with visual cultural production, their work, too, is visually charged and informs my notion of antiextractivist aesthetics.[76]

With chapter 2, titled "The Art of Peace and Its Extractivisms," the book begins to explore the role that contemporary art produced in sites of extractivism may play in responding critically to the current neoliberal juncture in the history of modernity/coloniality and its environmental politics. Existing debates on this role comprise two strands of scholarship. The first strand—one I have discussed in detail above—focuses on issues of overt environmental significance such as climate change, associating critique with the problematization of Eurocentric aesthetics for its links with colonialism and racialized humanisms. The second strand focuses on neoliberal geopolitics, appraising contemporary art's critical potential against postpolitical approaches to democracy, peace, and prosperity.[77] In this chapter, I bring these two strands together empirically as well as methodologically. I consider how the politics of ecology in northern Kurdistan is inextricably intertwined both with the state-endorsed practices of racialized violence of the twentieth century and with the neoliberal approaches to democracy and peace of the twenty-first. I do this by thinking with a body of work that Amed-based contemporary artist Cengiz Tekin produced in the late 2000s and early 2010s, a period associated with the deceleration of militarized violence. I show how extractivist politics in northern Kurdistan proliferated throughout the neoliberal-democratic transition from "war" to "peace," structuring the paradigm of peace upon that of war such that extractivism's influence extended to spheres beyond resource extraction and land appropriation.

Challenging the racial and colonial underpinnings of the philosophical category of the aesthetic and the postpolitical workings of neoliberalism is doubtless an important indicator of art's critical potential vis-à-vis what this book terms *extractivist aesthetics*. But I argue that a fuller appraisal of this critical potential also requires asking if and to what extent artworks point audiences toward the ways extractivism operates through the world of professional visual cultural production as well as through industries such as mining, agriculture, and construction. Tekin's work highlights these questions by pushing against the limits of the regionalist agency that the contemporary art world grants to him as a Kurdish artist. By *regionalist agency*, I mean an artistic platform where the artist is expected to produce work on issues in his home region by treating them as exceptionally regional: in Tekin's case, as unique to Turkey's Kurds and northern Kurdistan. Tekin, I argue, questions this expectation by pointing up the artistic (Eurocentric) canon's complicities in extractivism whether past or present. Engaging with extractivism in Kurdistan not simply as a regional affair to be laid bare by an artist from the region, but rather as one that implicates the artistic canon and the art world at large, places the antiextractivist imperative with art's audiences instead of individual artists and artworks.

Chapter 3 carries the book into the post-2015 period that witnessed the Turkish state's violent counterinsurgency campaign in Kurdish towns and cities, and the repressive measures that followed. Titled "War's Hypervisibility and Humanitarian Extractivisms," the chapter considers two series of images of urban warfare produced by state-affiliated actors and circulated widely on social and conventional media. The first comprises images of graffitied walls and domestic spaces, which were disseminated via Instagram accounts supportive of the counterinsurgency forces. The second comes from a factual television series titled *Bear Witness*, which combined true crime, citizen journalism, and military surveillance and which Turkey's state television TRT (Türkiye Radyo Televizyon Kurumu) produced and broadcast simultaneously with the counterinsurgency campaign. I argue that the visual ecologies formed around both the TV series and the Instagram images exposed the state forces' role in violent conflict, but only to obfuscate questions of institutional culpability and responsibility for wrongdoing. These visual ecologies portrayed the war as taking place between two insurgent groups (i.e., militants and vigilantes) rather than between one insurgent group and the state, shifting judicial focus away from war crimes to the images that documented them and repositioning the state as a neutral humanitarian actor rather than a warring party. This portrayal was extractivist in that it marked entire neighborhoods as wreckage in need of relief and repair by wholesale demolition and construction—two prominent drivers of Turkey's extractive economy—and reinforced the colonial imaginary of Kurdistan as a lawless territory impermeable even to the authorities, except for "humanitarian" reasons. My argument here contributes to recent scholarship on the role image production and circulation play in counterinsurgency's violence.[78] Whereas scholars have tended to understand this role as an extension of establishmentarian (nation-statist and militarist) allegiances preexisting violence's images, or of "seeing like a state," I show how it is generative rather than extensional.[79] Image production and circulation actively dress establishmentarianism in antiestablishmentarian garb here by redistributing the agency involved in state violence across media publics, who are led to see not like the Turkish state but rather like an international humanitarian force or at times even to see in spite of the state.

The last two chapters return to artistic practice. Titled "Testifying to Survival Environmentally and Nonextractivist Aesthetics," chapter 4 treats a visual practice that helps problematize the extractivism at work in the same urban settings discussed in chapter 3. This practice comprises a series of visual realist films that contemporary artist belit sağ produced using footage she shot in Cizîr (officially Cizre in Turkish), a border town on the Tigris River. sağ filmed here in the wake of the first wave of counterinsurgency operations. Once the fighting ended, the very neighborhoods sağ had filmed became the subject of a government project that promised reconstruction, including stretches of the riverbank where body parts were discovered to have been dumped. I consider sağ's work to evidence a constant grappling with extractivism both as an artistic theme and as part and parcel of the very visual ecologies in which art and artists operate. As such, sağ's films call for a rethinking of recent debates on visual realist work that have considered it a potent medium for witnessing and bearing witness to violence. These debates tend to focus on the extent to which visual realist work aids survivors' pursuit of resubjectivation and rights defenders' quest for justice in court.[80] Meanwhile, the politics of artworks themselves and the artistic decisions behind them are often put on the back burner. Considering sağ's work for the ways it aesthetically engages extractivism complicates these tendencies, an engagement I term *testimony as environment*. The term bridges historian Marc Nichanian's dyad of "testimony as monument," testimony that is about figuration, perspective, and imagery and that, as such, is what Nichanian favors against "testimony as document," testimony that is fixated on the realism and the documentability central to statist historiography.[81] sağ's work offers testimony as environment because, by foregrounding the role of relationality and positionality in the recovery of agency during and after state violence, it both grasps the spatially homogenizing character of the violence and avoids reproducing this homogenization.

Chapter 5, titled "Haunting as Ecology and Counterextractivist Aesthetics," situates the war in northern Kurdistan within a longer yet context-specific history of state violence. Stretching further back than the Republic of Turkey, this history encompasses the late nineteenth- and early twentieth-century episodes of violence that targeted Ottoman non-Muslims across what is now Turkey and that amounted to genocide. The genocide has since come to be commemoratively located in 1915 by Armenians and Assyrian Syriacs whose ancestors were its primary victims and survivors. While the Turkish state has long refused to acknowledge the genocide, a growing number of Turkey's academic and cultural producers have done so over the past few decades. In the lead-up to the genocide's centenary in April 2015, the country saw unprecedented scholarly and artistic interest in this violent history, and even a grassroots commemoration held just off Istanbul's Taksim Square, Turkey's premier public space. A few months later, violence broke out in northern Kurdistan. In this chapter, I discuss two moving images where war and the genocide are imbricated. This imbrication merits critical attention not only because it introduces the genocide into considerations of war but also because it reframes extractivist aesthetics as a question of technique. The reframing is thanks to the artists appropriating the abstracting propensities associated with extractive logics to invite critical reflection on extractivism—an appropriation that epitomizes what I term *counterextractivist aesthetics*.

The moving images are from auteur Gürcan Keltek's film *Meteors* and contemporary artist İz Öztat's video *Recounting Nightmares to Running Water*. Keltek's film makes extensive use of found footage documenting the state's violent counterinsurgency campaign, which he sourced online and at a remove from the region. Öztat produced her video in early 2015 using water she had then recently harvested in Istanbul; proceeding to explore hydroextractivism farther afield, including in northern Kurdistan; and subsequently continuing the watercolor series as a way of registering from a distance the violence that broke out in 2015–2016. I note that, in its own way, each work uses chromatic minimalism to foreground materiality rather than content—the water collected from the rain and the footage found online. While this minimalism may seem to aim at universalizing the artistic subject matter, it ends up releasing a particular, Turkey-specific ghostliness that imbricates early twentieth-century genocide against non-Muslims and in particular Armenians with the war waged on northern Kurdistan. This ghostliness opens violence to debate as a structural yet differentially experienced force, where the structures and experiences in question include those involving the production and circulation of artistic images. I build here on recent scholarship on haunting as a way of accessing the structural role that violent histories play in seemingly nonviolent presents, while also reconsidering scholars' orientation toward absence and its recovery.[82] I term the ghostliness released by Keltek's and Öztat's works *haunting as ecology*, arguing that what is haunted here is not traceable through already-existing absence or presence alone. Tracing it, rather, requires asking how absences and presences are produced and distributed in the first place, who has the agency to shape this production and distribution, and the extent to which the answers to these questions facilitate or inconvenience colonial and racial-capitalist environmental politics.

Earthmoving closes with a chapter that reflects on my post-2010s collaborative engagements with the Amed-based independent arts space Loading and on some of their artistic outputs. Observing in these outputs an attempt to speak to recent extractivism-related developments elsewhere in Turkey,

I discuss what it might mean to engage with other extractivisms from the vantage point of Kurdistan, understood here as a perspective that is more about the aesthetically charged work that collectives are willing to undertake together than about any origins they might share. Understood in this way, the question ensnares my own research and writing. The final chapter therefore addresses extractivism's implications for the relations between the production, circulation, and transfer of knowledge between geographies, disciplines, subject positions, and practices aligned differentially with respect to coloniality and racial capitalism, and their context-specific manifestations in various yet interconnected sites.

EXTRACTIVISM AS A METHODOLOGICAL AND EPISTEMOLOGICAL QUESTION

In this book I deliberately use and refer to aesthetics as a theory. Echoing recent scholarship of relevance, I understand aesthetics not as "the material and textual forms aesthesis (sensibility) takes" but rather as a theory that helps unpack the politics of those forms; a theory that requires "critical and political work" in order "to problematize" what it theorizes.[83] Aesthetics is neither intrinsically emancipatory nor necessarily tantamount to depoliticization; its politics is not self-evident.[84] If anything, the birth of the aesthetic as a philosophical category in eighteenth-century Europe was inextricably linked with colonialism, legitimizing the evisceration of socialities, relationalities, knowledges, and modes of existence found among the colonized.[85] A series of dualistic categories underpinning Kantian notions of the aesthetic have been implicated in climate change and attendant environmental disasters: humans versus nonhumans, reason or judgment versus embodiment or corporeality, and speech or text versus tactility or nondiscursive sociability.[86] Non-Kantian approaches are not unproblematic, either, insofar as they have simply reversed what category within each dualism is privileged, rather than undone them altogether.[87] If this wealth of criticism seems reason enough to abandon aesthetics altogether, another response is to use aesthetics deliberately *as a theory* to stay with coloniality as an ongoing phenomenon and as one that implicates theorists. Opting for this response, I attribute the colonial and decolonial politics of aesthetics not to one theoretical category or another alone but rather to already existing *relations* between socialities, relationalities, knowledges, and modes of existence that Kantian and some non-Kantian approaches have dualized.[88] This relational understanding incorporates ethics as well as politics into aesthetics, insofar as "the ethical" is "the *relational* framework within which sense, action, and speech become possible."[89]

Approaching extractivism as per this understanding of aesthetics—as a relational, ethically framed politics—means that it is not simply a research topic but also a methodological and epistemological question for its researchers. The book's final chapter expounds on this idea; here I limit myself to providing some background on how I have come to approach extractivism as such. As mentioned at the outset, many of the insights I discuss in this book are grounded in the extensive periods of time I have spent since 2018 with and among Amed's artistic and architectural communities, which are immersed in the politics of ecology. These periods followed on from previous research I had conducted in the city in 2012 on how memory activists employed urban space to remember 1980s and 1990s state violence.[90] Understood conventionally and in a practical sense, my methods have remained consistent between the early 2010s and the late 2010s: ethnography, textual analysis, notes from conversations with interlocutors, and thick description of sites of violence and defiance. But, in terms of the politics of methodology, there was one major difference: central to my research in the late 2010s was a relation of reciprocity and collaboration with those working on the politics of ecology in Amed, rather than one of treating them as sources of empirical material only.

In late 2018, I was invited by the Amed branch of the Chamber of Architects (Mimarlar Odası)—a leading NGO campaigning on matters of urban political ecology—to coordinate on their behalf a series of workshops leading to a summer school, which took place throughout the first half of 2019. The summer school's main venue was the independent, artist-run space Loading, founded and run by two Amed-based internationally exhibiting contemporary artists, including Cengiz Tekin, whose work I discuss in chapter 2. Loading was founded in 2017 at a time when the two artists were reeling from the state's violent counterinsurgency campaign, having been expelled from their day jobs as art teachers in state schools simply because they signed a petition calling for an end to the war. Loading's cofounders suggested that I extend my stay in Amed to be their inaugural researcher in residence. Throughout the summer and early fall, I coordinated a series of workshops under Loading's aegis, collaborating in each with an Amed-based woman trained in an aesthetically charged technical profession (i.e., architecture, landscape design, and horticulture). After returning to London, where I lived and worked at the time, I continued collaborating with Loading to lead a new workshop series on the relations between violence, ecology, and photography (discussed in the book's final chapter), culminating in an online exhibition. Admission and enrollment were free of charge for these various events I led or coordinated throughout 2019 and 2020 on behalf of Amed's artistic and architectural communities. Meanwhile, I coauthored a book chapter on the destruction and reconstruction of Amed's historic city center, with the architect who had been the one to invite me on behalf of the architects' professional organization to coordinate the summer school in 2019.[91]

Calls to decolonize research methodologies, which at the time of writing have become more audible than ever, had already gained momentum in the late 2010s, especially among scholars of racial and environmental politics and in ways that bear upon scholarly work both in situ—or in what is often called "the field"—and elsewhere.[92] As I—a scholar who hails from Turkey but who is not Kurdish—accepted the architects' and then Loading's invitations, I was particularly mindful of self-reflexivity's centrality to decolonizing "fieldwork," which involves asking whether the researcher's presence is welcomed by those inhabiting the "field" and whether the research harms or benefits them.[93] This point about work in situ is what the book's final chapter will address. Now, as we prepare to embark on the book's core chapters, where critical analysis and argumentation are articulated, I wish to consider the phase of scholarly work where this very articulation takes center stage: writing. Recent debates on the colonial politics of citation as a question of how to write not just on but with decolonial struggles are especially instructive here.[94] While efforts to decolonize citational practice have engendered much-needed bibliographical revisions such that hitherto excluded voices are now included, Max Liboiron and Rui Li argue that many of the hierarchies that structure critique itself have continued to persist: "This type of inclusion does nothing to change the regime of perceptibility or power dynamics so that diverse forms of knowledge can know and be credited on their own terms."[95] I broadly echo this point albeit with a nuance. I wish to distinguish between two kinds of nonacademic practice featured in this book as productive of the kind of diverse knowledges mentioned by Liboiron and Li: activist practice and artistic practice. I wish to keep in focus the specificities of each.

Where I discuss activist practice in this book, as in chapter 1, I do so with a certain eschewal of empirical analysis. Instead, I derive from activism my conclusive arguments about how best to undermine the kind of extractivist aesthetics analyzed in chapters 1 and 3. In the case of artistic practice, however, I do the opposite and engage in detailed analysis and interpretation of artworks, as in chapters 2, 4, and 5. This distinction I make between activist and artistic practice derives from a particular understanding of scholarship's relationship to political work. Choosing to consider aspects of activism as examples of a decolonial imaginary and practice without first subjecting them to empirical analysis in the conventional sense is my attempt to do their political work and agency justice. This is where I find the current interest in upending the hierarchy of analysis over description—and that of the analyzer over the analyzed—useful and relevant.[96] Choosing to subject artistic practice to my own "creative critical interpretation," often without taking into account artists' intentions, on the other hand, derives from two objectives.[97] The first is to avoid "assuming the power of art" in the realm of politics proper, an assumption that detracts attention from the political work of organizing and mobilizing that is required for overcoming colonialism and racial capitalism.[98] The second objective is to remember that the "relevance and effects" of artistic practice are constituted in analysis and discourse as well as in artworks.[99] My twofold aim, in other words, is both to avow scholarship's responsibility in constituting the critical significance of artistic practice—rather than landing it on the shoulders of artists alone—and to avoid the assumption that work done within a global cognitive capitalist market, whether in contemporary art or academia, could ever compensate for the political work required for critique to have tangible implications.[100]

1
EXTRACTIVIST AND ANTIEXTRACTIVIST AESTHETICS

IN JUNE 2019, GERMAN STATE-OWNED broadcaster Deutsche Welle published a video news segment in Turkish titled "Swallow Sensibility" (figure 1.1)—sensibility of the needs of the hole-nesting bird the swallow. The segment featured the owner of a sand-quarry-cum-concrete-plant located on the banks of the Tigris River. The video was captioned as follows:

> *Despite losing 100,000 lira a month, they did not remove the birds' nests.* All work came to a halt when swallows nested in 5,000 tons of sand stored at this concrete plant located in Diyarbakır's Bismil district. Rather than remove the swallow's nests, the owner, Halil Başaran, hired new equipment to quarry sand from scratch and bought sand from elsewhere to be used in ready-mix concrete.[1]

The story spread across Turkish media of various political persuasions, including state-owned and pro-government outlets otherwise critical of Turkey's recent coverage by international broadcasters like Deutsche Welle.[2] *Sabah*, a major pro-government newspaper, titled it "Humanity in Action."[3] The story incited much commentary online, where the tendency was to interpret the quarry owner's "humanity" or "sensibility" as characteristic of

FIGURE 1.1. Screengrab of the news segment "Swallow Sensibility" published by Deutsche Welle Turkish.

"the Kurds" or "the people of Diyarbakır" and "their chivalry" and "nobility."[4] Some articulated this interpretation in greater detail than others:

> If we could all be as decent as the Kurds, then this country wouldn't be in this condition. If you were abandoned on the street and knocked on people's doors to seek shelter, in much of the country, from the Black Sea to Central Anatolia, all you'd receive is a good beating. But, in the east and southeast, people will open their homes to you. That is, except the PKK . . . an imperialist pawn seeking to destroy the country. The PKK is the No. 1 terrorist organization requiring elimination. And eliminate them we shall—we'll soon drop bombs on your heads![5]

This "swallow sensibility" story, where events at an industrial quarry become the catalyst for celebrating a people for their benevolence yet at the same time demanding war against an organization fighting in their name, introduces an underexplored aspect of contemporary extractivism I unpack in this chapter: its political mobilization of senses and sensemaking, which I theorize as extractivist aesthetics. The term refers to the ways the value of parts of the earth and sections of its population is sensed and made sense of exclusively in quantitatively measurable and marketable terms. My use of aesthetics to theorize how politics is enacted through sensibilities and the senses is broadly (but, as this chapter will clarify, not exclusively)

Rancièrian. As such, it follows a growing number of geographers who have engaged his theory over the past decade and a half, particularly by applying his insights beyond their initial articulation within the arts.[6]

The scholarship on extractivism analyzes it primarily as a negational force—a point that I have already made in the introductory chapter and will further address in this one. Extractivism negates—renders insensible—the life and agency of those it targets to normalize the exploitation of their labor and the environments they inhabit. Parts of relevant scholarship have also problematized Eurocentric theories of aesthetics and their notions of humanity and sensibility for being based on the negation of that which is "nonhuman," "inhuman," or "insentient."[7] Here, I attend instead to the flip side of what scholars have amply problematized: the aesthetically affirmative extractivism that accompanies the negational. The "swallow sensibility" story implies what this might entail. The depiction of the sand quarry owner as the epitome of "humanity" and of animal-friendly "sensibility" involves less a negation of agency than an excessive affirmation of it. Extractivism's imprint is evident in the fact that this excessiveness is measured quantifiably—whether against the market value of the sandpile in which the birds have nested (100,000 Turkish lira a month, then equivalent to US$17,200) or its sheer weight (5,000 tons). The attribution of an unrivaled sensibility to "the Kurds" or "the people of Diyarbakır" collectively burdens the inhabitants of a geography affected by extractivism with the obligation to mitigate its quantitative consequences. Meanwhile, the hand of those who ought to be answerable for extractivism's toll, and duty-bound to alleviate its consequences, is obscured. The seemingly inevitable juxtaposition of "decent" Kurds with the PKK demonstrates that the specter of war haunts even the most generous praise of Kurds' humanity and sensibility, demarcating which sorts of Kurdishness are praiseworthy and which are not. Violence proves itself central to extractivist aesthetics not only where agency is negated but also where it is inflated. There is a violence at work in the ascription of an unjustly inflated agency to human and nonhuman constituents of geographies where extractivism operates and in the resulting obfuscation of the actual sociopolitical actors and processes that enable extractivist activity.

This chapter spans the two historical junctures that bookend the book's historical context: the late 2000s and the late 2010s. The late 2000s witnessed the riparian impact of the first two major Tigris dams—built upstream of central Amed—become apparent. This development prompted restorative efforts, including a project to transform the city's riverbank into a recreational landscape. Concurrently, a construction boom began that eventually doubled the city's urban area. Then, in the late 2010s, Amed witnessed profound changes in precipitation patterns, the failure of one of the dams upstream that resulted in floods, and a recession in the construction sector. The period between the late 2000s and late 2010s was also significant in that it began with the government's attempt to address the Kurdish question by granting the Kurds certain cultural rights alongside conducting peace talks with the PKK. But the period ended with a fresh episode of full-scale war in urban centers, followed by the state's clampdowns on the pro-Kurdish political movement. Within a decade, the neoliberal promises of peace and prosperity that had been bolstered by the construction sector and energy infrastructures like dams came to fail not only gradually but also increasingly spectacularly: war arrived in city centers, building activity stalled, a dam burst, and untimely downpours became frequent. What I term *aesthetically affirmative extractivism* becomes operative in precisely this kind of a context, where extractivist excesses become difficult to conceal and profit from—a twofold difficulty that is increasingly palpable not only in the region I discuss but also across today's extractivism-driven capitalist world. Extractivism, I argue, repurposes its own excesses for an affirmative ethics that overstates—glorifies, even—the agency of rivers and sand quarry owners alike, but in ways no less racialized than those involved in its better-explored negations of life and agency. I conclude the chapter by fleshing out the antiextractivist implications of my argument.

Extractivist Aesthetics (Affirmative as Well as Negational)

According to Rancière, aesthetics is "the system of a priori forms determining what presents itself to sense experience . . . a delimitation of spaces and times of the visible and the invisible, of speech and noise, that simultaneously determines the place and the stakes of politics as a form of experience."[8] Aesthetics addresses "the distribution of the sensible," or the establishment of the material terms on which one may partake in politics, "by first defining the modes of perception in which they are inscribed" and policing them through inclusion, exclusion, and separation. Regressive politics—in Rancière's terms, "statist practices" and "the police"—hinge on "a partition of the sensible that is characterized by the absence of void and of supplement," or the "exclusion of what 'is not.'"[9] Dissentient politics "consists in disturbing this arrangement" through "an intervention in the visible and the sayable."[10] These understandings of the politics of aesthetics inform the way I focus my analysis of extractivism on how northern Kurdistan's geography and inhabitants are rendered "sense-able" and rationalizable *collectively*—both *as* a collective and *by* collectives. I follow Rancière in understanding aesthetics as that which engages or forecloses sensibilities, and politics as an intervention in existing orders upheld by such engagement or foreclosure.

For many aesthetics-inflected critics of colonialism and racial capitalism in geography and allied disciplines, the sensibilities that are foreclosed in the Rancièrian sense have historically been marked as belonging to the nonhuman or inhuman. For these critics, challenging regressive politics demands not only that we incorporate back into the equation those whose sensibilities have been foreclosed but, more fundamentally, that we overcome the humanist ethics that make such foreclosures possible.[11] Indeed, recent and current iterations of capitalism have increasingly appropriated the logics of incorporation to co-opt (rather than outright disregard) life and agency.[12] Relatedly, the racial capitalist shaping of the earth that underpins climate change has drawn on whiteness less as a reified and straightforwardly delineable identity and more as "an onto-epistemic structure" that upholds "a broadly racialized landscape."[13] This landscape contains not only human and sociocultural elements but also non- and inhuman and biophysical ones, including those extracted from deep within the earth, all of whose "life" racial capitalism continually "strives to bring . . . into its preternatural ambit."[14] As a primary means through which racial capitalism reorganizes geography and geology, extractivism in its contemporary iteration may then draw on both the affirmation and the negation of agencies and vitalities that Eurocentric humanisms have historically foreclosed.

Two strands of existing scholarship on the politics of ecology provide insights into how these affirmations and negations work side by side. The older of these strands explores (and has developed coevally with) the late-capitalist neoliberal production of "nature" as both a socially constructed and a material phenomenon.[15] Central to this late capitalist production of nature, scholars show, is the setting aside of parts of the earth for "environmental protection" to then serve functions around leisure or cultural consumption that hinge on the colonialist geographical imaginaries of "wilderness," "wetlands," and "Indigeneity."[16] Late capitalist conceptions of nature therefore affirm colonial agencies and vitalities. The second, newer strand of scholarship explores racism as central to contemporary extractivism's negation of the life and agency of those it targets. Echoed here is the broader geographical-aesthetic critique of the racialization that operates today in former imperial metropoles and postcolonial cities by engendering "danger" and "endangerment."[17] This strand of scholarship demonstrates how the racialized negation of the "subaltern" and "inhuman" perpetuates the geographically uneven distribution not only of extractive activity but also of the production, circulation, and management of the waste and toxicity extractivism causes.[18] If, taken together, these two strands of scholarship acknowledge that extractivist capital and governance operate by affirming some sensibilities and negating others, they largely understand the physical sites of negation to be separate from those of affirmation.[19]

Revisiting existing scholarship in light of both modes of extractivist aesthetics, which I call the affirmative and the negational, then, raises a number of questions. How does the interplay between negation and affirmation operate to uphold and perpetuate extractivism's logic of quantifiability and the racialization that underpins it? Under what conditions does one mode of extractivist aesthetics become more prominent than the other, and how might the answer to this question inform antiextractivist pathways? I explore these questions below by attending to the ways the affirmative and the negational workings of extractivist aesthetics operate in Amed, not spatially separately but interdependently through the materialities of sand and water.

SENSING THE TIGRIS VIA EXTRACTIVISM

The first historical juncture relevant to my discussion is the mid-2000s, when Kurdish and pro-Kurdish mayors had just been elected to office across northern Kurdistan in Turkey's 2004 local elections. They included Amed's Osman Baydemir, a Kurdish lawyer and member of the Kurdish Peace and Democracy Party who served as mayor of Diyarbakır Metropolitan Municipality until 2014. In late 2006, the municipality launched the Tigris Valley Landscape, Planning, Urban Design and Architecture competition to tender designs for its Tigris Valley Project. Baydemir described its objective as "bringing the Tigris to life."[20] This objective was a response to the riparian impact of the first Tigris dams, built as part of the Turkish state's so-called Southeastern Anatolia Project. Dovetailing with a century of attempts by Britain and then Turkey to render the Tigris and the Euphrates navigable and measurable, this Kurdistan-specific project had entered implementation in the mid-1980s.[21] Two of the three dams that inaugurated the project had been on the Tigris, specifically on its northernmost headwaters, about fifty kilometers upstream of central Amed.[22] Upon their reservoirs becoming fully impounded in 2000, the two dams' impact had become palpable, with water-land relations in and around Amed changing immensely. Floodplains stretching north of the city were no longer being flooded, transforming into soil proper the historically diverse coastal zones of sand, aggregate, and gravel formerly produced by the dramatic and seasonal river regime shifts resulting from the region's semiarid climate.[23] Varieties of gravel watermelon and sand peach named after their specific terroir, as well as melon and cucumber varieties unique to Amed and grown just downhill from the city center, were now uncultivable. Over time, the Rafetus softshell turtles historically found in great numbers along the Tigris became "endangered" (as rated by the International Union for Conservation of Nature) due to the disappearance of the sand that once characterized the Tigris's floodplains and that is integral to the livelihood of this animal.[24]

Precisely how Baydemir's objective of "bringing the Tigris to life" would materialize was prescribed in the competition guidelines: by erecting barriers along the length of the two bridges bookending the stretch of river that Amed's historic center overlooks.[25] Taming "the river's irregular regime," these barriers would volumize the water to enable views for all to enjoy and thus "reunite the city with the Tigris" on which it had previously "turned its back."[26] The winning entry was geared toward recreation, proposing a water sports center and foregrounding the idea of the river as a "vista." The Tigris-as-vista would be made accessible for all to enjoy from viewing terraces to be constructed on the slope between the walled city and the riverbank. The vista would be further enhanced by glowing buoy-mounted lights suspended on the water, reminiscent of a now-lost multifaith and multiethnic ritual historically held there to celebrate the watermelon harvest by using melon rinds as lanterns and floating them down the river (figure 1.2).

The municipality proved unable to entirely execute the Tigris Valley Project during the early 2010s; the central government withdrew the cooperation it had pledged for the two barriers key to the idea of "bringing the Tigris to life" and at the same time began claiming the project as its own.[27] Then, during the mid-2010s regional state of emergency declared in the name of counterinsurgency, the government used emergency rule to push ahead with the project, completing phase one in summer 2020. Meanwhile, the project became the subject of much criticism. Pro-Kurdish voices, in particular, protested its few elements that Baydemir's mayoralty was able complete—especially the panoramic observation terrace that included an upscale café with a view—for "damaging the natural landscape" and furthering the Kurds' "urban and spatial assimilation."[28] While such architectural consequences as the terrace and the café are questionable for reasons of environmental and racial injury, I suggest that they were each the result of a much more profound influence that extractivism exerts across the political spectrum as a value system based on quantifiability. This influence is

FIGURE 1.2. Computer-generated rendering of the winning entry in the Tigris Valley design competition (reproduced by permission of SekizArtı Architecture and Urban Design).

evident in how actors like the Baydemir administration—despite their contrasts with the Turkish state—sensed the river's life in terms of the *amount* of water it retains visibly and continuously, a sensibility manifested in the additions of the terrace, the café, and the floating, buoy-mounted lights stretched between the riverbanks, all of which capitalize on the water's visible and continuous profusion. This is as aesthetic an influence as it is a political one.

DAMS, DOWNPOURS, AND THE RIVER'S AGENCY

The second historical juncture relevant to my discussion is the late 2000s. The profundity of extractivism's influence on sensing and making sense of the Tigris's life in quantifiable terms is evident in how, despite the criticisms raised against the Tigris Valley Project, its logics remained forceful throughout the 2010s. Consider two instances from the tail end of the 2010s, which, due partly to the dams' climatic impact, were marked by unusually heavy rainfall in Amed.[29] In December 2018, following a sudden downpour, a floodgate in one of the two dams upstream of Amed collapsed, and the city's riverbanks were flooded. Some journalists celebrated the incident for having revitalized the river after all those years in which it had "flowed submissively," remarking that "such is the Tigris' might" and "free-spiritedness."[30] Popular social media users posted historical photographs alongside those of the incident as evidence of the river's revitalization.[31] During a subsequent episode of downpours in May 2019, the dam's operators this time preemptively opened the floodgates. As the water increased to a level unseen since the construction of the dams and the snowmelt that had accumulated in the reservoirs rapidly discharged southward, the Tigris began to flow under Amed's UNESCO-listed bridge in a way that newspapers from across the political divide celebrated as unprecedentedly "clear" and "voluminous."[32]

In both these sets of responses to an unforeseen manifestation of the mutual impact between dams and the weather, the vitality of the Tigris—known historically for dramatic seasonal changes in color, volume, and width—was perceived as per extractivism's valuing of the earth in terms of the quantity of resource extractable from it. Moreover, unlike the late 2000s, in the late 2010s, the Tigris's quantifiably perceived vitality was not only a *static* characteristic demonstrable by the river's looks. Vitality figured here also as a *dynamic* characteristic, considered evident in the Tigris's *agency*: how the river flowed despite attempts to submit it to authority. A similar dynamism also figured prominently in the contemporaneous "swallow sensibility" story (dating from the same period of unusual downpours in late 2018 and early 2019), which praised the quarry owner for demonstrating "humanity in action." I wish to revisit that story to further unpack the sort of conditions within which extractivism mobilizes life and agency in its own way.

SAND, RECESSION, AND THE LOCALS' AGENCY

The sand quarry in Bismil is but one among many private industrial quarries that have appeared in the region since the late 2000s. Understanding how these quarries came about requires discussing a piece of legislation known as the Coast Act (Kıyı Kanunu). The legislation is dedicated to coastal protection and was passed in 1984 when the contradiction between tourism and construction—two sectors central to the economic neoliberalization enforced by the 1980 military junta—became salient. The Coast Act sought to resolve this contradiction by outlawing construction activity (except where it is "in public interest") along Turkey's coastlines, including the banks of major rivers like the Tigris and Euphrates and the Mediterranean, Aegean, and Black Sea shores. Between 1984 and 1990, the Coast

Act was repeatedly amended to enhance its protectionism. For instance, its geological definition of what constitutes a coast was expanded, and its programmatic specification of what qualifies as construction "in the public's interest" was narrowed.[33] But there was one important exception to these protectionist enhancements: an amendment to the Coast Act passed in August 1990, titled "The List That Specifies What Part of Our Watercourses Are Identified as Rivers." The amendment defined the Tigris as originating in Bismil, a district of Diyarbakır Province one hundred kilometers downstream of the river's northernmost headwaters, where the first two dams on it were built.[34] Note that their construction had already been underway for a few years by the time the amendment was enacted. Central Amed lies halfway between the dams and Bismil. The amendment therefore annulled the "riverness" of the Tigris in and around Amed—the primary area of the dams' impact on floodplain geomorphology once they went into operation—and allowed, among other physical interventions, sand quarries to be dug there.

As a growing body of scholarship has shown, the violence of abstraction underpins prevalent hydrological approaches today. Examples range from the colonialist "invention of rivers" that imprisons myriad conditions of "wetness," to the modernist notion of "water" that homogenizes diverse waterscapes and deprives them of context-specificity.[35] The amended Coast Act's redefinition of the Tigris evidences the geographically uneven ways such abstractions are distributed. Their violence, in other words, has a racialized and racializing character that is constituted not in abstraction per se but rather in its uneven distribution. Affected most severely by this unevenness is the uppermost stretch of the Tigris upstream of Bismil, the scene of the swallow sensibility story and the Tigris's origin according to the Coast Act. The quarries dug there grew in both number and size with Amed's construction boom around the turn of the 2010s, which expanded the city's urbanization westward along six-lane inner-city roads that Baydemir's municipality built. Today there are more than twenty such quarries in the valley's uppermost one hundred kilometers, the area that has been deprived of river status. The quarries have caused immense and often irreversible damage to the riverbank and the riverbed (figure 1.3). One of the first and most conspicuous of these quarries appeared as an offshoot of the Tigris Valley Project launched in 2007. The project's first feature to be constructed was the two lakes that the winning competition entry had intended for water sports. What materialized following the breaking of ground there in 2008, however, was not lakes but rather quarries feeding sand into Amed's booming construction industry (figure 1.4). When there was no more sand to quarry, the hollowed-out pits were turned into industrial fishponds. Use of groundwater for this purpose further weakened the already sedimented river, at times encroaching on the riverbed itself. Meanwhile, many quarries that are less visible from central Amed have remained operational, including the one featured in the "swallow sensibility" story. As the construction industry went into recession in the late 2010s, sand dug from these quarries began piling up. The unusual downpours Amed experienced between late 2018 and mid-2019 worsened the recession's impact on the industry. Not only did the rain further decelerate construction activity in and around Amed; it also damaged the quality and the market value of the sand piled up in quarries.

These are the crisis conditions that threw into sharp relief extractivist excesses like the sandpile featured in the swallow story. Note how these excesses have been repurposed as measurable evidence of an excessive ecological sensibility and agency—attributed first to the quarry owner and then, through a racialized ethics, to the people of Amed and northern Kurdistan in general. As such, they recall Kathryn Yusoff's proposal to understand human "identity" as "always in excess of itself."[36] For Yusoff, this "excess" has "non/inhuman" as well as "social" constituents and as such renders subjectivity a "geologic" and "distributed affair" involving "a wider ecological and mineralogical field."[37] In addition to helping problematize the neglect of non- and inhumanity that characterizes the Rancièrian notion of aesthetic "surplus" and some of its recent uptakes by geographers,[38] Yusoff's proposal critically reconsiders the contemporary question of extractivism-driven growth. Many "Anthropocene-inflected" responses to this question have emphasized resource "scarcity" and planetary "limits" as barriers to growth. Yusoff reformulates the question instead as one of "abundance" or "what to do with the accumulated excess when growth is no longer biophysically possible."[39] That extractivism's excesses in the form of sand and water figure prominently in both the sand-quarry story and the floods discussed in this chapter indicates the urgency of Yusoff's reformulation. It indicates that contemporary extractivism continues to gain momentum even when its excesses become spectacularly visible. While critics may wish to read these excesses as barriers to growth, extractivism continually repurposes them for its aesthetics—for extending its influence into ways in which human and nonhuman life and agency are rendered sensible (affirmed) and insensible (negated). Any critique of extractivist growth must therefore be accompanied by criticism of extractivism as sensemaking.

It is all the more important to take seriously the affirmations of life and agency explored in this chapter, precisely because they are intertwined

FIGURE 1.3. A stretch of the riverbank twenty-five kilometers north of central Amed as seen in 2019, plundered by successive enterprises in sand mining (author's photograph).

FIGURE 1.4. Google Earth images showing a sand quarry turned lake (see just right of top center of each image), located directly across the river from central Amed (left, 2013; right, 2019).

with the negations. Just two months before the swallow sensibility story came out, a young man drowned near that spot while fishing.[40] Over the 2010s, drowning due to quarry-induced riverbed and riverbank deformation caused an increasing number of deaths along that stretch of the Tigris in the spring and summer months. It affected both people and their livestock—animals fell into former sandpits and died while drinking the water accumulated in them—and prompted protests by villagers otherwise inactive in party politics.[41] Quarry-related deaths occurred in a militarized context, too: at the outset of the fighting that flared up in 2015, access roads that quarry owners had opened during the peace talks period became instruments of war due to their being under-surveilled territory conducive to insurgents' movement.[42] "Nature," as Derek Gregory has shown, "is a medium through which military and paramilitary violence is conducted."[43] Amed's quarries help nuance Gregory's insight: they indicate that in racialized geographies such as northern Kurdistan, redesigning "nature" is not simply a means to a violent end but constitutes violence in its own right.

In sum, whether in negating or unjustly affirming the life and agency of racialized peoples and the geographies they inhabit, extractivism is underpinned by a symbolic and systemic structure that reduces the worth of those it targets to the marketable value of an extractable resource. As such, contemporary extractivism manifests in affirmations of life and agency at least as often as it does in negations. The instances discussed in this chapter, where the vitality of the Tigris, the sensibility of Kurds, and the agency of both were excessively affirmed—albeit only in quantifiable terms—evidence this point. Recall the crisis conditions that framed these instances: a dam shutter breaking open and downpours combining with recession to cause disused sand to pile up in quarries. What I have conceptualized as aesthetically affirmative extractivism, then, looms particularly large whenever extractivism experiences a crisis. Given that the contemporary juncture in the history of racial capitalism is one where crises recur increasingly frequently, the concept warrants critical attention beyond the immediate context explored above. Each crisis reduces, if temporarily, the profitability of extractivism's excesses while also laying bare their excessiveness—a recent and globally mediatized example being the amount of oil that continued to be extracted during the first months of the COVID-19 pandemic despite the dramatic drop in fuel consumption. Given that a basic concern for the environment is now part of the mainstream, such crises, I argue, render extractivism's excesses conducive to an ecological sensibility that values life and agency through the racialized logic of quantifiable measurability. These crises call for a critique of extractivism focused not on resource scarcity versus abundance but rather on the politics of quantifiability that underpins this dichotomy.

ANTIEXTRACTIVIST AESTHETICS

I intend my argument to have antiextractivist implications. I unpack these implications here in the hope of furthering recent scholarship on aesthetics and its critical potential against extractivism. I do so by thinking with Amed's eco-activists. Their practices, I argue, help us to imagine an antiextractivist aesthetics that shifts us away from valuing life and agency as per racialized metrics, to valuing life and agency in terms of unquantifiable relationality. Indeed, extractivism scholarship has also considered the latter sort of valuation for its critical potential, associating it particularly with "indigenous" or "local" senses of and attachments to place.[44] My argument's antiextractivist implications both confirm the significance of these associations and nuance them. The nuance is that the antiextractivist imaginaries I chart practice a kind of localism and attachment to place whose criticality derives from an ability to zoom into and out of one's own locality and indigeneity.

Consider eco-activist Ferat Demiroğlu's interviews with villagers living near the quarry shown in figure 1.3, the context being his six-episode ecology-themed series broadcast in 2015 by the Kurdistani channel Özgür Gün TV. Villagers lambaste the quarry for having damaged their quality of life as well as for having taken a toll on flora, fauna, and the landscape, noting that the damage has been experienced differentially along generational, occupational, and gender lines. The minibus driver who connects the village to the city center complains about roads wrecked by earthmoving equipment. A subsistence herder laments that his livestock are drowning. A homemaker grouses about dust constantly accumulating inside her home. A subsistence farmer objects to the dust accumulating all over the vegetables in his garden. These stories indicate an antiextractivist aesthetics that, by zooming into the everyday and grappling with the uneven effects of affairs otherwise sweepingly deemed "local," values life and agency as unquantifiable relationalities. The Amed-based ecology collective Bûka Baranê's (Kurmanji for Rain Bride) response to a private housing estate built in 2012–2014, right across the valley from the historic city center on a previously undeveloped hilltop overlooking the Tigris, is equally instructive in this regard. Protesting the estate and the municipal authorities who had given it planning permission, many in the pro-Kurdish movement demanded its demolition. In contrast, Bûka Baranê demanded that the estate be employed to house refugees, who were then only just beginning to arrive in Amed from war-torn Syria. "The project's urban-ecological damage is irreversible," reasoned the collective; the valley and its inhabitants had already been exploited for materials and labor, and demolishing the estate would only create more toxicity and waste.[45] A further downside to demolition that Bûka Baranê could not have foreseen manifested in March 2018. The *kayyım* (mayor appointed centrally by the government during and in the wake of its recent counterinsurgency campaign) did in fact demolish the estate and then used the quantifiably measurable ethical leverage he derived from the demolition to push ahead with the Tigris Valley Project. Rather than performing a local ecological sensibility by calling for the literal clearing away of extractivism's excesses, Bûka Baranê had proposed to expropriate them as a material resource for the dispossessed. The proposal gestures toward an antiextractivist aesthetics in that it considers awareness of extractivism's long-standing attempts to dispossess one's locality and fellow locals as a basis from which to zoom out and connect with others whose dispossession may require a more urgent and direct response than one's own.

In both these instances, activists traverse and collapse different temporalities in ways that challenge extractivist politics: by homing in on processual and yet differentially experienced details of the "local" everyday; by attending to urgencies arising from one's larger regional neighborhood. This interweaving of the long-term with the urgent and the quotidian with the processual helps to rethink the Rancièrian formulation of disruption as the articulation of progressive politics. Rancièrian aesthetics has been criticized for premising the very possibility of sensing, acting, and speaking in progressively political ways on a Eurocentric humanist ethics that privileges certain agencies at the expense of others historically foreclosed by racialization and colonialism.[46] The cases I have discussed in this chapter—especially the instances of activism that have concluded it—echo this observation regarding the hierarchical ethics that underpins Rancièrian aesthetics. But the chapter also indicates that what might actually be at stake in this hierarchical ethics is not agency as a formalizable phenomenon—forms of sensing and making sense that have historically been disadvantaged. Rather, the issue might involve a more fundamental notion of agency: the very agency to continually make, unmake, and remake new forms of sensing and making sense. This is a kind of agency whose challenge to extractivist power dynamics derives from the ways it escapes formalization aimed at the representation of locality or identity. The next chapter expands on the implications of this understanding of agency as I continue to approach the question posed by Eurocentric aesthetics-as-politics not in terms of *whether* a certain sensibility is problematized but in terms of *who* is granted the agency to problematize it and *to what extent* this problematization challenges or confirms extractivist power relations.

2

THE ART OF PEACE AND ITS EXTRACTIVISMS

PANORAMA (2007), A PHOTOGRAPH BY contemporary artist Cengiz Tekin, depicts a man standing on a rock, gazing out from on high over a stretch of the upper Tigris valley that skirts the artist's native city of Amed (figure 2.1). The valley he surveys bears the ecological imprint of the city's thriving construction sector in the form of new infrastructural works and riverbank quarries that extract the sand feeding into hundreds of construction projects rising across the city. Amed is the officially unrecognized capital of a region whose twentieth-century history saw violent Turkification policies and the backlash they triggered, leading in the 1980s to a bloody war between state forces and Kurdish insurgents. The thriving construction sector *Panorama* depicts was facilitated by the mid-2000s political context of peace talks and democratization initiatives the Turkish government addressed to Kurds. But a straightforward paradigm shift from war to peace is not all there is to this landscape. The man gazing triumphantly out across the valley sartorially resembles state-sponsored paramilitaries who tortured, disappeared, or assassinated hundreds of Kurdish intellectuals and activists throughout the 1990s. This resemblance is reinforced by two elements: the work's titular allusion to the 1990s state TV show *Panorama from Anatolia* (*Anadolu'dan Görünüm*), which propagandized the military's campaign in northern Kurdistan, and a second man lying lifeless with his head crushed under the weight of the first man's boot. An art history reference further consolidates the implication that nationalist

FIGURE 2.1. Cengiz Tekin's photograph *Panorama*, c-print, 90 × 130 cm (reproduced with the artist's permission).

violence has not disappeared from but rather remains constitutive of this new landscape where peace and prosperity are forged at ecology's expense: the photograph visually quotes the painting *Wanderer Above the Sea of Fog* (1818) by German Romantic Caspar David Friedrich, whose landscapes enthused both Prussian nationalists in the nineteenth century and Nazis in the twentieth.[1]

What role might contemporary art produced in sites of extractivism play in responding critically to extractivist aesthetics at the current neoliberal juncture in the Anthropocene? As detailed in this book's introductory chapter, I follow decolonial scholarship in complicating the imaginary of a homogeneous "humanity" (*ánthrōpos*) that characterizes the Anthropocene thesis and in emphasizing instead the differences between the authors, proponents, victims, survivors, and opponents of colonialism-driven racial capitalism—the main motor of what is now called "anthropogenic" climate change. Many adopting such an emphasis have gone on to develop new concepts—for example, Capitalocene, Plantationocene, Chthulucene, Eurocene, and Misanthropocene—as alternatives to the Anthropocene, each tending to identify its own singular historical origin for the problem it centers.[2] I diverge from this tendency. Here I take my cue from Kathryn Yusoff, who observes that racial capitalism has from its beginnings been characterized by both continuous formal innovation and an obsession with singular origins.[3] Responding to the concept of the Anthropocene by adding to the litany of alternative terms dovetails with the impulse to formally innovate. Basing each term's critical analytical contribution on revision of the correct historical origin of this geological era mirrors the obsession with singular origins. Contrarily, Yusoff proposes appropriating the room for critique that the concept of the Anthropocene has doubtless facilitated across the humanities and the social sciences. She does so by pluralizing the Anthropocene's homogeneous imaginary—by reformulating it as Anthropocenes—and by working from its empirical focus on geology to problematize geology as a discipline: geologic theories, methodologies, and epistemologies. I take my cue from her pluralization of the term and her materialist understanding of Anthropocenes' *geo*politics as literally earthly politics, while also redirecting her disciplinary problematization to visual culture and its theorizations. Diverging from the flurry of debates over the past decade that have sought to probe what art in or of the Anthropocene might look and feel like, I interrogate art's own Anthropocenes: the ways in which "the Anthropocene" implicates art, including its histories and theories.[4] I focus the specific historical juncture in which I discuss this question on neoliberalism. I do so in conversation with recent scholarship that treats the critical potential of art's geopolitics against postpolitical approaches to democracy, peace, and prosperity that have characterized neoliberalism. The book's methodological focus on extractivism helps me interweave this scholarship and the kind of decolonial approach to the Anthropocene mentioned above.

My discussion draws on a series of photographic works that contemporary artist Tekin produced in the late 2000s and early 2010s. I consider them generative of insights into extractivism in northern Kurdistan at a historical juncture dominated by a neoliberal project that promised peace, democracy, and prosperity against a background of state violence. *Panorama* helps foreshadow my main argument in this chapter. The work portrays Amed's thriving construction sector—the hallmark of the city's reputed postconflict prosperity—as not only environmentally destructive but also grounded in the racialized violence of ethnonationalist state-building. The image formally references a nineteenth-century style whose framing of landscape has associated it with some of nationalism's most violent iterations in Europe.[5] If *Panorama*'s exploration of the relationship between the politics of violence and ecology as an art historical question critiques the (Eurocentric) canon, it does so through reflexive appropriation rather than outright disavowal. This shifts the question of criticality from whether or how the canon is problematized to *in what specific neoliberal contexts* (of both art and politics at large) and *by whom* it is problematized, as well as *who* is considered capable of critique and, as a result, *whose worldviews* are assigned critical agency. I explain how Tekin produced the body of work discussed in this chapter at a time when the artistic platform he found on the national and international scene came with a certain expectation to treat his subject matter as unique to Turkey's Kurds. I term this limited platform granted to Tekin as *regionalist agency* and show how his work challenged it by not simply portraying extractive violence in Kurdistan but also pointing up the complicity of artistic canons (both old and new) in extractivism. My scholarly contribution, then, involves emphasizing sociopolitical subjectivity and agency when addressing art's critical geopolitical potential vis-à-vis extractivism, particularly as it operates within the current neoliberal juncture in the history of colonially driven racial capitalism. Understanding extractivism as operating through cultural industries like art as well as overtly extractive industries like mining and speculative construction, I argue that the question must be approached not only by considering art as food for geopolitical thought and practice but also by attending to how racial geopolitics unfolds through the art world itself.

CONTEMPORARY ART, ECOLOGY, AND AESTHETICS-AS-GEOPOLITICS

The past two decades have seen a growing literature on contemporary art's geopolitical implications that employs the framework of aesthetics. I discern in this literature two themes that resonate with my analytical aims: ecology and neoliberalism. Having used part of this book's introductory chapter for an in-depth discussion of the literature that engages the first theme, I recap here only its main point. This point is that the philosophical category of the aesthetic has from the outset been employed to legitimize the racialized compartmentalization of the earth's inhabitants and their ways of sensing and making sense of the planet. Any critical attempt to theorize the politics of ecology through aesthetics therefore requires self-reflection concerning theory's own embroilment in what it theorizes. This literature, which dovetails with recent decolonial and posthumanist turns in the humanities and social sciences, is useful to think with, because it explores how Eurocentric approaches continue to permeate the politics of ecology not only as an empirical question but also as one that implicates theory and theorization. I, too, explore this question as such, but by staying with the theory of aesthetics rather than by disavowing it. I maintain that even such a disavowal would not suffice to entirely disentangle scholars like me from our embroilment in histories of racial capitalism and colonialism. In referencing scholars like myself here, I have in mind those who inhabit the institutions of Anglophone academia, disseminate their work on its platforms, and use its languages.

The strand of scholarship focusing on neoliberalism explores art's aesthetics-as-politics across various sociospatial scales. One such scale concerns postindustrial urban space and its financial commodification. Art is considered complicit in this commodification's concealment of existing socioeconomic conflicts and its production of new ones, where complicity derives not simply from artists' presence in gentrifying neighborhoods but also from the formal, representational, and performative techniques they employ.[6] However, since such techniques are also mobilized by the very technocrats and profiteers driving neoliberal urbanization, artists' proficiency in them is considered to possess the potential to challenge this mobilization.[7] Practices that physically intervene in urban space to create concrete opportunities for subverting neoliberal urbanization are considered to be among the foremost manifestations of this potential.[8] At scales larger than the urban, the neoliberal geopolitics of conflict have involved wars waged or endorsed by Western powers in the name of spreading democracy throughout the post–Cold War world and establishing global peace. Art's critical potential in this context is seen as leverageable not simply by confronting Western audiences with war's violent reality but by further problematizing the drive for solutionist intervention and consensus that characterizes the very notions of democracy and peace touted by the proponents of these wars and by indexing the dissentience-oriented political work that needs doing outside the gallery or museum.[9] Methodologically, then, this literature appraises art's aesthetics-as-geopolitics against those "postpolitical" notions of democracy, peace, and prosperity that are used in legitimizing neoliberal policies, notions that both inflict and mask various forms of marginalization and violence in cities and beyond.[10]

I interweave these two strands of literature by connecting the two issues they have tended to explore discretely: (1) how theorizations of art through the aesthetic are implicated in racial and colonial humanism's ongoing impact on the aesthetics-as-politics of ecology and (2) how neoliberal notions of democracy, peace, and prosperity permeate art's aesthetics-as-geopolitics not simply as a question to be represented or resolved but as an artistic-methodological one requiring constant reflection. Operationalizing the concept of extractivism facilitates this interweaving. Recall here this book's conceptualization of extractivism as a racialized and racializing practice that values parts of the earth and its inhabitants only in terms of the quantifiable and marketable value of the resources and labor extractable from them and that does so not merely through conventional extraction (mining, agriculture, construction) but also through a number of other industries based on symbolic and epistemic production, including art. The ongoing implications of art's extractivist workings (and potential antiextractivist ones) have most recently and comprehensively been explored by Macarena Gómez-Barris.[11] Focusing on South American regions inhabited predominantly by Indigenous peoples, Gómez-Barris's analysis of extractivism centers on the politics of visibility and invisibility. If "historically, the extractive view rendered Native populations invisible," the "vertical" or "planetary" gaze it instituted enables extractivism in novel ways today: for instance, by making extraction and extractors invisible through "opaque nodes of digital information . . . hidden away from public debate," while "rendering natural deposits of human and nonhuman life transparent" to extractive activity.[12] Gómez-Barris is careful to avoid reproducing extractivism's planetary gaze through her own critical analysis, hence her extensive discussion of art from within "the extractive zone" that challenges "Eurocentric, high modernist, and totalizing visions of differentiated planetary life" by using countervisualities such as "shadow play," "seeing from below," and "listening to the water."[13]

Gómez-Barris's attention to the racialized visibilities and invisibilities that feed into and result from conventional extraction, not least through artistic practice, informs my conceptual operationalization of extractivism for empirical analysis. I follow especially her attention to art that addresses extractive activity from within zones of extraction and to the increasingly complex workings of contemporary extractivism that escape erstwhile visual geopolitical dichotomies of visibility versus invisibility. As I discuss examples of Tekin's art that both show and operate from within Amed's landscapes, where extractive activity has not only survived but also thrived during the transition from decades of racialized violence into a neoliberal project of peace, democracy, and prosperity, I am guided by two interwoven questions. How might such art help locate the Anthropocene in both the history of racial capitalism and its current neoliberal iteration? And how might this kind of art help grasp the geological and geographical politics that both derives from that history and assumes new features in its present iteration? The way I explore this question is undoubtedly informed by the time I have spent with Tekin in Amed as part of the many collaborations I have been involved in there. Specifically, I visited relevant sites with Tekin, including his native neighborhood on the Tigris, and also spent time in Loading (the independent, artist-run space he cofounded in Amed in 2017) during collaborations conducted under its aegis. My story therefore resonates with the growing interest in critical insights obtainable through collaborations between geographers and artists.[14] But in my case, collaboration functioned less as an empirical source and more as the reciprocity through which I related to the artist and his hometown: it sooner informs my methodological-political premise than animates my claims to analytical credibility or legitimacy.

EXTRACTIVIST EXPANSIONS DURING THE PEACE PROCESS

The artworks I discuss in this chapter were produced between the mid-2000s and the mid-2010s. It is useful to recall from the book's introductory chapter a few characteristics of this context that will be relevant to my discussion. The best known of these is the de facto peace process the period witnessed after two decades of intense fighting and emergency rule across northern Kurdistan. As this process got underway in the mid-2000s, the impact of the first two dams built on the Tigris for the state's

Southeastern Anatolia Project was beginning to become palpable along the riverbank in and around Amed. This included not only the direct geomorphological impact the dams had but also the exposure of the riverbank about fifty kilometers on either side of Amed to physical interventions, including industrial sand-mining activity. The exposure was due to an amendment to the so-called Coast Act that redefined the Tigris as originating from one hundred kilometers downstream of its northernmost headwaters. The sand coming from these quarries fed Amed's construction boom in the late 2000s and early 2010s, when the size of the city's urban center virtually doubled through various enterprises, including controversial ones involving Kurdish-run municipalities and businesses. Among such controversial projects was one avowedly aiming to preserve architectural heritage in Amed's historic center but effectively requiring the expulsion of residents in the run-up to its UNESCO World Heritage Site bid, which it eventually gained in 2015. Many of the residents slated for expulsion had moved there in the 1980s and 1990s looking for work or shelter from the war that was unfolding in the city's rural hinterland. In the early 2010s, the Turkish state also undertook a number of large-scale infrastructure projects that straddled both civilian and military uses—high-tech outposts, airports, and hydropower dams—and that flooded areas previously used as passageways by guerrillas.

Amed's period of "peace" witnessed significant developments in contemporary art, too, preluded by the city's first-ever contemporary art exhibition, titled *Art and the City* and staged in 2001 by a group of local artists, including Tekin.[15] Most of the group's members had met in the late 1990s while studying fine art at Çukurova University in the eastern Mediterranean city of Adana, five hundred kilometers west of Amed. In 2002, Amed's first contemporary art exhibition venue, Diyarbakır Arts Center, was founded by Anadolu Kültür (literally, Anatolia Culture), a nonprofit company based in Istanbul and spearheaded by western Turkish individuals from the worlds of business, art, and cultural policy. Still active, Anadolu Kültür aims to "develop civil initiatives nationwide" by organizing "cultural programs across Turkey in partnership with nongovernmental organizations and local institutions."[16] In fact, Diyarbakır Arts Center was the reason Anadolu Kültür was founded in the first place and remains one of only two Anadolu Kültür institutions, the other being a central Istanbul exhibition space established six years after the one in Amed. Using funding from the European Union and its prominent member states, Diyarbakır Arts Center focused in the mid-2000s on bringing contemporary art exhibitions held in western Turkey and Europe to Amed, including the displays it hosted as part of the Istanbul Biennial in 2005 and 2007.[17] Throughout the same period, the generation of Amed-based artists who had organized the city's first-ever contemporary art show in 2001 began exhibiting in Turkey and internationally. But they were largely absent from Diyarbakır Arts Center's programs, even though the institution frequently relied on them to chaperone artists and curators visiting Amed on tours of the city's cultural sites and in other social events.[18]

If, in the mid to late 2000s, Amed's first generation of contemporary artists found a wider platform outside their hometown than inside, this process was not entirely frictionless. Some of the frictions are visible in Tekin's experiences. Between 2005 and 2007, the North Rhine–Westphalian government's cultural exchange program, Transfer, partnered with a group of Turkish universities to organize a series of exhibitions involving artists from this German region and from Turkey, including Tekin and another Amed-based artist. When a press release in 2006 called the artists' hometown a "Kurdish city," all Turkish partners but one withdrew from the project, displaying the nationalist reflex that sees any reference to Kurdishness as separatism.[19] Then, in 2008, Turkey's first-ever, then-nascent modern and contemporary art museum, İstanbul Modern, hosted an exhibition showcasing the Austrian corporation Verbund's collection, whose only two artworks from Turkey included a video coauthored by Tekin and another Amed-based artist. An exhibition review in one of Turkey's most popular national dailies opined that the exhibition's curator "foregrounded the artists' Kurdishness before their Turkishness" and their inclusion must have been a last-minute decision driven by the collector's business interests as a hydropower company looking to enter Turkey.[20] The Amed-based artists were then excluded from the exhibition catalog. Throughout the late 2000s and early 2010s, Tekin also experienced friction with non-Turkish actors due to perceptions of identity. Cases in point are the invitations he received to participate in the 2009 Venice Biennale collateral exhibition, *Planet K*, which sought to serve as a pan-Kurdish pavilion, and in the 2013 show *Amed* held at Vienna's Welt Museum, which showcased the city's "culture," including its "copperware."[21] Tekin declined these invitations on grounds of their essentialist approach to identity, which he saw evident in politicians sitting on their curatorial boards simply by virtue of being Kurdish, or in their conceptual framework resting solely on showcasing localism.[22]

In short, if throughout much of the twentieth century extractivism involved overtly violent racialization in northern Kurdistan, once overt violence decelerated at the turn of the 2010s, it remained operational, expanding its social reach by permeating such cultural realms as contemporary art, not least during the latter's formative years in Amed and the region. Noteworthy in this respect were the struggles that Tekin and some of his fellow first-generation Amed-based contemporary artists experienced in being recognized for their art rather than for being from Kurdistan or Amed. Whether resulting from the celebration or deprecation of this aspect of the artists' identity, these struggles were rendered all the more complex because Tekin and his confreres were not simply ignored; they were expected to perform types of labor that reduced their worth to that of a local representative. This methodologically extractivist expectation at times also embroiled Tekin in conventional extraction (e.g., resource extraction), such as when it deemed him little more than window dressing for a hydropower company's business interests or a local material cultural artifact alongside copperware.

INTERROGATING EXTRACTIVISM AS A CONTEMPORARY-ARTISTIC QUESTION

It was against this background and in this context that Tekin produced a body of work that contributes to a critical geopolitics of the Anthropocene. As foreshadowed in the introductory chapter, my argument is that this contribution hinges on methodological reflexivity concerning how artworks address the geopolitics of both art and life, how they address the geopolitics of visually charged ideologies and their practical, material consequences. Tekin's work enables this reflexivity by mobilizing two art-historical devices: style and medium. Concerning style, recall the artwork that introduced this chapter, *Panorama*. Its extraction-afflicted landscape references not only Amed's recent history of war driven by Turkification policies and its present-day construction boom but also Romanticism and thus art's own historical implication in violent nationalisms and their geological imaginaries of identity and civilization. In arguing that *Panorama* mobilizes "style," then, I mean neither a taxonomy nor an individual technique but rather a visual quotation of existing artworks recognizable to those versed in art history as emblematic of historical movements or schools.[23]

Two further works mobilize style in a manner akin to *Panorama*: *Still Life* (2007) and *Here Is No Water, Only Rocks* (2010). *Still Life* references van Gogh's 1890 painting *Wheatfield with Crows*, one of his final works before he died at the age of thirty-seven by suspected suicide, which portrays the fields where he received the fatal gunshot. Tekin captures a man lying lifeless in a wheat field, with a pistol in his right hand (figure 2.2). If the formal reference to van Gogh evokes death by suicide, the setting and the man's outfit

FIGURE 2.2. Cengiz Tekin's photograph *Still Life*, c-print, 130 × 180 cm (reproduced with the artist's permission).

foreground the evocation's sociopolitical significance. The fallen man's outfit recalls 1990s urban Kurdish insurgents. The location, northern Kurdistan, is one where war may have decelerated but its architectures continue to tower over the landscape, as indicated by the watchtower-like structure at the top right. The wheat that dominates the scene figures prominently in mainstream histories of civilization as state-building.[24] Indeed, it has earned Kurdistan the celebratory status of a civilizational cradle.[25] That the work pairs this celebratory reference to civilization with invocations of war and late nineteenth-century landscape painting's pastoral reverie is significant. It indicates the role that geography and its representations—whether historiographical or artistic and however benign—have played throughout modernity in disciplining heterogeneous lands and peoples into monoliths.[26] This pairing also speaks back to the work's art-historical reference: it invites reflection on the political-ecological context of van Gogh's psychological tribulations, which originated from his time in a Belgian coal-mining town with appalling labor and environmental conditions and which ended in Provence where he sought refuge from industrialization, to no avail.[27] Pairing this context and that of 2000s northern Kurdistan draws attention to the historical and geographical inequalities that both predetermine one's ability to opt for an anti-modernist pastoral escape and differentiate the lived experiences of typological landscapes such escapism involves—even those as seemingly uncomplicated as a wheat field.[28]

At first glance, *Here Is No Water, Only Rocks* offers a view of Amed's renowned basalt-dominated rocky landscape (figure 2.3). A detailed look, however, reveals the children hidden behind the rocks, gazing back at viewers. If the title's emphasis on waterlessness evokes extractivism's impact on the upper Tigris, an impact that became palpable in the 2000s, its reference to rocks, coupled with the work's visual incorporation of children, links this environmental issue with war's ramifications in the same decade. Specifically, the link made here is with the phenomenon known as "rock-throwing children" (*taş atan çocuklar*), Kurdish youth who constituted the single most persistent political force on the streets throughout the 2000s as they protested the presence of the Turkish army in the region's urban centers. If these children were able to challenge the mainstream characterization of the decade as sweepingly beneficial and of peace as deliverable top-down, the media's portrayal of them—heavily reliant on visuals—"depoliticized" and "infantilized" both their challenge and the shortcomings it exposed in the "peace process."[29] That the children face the camera reverses the media-endorsed gaze. That they do so from behind the rocks burdens viewers with the responsibility of an inquisitive gaze. At a level broader than this, the work's title and the landscape it portrays evoke the theme of water and rocks that figured prominently in northwestern European painters' late eighteenth-century uptake of the picturesque and that contributed to the rise of nationalisms in their home countries—for instance, in England through artists like Cozens and, subsequently, Turner.[30]

A second triplet of works mobilizes the artistic device of medium and comprises *Normalization* (2009), *Sand* (2012), and *Here Is a Base Station* (2013). *Normalization* portrays a seemingly ordinary day in the life of a family inhabiting an old house: they sit on a sofa in their living room, likely facing the TV that is the room's focal point (figure 2.4). Upsetting this ordinariness, however, is the hole being dug in a corner of the room, already to a substantial depth. If digging in the ground is always already evocative of extractivism, here it assumes a context-specific meaning due to the violent episode that served as a prelude to the founding of the Republic of Turkey: the state-organized violence that targeted Armenian and Assyrian Syriac populations throughout the late nineteenth and early twentieth centuries and that amounted to genocide. Indeed, the house *Normalization* captures is located in Eğil, a district forty kilometers north of central Amed where a significant Armenian population lived prior to the genocide and

FIGURE 2.3. Cengiz Tekin's photograph *Here Is No Water, Only Rocks*, c-print, 80 × 150 cm (reproduced with the artist's permission).

FIGURE 2.4. Cengiz Tekin's photograph *Normalization*, c-print, 90 × 120 cm (reproduced with the artist's permission).

where one of the first two dams built on the Tigris in the 1990s is located today. The genocide resurfaced in the public eye in the 2000s when deceleration of armed conflict led growing numbers of tourists to visit historic towns and cities across northern Kurdistan—a process then widely called "normalization" (*normalleşme*), as per the work's title. Such towns and cities began to capitalize on Armenian and Assyrian Syriac architectural remnants to expand their heritage tourism offering, while also witnessing the proliferation of treasure hunters who, often with the authorities' condonation, dug up former non-Muslim homes for riches reputedly buried under them.[31] The specific manner and locality in which *Normalization* features digging, then, situates the region's recent experiences of extractivism within its longer-standing histories of genocide.

Unpacking precisely how *Normalization* self-reflexively mobilizes medium requires revisiting the global art world of the 2000s and the rise of artistic and curatorial methodologies such as *relational aesthetics* and *useful art* that proposed to fundamentally reconsider contemporary art's politics of medium. Uniting these otherwise discrete methodologies was a non-representational approach to artistic medium. Relational aesthetics based its political offering on situations that engage audience participation and embodiment rather than on artistic representation, intention, and expertise.[32] Useful art did so by refusing to simply represent sociopolitical problems or their potential answers, instead prioritizing the delivery of workable, context-specific, and situated solutions to them.[33] Importantly, a shift from visual representation to an experiential convergence between art and life outside art animated both relational aesthetics and useful art. This shift manifested in relational aesthetics through art's reframing of life, and in useful art through its measurable amelioration of life. This shift also drew criticism to both methodologies for dovetailing with neoliberalism. Useful art was criticized for dovetailing with the neoliberal state's deflection of its duty to resolve social issues.[34] The criticism of relational aesthetics was that it dovetailed with the experience economy's commodification of social relations, or with the postideological celebration of "participation" as singularly sufficient for progressive politics.[35] These critiques notwithstanding, the two methodologies have remained influential outside of the art world's epicenters, including in Turkey and especially on works exploring violence and ecology.[36] Specifically, usefulness and relationality have characterized Western actors' contemporary artistic enterprises in northern Kurdistan, as epitomized by Diyarbakır Arts Center in the mid to late 2000s. Its founders ascribed to the center the pragmatically useful roles of introducing art to the region, motivating its young creatives, and educating its citizens, while project coordinators articulated their mission in terms reminiscent of relational aesthetics, using such phrases as "opening up a public forum" for "expressing oneself through art" rather than "doing politics."[37]

Normalization's politics of medium merits reconsideration against the backdrop of this surge of contemporary artistic interest in nonrepresentational methodologies. Consider the work's attitude toward art's usefulness. Because Tekin is, as a matter of principle, against photo manipulation, *Normalization* required a house he could actually excavate. He subsequently found a family that wanted their house repaired and then used a significant portion of his budget for the repair work. If the excavation seen in *Normalization* was pragmatically useful, the artist has hitherto avoided publicly disclosing this aspect of the work and thus deriving any sort of artistic significance from it. Nor is the work indifferent to relationality. For instance, its visual treatment of ordinary citizens (the family whose home it portrays) as more prominent photographic subjects than the excavation worker echoes relational aesthetics' skepticism toward expertise and its interest in platforming participants who are not artists. The work moreover centers an act—digging—that has been deployed by contemporaneous relational aesthetics-inflected and extraction-themed artworks like Ahmet Öğüt's *Black Diamond* (2010), which invited audiences to discover a diamond hidden in a coal heap at a prominent Istanbul contemporary art venue, and Michael Sailstorfer's *Folkestone Dig* (2014), which buried gold bars under a beach in southeast England, both awarding their trophies to discoverers.

But contrary to relational aesthetics' celebration of immersive participation, *Normalization* does not portray the family members sitting against the wall as engrossed in the excavation, despite the occasion's anomalousness—one goes about his daily business on the telephone, the older man is entirely indifferent, and the woman and child are glancing over the hole distantly. It instead orients them all toward a television set, a most prominent visual-representational apparatus. This portrayal, combined with Tekin's insistence on the representational medium of photography, prompts critical reflection on methodologies that premise contemporary art's political significance solely on nonrepresentation. In fact, this insistence has led figures from the western Turkish contemporary art scene to deem his work limited in its exploration of such materially engrossing issues as violence and ecology, deprecating it for remaining two-dimensional and representational.[38] My point is that *Normalization* escapes precisely those deprecations whose approach to the politics of medium dichotomizes representation against nonrepresentation or multidimensionality.[39] But there is another, analytically more propulsive argument to make here about how the encounter with the Western contemporary art scene, increasingly pervasive in Amed, presented the city's artists with condescending expectations regarding what artistic media they ought to use. My argument is that these—often uneasy—encounters require attention when appraising art's aesthetics-as-geopolitics in such ostensibly postconflict contexts as northern Kurdistan around the turn of the 2010s. For they indicate the important role that cultural spheres like art play in extending the unequal power relations shaped during periods of overt conflict into those regarded as postconflict.

Sand, the second work that engages self-reflexively with the question of medium, echoes *Normalization* in that it also portrays the everyday setting of a family's living room (figure 2.5). A little girl is seated calmly, as if on a break from play, while a middle-aged man is hanging a framed sunset photograph on the wall. All seems quotidian except the wall-to-wall sand that covers the floor. In contrast to *Normalization*, however, this is the living room of a modern home, the kind that has proliferated in Amed since the late 2000s, when the city began experiencing a construction boom. In the framed photograph hung by the man, the sun is setting over water, fulfilling the promise of a pleasurable waterscape vista that figured prominently in local authorities' plans to embank the city's Tigris coastline for recreational purposes. That this is a modern living room in an increasingly built-up city associates the sand less with the beach than with Amed's booming construction sites, which were fed by tens of giant quarries dug along the Tigris. *Sand* draws a stark separation between waterscape and sandscape, not only spatially but also sensorially. The sandscape is treated as the stuff of embodiment, whereas the waterscape is relegated to the visual domain. The residents of this expanding city may have been promised a pleasurable experience of the river to offset urbanization's ills, but extracted sand is all they get. The resulting gloom becomes more palpable the longer one studies the scene, not least because of how, on closer inspection, both the girl and the man look world-weary, going about their tasks with a listless automation, uninspired by the view from their sandy, whitewashed living room. Their demeanor is far removed from the comfortable embodied feeling of warmed and happy bodies soaking in sun and sea referenced by the framed sunset and the sand underfoot. The near mise en abyme of a watery sunset view observed from a cold whitewashed living room beach confronts viewers with their own appetite for viscerally pleasurable views. In hanging this frame, does the man seek to brighten his home in an otherwise monotonously urbanizing city? Or does he aim to feed the contemporary art viewer's quest for packageable and consumable images, diverting this objectifying gaze away from his family? *Sand* highlights not only the symbiotic relationship that binds recreation-oriented preservation to profit-driven construction so central to capitalist urbanization, but also photography's fundamental role in sustaining this extractivist symbiosis.

FIGURE 2.5. Cengiz Tekin's photograph *Sand*, c-print, 70 × 100 cm (reproduced with the artist's permission).

Finally, *Here Is a Base Station*, a series of nine photographs produced as postcards, shows cellular base stations mounted in the brand-new neighborhoods that had formed in the early 2010s around arterial roads the municipality had built in the late 2000s, doubling Amed's urban area (figure 2.6). The stations were built to resemble the iconic bastions and rectangular minarets that are among Amed's heritage landmarks, but at the outset bore no signage regarding their function. Given the health risks base stations pose within a certain radius, the guise prompted Amed's residents to lobby the municipality for appropriate signage. Note that this was a time when Amed's first pro-Kurdish mayor, Osman Baydemir, was completing his second term in office—a period considered elsewhere to have witnessed "urban activism" coalesce with "municipal power" into a single "bloc" in the city.[40] Complicating such a coalescence, the campaign around base stations brought Baydemir face-to-face with the novel challenge of a popular, nonpartisan demand.[41] The same mayor's tenure saw major enterprises in not only urbanization and infrastructure but also heritage tourism, as evidenced by the renovation of Amed's Armenian and Assyrian Syriac churches and its ancient, now UNESCO-listed walls. These enterprises are not irrelevant to the postcard format of *Here Is a Base Station*. Recall

FIGURE 2.6. From Cengiz Tekin's photographic series *Here Is a Base Station*, postcards, 12 × 17 cm each (reproduced with the artist's permission).

that the postcard was invented in mid-nineteenth-century western Europe simultaneously with the industrialization of tourism, heritage, and urbanization, and that visuals promoting these industries, not least on postcards, enlisted Romanticist landscape painting and eventually photography, helping these burgeoning visual cultural enterprises prosper.[42] The work not only suggests an expanded notion of extractivism as a force that operates through heritage, tourism, infrastructure, and urbanism; it also prompts critical reflection on the visual arts' historical role in enabling extractivism's operations as such a force.

UNFORMALIZABLE CHALLENGES TO THE EXTRACTIVIST GAZE

Tekin's artistic decisions appropriate the Eurocentric canon to enable multiple layers of reflection on the ways state violence, colonialism-driven racialization, neoliberal projects of peace and democratization, and industrial commodification of the earth have intersected in northern Kurdistan and beyond as well as in and through the art world and outside it. In a context where a long history of racial violence and colonialist enterprise combines with newfangled essentialisms that confront artists like Tekin with various if mutually conflicting expectations regarding who they ought to be, what they ought to represent, and what sort of value their art ought to proclaim, engaging the canon by staking a self-reflexive claim to it has critical geopolitical significance. This significance resonates with and expands on the trope of "Turkishness" as a way of "gazing at the Kurd" to "see anything but a Kurd" that has figured in Mücahit Bilici's essays on "Turk–Kurd relations."[43] It engages critically with multiple gazes arising from the imbrications of colonialism, Turkification, and neoliberal marketization, which may as much impose essentialist ideas of Kurdishness on, as altogether refuse to see a Kurd in, the subject being gazed at, but which all objectify this subject as an extractable resource. The critical engagement Tekin's work prompts does not simply reverse such gazes but signals their complicity in racial geopolitics. To return to my main concern, Tekin's work and experiences demand approaching art's critical geopolitical significance to current debates around the Anthropocene not simply as a question of whether visual and epistemic canons or Eurocentrisms are critiqued or not. The imperative, rather, is to ask who is considered capable of expressing such critique in ways they see fit—including in appropriative ways—and how this contestation over agency implicates artistic practice (and its theorizations) in the very object of criticism.

If this imperative is, as I have suggested, largely underexplored in the literature on art's geopolitics, a couple of exceptions exist that are perceptive even as they remain inexhaustive. One is a brief rejoinder where geographer John Paul Catungal draws on the Canadian First Nations artist Kent Monkman's work to propose "situatedness" as central to art's decolonial potential.[44] Catungal's proposal resonates with my analysis: both he and I focus simultaneously on the problematization of Eurocentric canons and on who gets to problematize them. Such a double move recognizes the critical significance of self-reflexive appropriations (rather than straightforward dismissals) of the canon that mobilize "agentive depictions of Indigeneity in the landscape to unsettle the settler colonial and racial aesthetics of landscape art."[45] Consider, too, Divya Tolia-Kelly and Rosanna Raymond's work on "decolonizing museum cultures," which approaches decolonization as an infinitely open-ended imperative to contest the unequal distribution of agency and the relations of power structured by racial capitalism, rather than as definitively accomplishable through artistic and curatorial practice or theorization.[46] These emphases on the situatedness and open-endedness of the decolonial imperative resonate particularly strongly with critique of the Anthropocene thesis's individualist (whether heroic or villainous) imaginary of the human for conjuring white male European colonizers as the sole bearers of sociopolitical agency and thus foreclosing other agencies and subjectivities.[47]

In interweaving, through the concept of extractivism, the racialized geopolitics of quantifiable valuation and objectification that permeate various industries—both those of conventional extraction and cultural ones like art—my intention has been to call attention to these agencies and subjectivities and the work they might do collectively. If Tekin's art signals the complicity of the art world and its audiences in racial geopolitics instead of supplying them with formally radical visualities that undo for them the extractive and Eurocentric gaze, then the effect is not a damning verdict. It is rather an invitation to think and work together by shouldering a part of the decolonial imperative proportionate to one's capacity and positionality. This invitation has particular urgency in what Derek Gregory has conceptualized as the "colonial present." For Gregory, the coloniality of this historical juncture turns on "a nostalgia" not only for the very cultural forms that "colonial modernity has destroyed" but also for the colonialist "privileges and powers" of formalizing both "good" and "evil" in objectified existences and practices other than one's own.[48] I have sought to do my part in addressing this urgency by appraising art's critical geopolitical significance as unformalizable. In so doing, I respond to the invitation that marks Tekin's work and that calls on each viewer to contribute their share to the collective work of undoing extractivism, rather than assume it is accomplishable by artworks or artists themselves.

This chapter has discussed a body of visual cultural production that chronicles the ways extractivism operated throughout a period that saw the deceleration of overt violence. With the next chapter, the book proceeds into the post-2015 period and a fresh episode of full-blown war. Chapter 3 begins by unpacking the period's extractivist aesthetics. It dissects a set of visual cultural practices that sought to get audiences to sense and make sense of the state's role in the war not as a warring party but as a neutral humanitarian actor, thereby repurposing for wartime the extractivism-driven claim to prosperity discussed here.

3
WAR'S HYPERVISIBILITY AND HUMANITARIAN EXTRACTIVISMS

> Do you want to access the truth? Do you want to *find* the truth? Then go first to the source of the event and find the human in there. Touch them. Listen to them. See things through their eyes. *Bear witness* to the events. *Bear witness* so that you can assume responsibility, both ethically and conscientiously, so that you can't just ignore, turn back, leave. *Bear witness* so that the truth may be appreciated.[1]

SO GOES THE OPENING MONOLOGUE of Turkey's factual television series *Bear Witness* (*Şahit Olun*), which in Turkish uses the second person plural imperative, as if to command its viewers to bear witness. The show was launched in conjunction with the state's violent counterinsurgency campaign in northern Kurdistan, during which PKK-affiliated groups set up ditches and barricades in the streets and the government declared successive, localized, round-the-clock curfews in Kurdish towns and cities.[2] Broadcast online and on the state television company TRT's documentary channel, the series was hosted by an ex–special forces commando turned risk management consultant.[3] In each episode, the host follows counter-insurgency units and special police forces across the urban spaces where fighting restarted in August 2015 after more than two years of ceasefire and peace talks. The fighting is chronicled by way of dashcam footage, handheld cinematography, and aerial videography, combining in one fell swoop the genres of true crime TV, citizen journalism, and military surveillance. This stylistic and methodological hybridity is reflected further in the conceptual framework, aspects of the narration, and the characters involved. Instead of portraying the conflict as one between the stock categories of gallant soldiers versus helpless terrorists, the show zooms in on the ostensibly precarious lives of the security forces in their everyday architectural spaces. Rather than present a scripted and detailed elaboration of the images, the verbal narration is intermittent, disjointed, and subordinate to its visual counterpart. As indicated in the opening monologue, *Bear Witness* purports to be less about the overtly political claim to sovereignty that characterizes conventional state propaganda than about grand, ethically and conscientiously charged concepts such as responsibility and truth. In this chapter, I repoliticize the ethics of responsibility and truth being invoked here by taking seriously the visual nature of the invocation.

In reconnecting the ethics of responsibility and truth back to the politics it is invoked to mask, I use the series *Bear Witness* together with a set of images from Kurdish towns and cities that depict counterinsurgency forces inside and outside houses and that circulated widely on social media. First, I analyze *Bear Witness* as an indicator of how the state reconceives sovereignty through urban warfare and its embedded reporting. Embedded war journalism—the approach to filmmaking through which the series seeks to undergird its ethically charged messages—has now become a genre unto itself globally, and a number of recent precedents to *Bear Witness* exist in Turkey.[4] But the show's hybridization of reality TV, gonzo reporting, and high-tech aerial surveillance is noteworthy. It draws on both a global fascination and a context-specific familiarity with these genres due to their prominent role during and after the 2013 Gezi Park protests against the Erdoğan government and a series of events that took place in the run-up to the counterinsurgency campaign, including the Suruç and Ankara bombings, the Tahir Elçi assassination, and the downing of a Russian jet fighter.[5] This hybridization, I argue, helped *Bear Witness* forge an image-heavy rather than verbal ethic—a hypervisibility that promised direct sensory experience of urban warfare rather than documentation to be cognitively perceived and interpreted.

Then I turn to social media images that circulated through unofficial and often anonymous accounts portraying counterinsurgency forces in ravaged domestic spaces and streetscapes. I document how the themes, formal characteristics, and means of circulation constituting the ecology around these images mimicked dissident visual ecologies that evolved around and were popularized by recent antigovernment practices such as the Gezi protests. They therefore fabricated an antiestablishmentarian aura energized less by loyalty to the state than by grassroots support for something with the look and feel of insurgency. The hypervisibility of these images, I argue, oriented the primary realm of crime and accountability away from war crimes themselves toward the visualities documenting them.

In his work on the Israeli military's destruction of Palestinian homes as part of its counterinsurgency operations, Eyal Weizman discerns a shift in the state's consolidation of sovereignty through siege warfare. The site of siege is no longer the borders of another state, Weizman suggests; it now also involves the walls of homes, rendering the likelihood of being sieged omnipresent for certain populations.[6] As Paul Virilio has shown, today such omnipresence involves not just siege warfare but also the often simultaneous and prolific circulation of its images across homes located beyond the "theaters of war."[7] While, until recently, the politics of this circulation was predominantly understood as per Susan Sontag's argument that omnipresence leads to indifference or Jean Baudrillard's notion that it constitutes a "hyperreality," this understanding is increasingly uncapable of addressing today's world, where images of war participate in rather than simply visualize the reality of violence and as such are available for use toward various political ends.[8]

In this chapter, I argue that the visual ecologies formed around *Bear Witness* and counterinsurgency-affiliated social media posts point to a hypervisibility that is neither tantamount to a Baudrillardian hyperreality nor easily associable with a politics deriving directly from war's visibility or invisibility. The hypervisibility I trace makes the war visible both excessively and with a specific kind of politics that involves images' inseparability from the violence, rather than their serving as a discrete realm. I argue that, in mid-2010s northern Kurdistan, this hypervisibility involved a visual paramilitarization of both counterinsurgency personnel and the act of supporting them. This twofold paramilitarization hinged on a portrayal of the war as taking place between two insurgent groups (PKK-affiliated militants and vigilantes revolting against them) rather than between one militant group (the PKK) and the state. In this way, the state came to be positioned as a neutral humanitarian actor uninvolved in the war itself and best equipped to restore order before and after hostilities.

EMBEDDED JOURNALISM PORTRAYING THE STATE AS A HUMANITARIAN ACTOR

"In this broadcast, we will say very little but show a lot," opens episode 7 of *Bear Witness*. Indeed, the series is considerably discourse-light in comparison to conventional warfare coverage by outlets affiliated with states participating in wars. Use of such terms as "terror" and "terrorist," which figures prominently in conventional state-affiliated coverage, is brought to a minimum here. Instead, *Bear Witness* uses generic categories like "humanity" and "people" to speak of those involved in or affected by the war. Similarly, it avoids overt references to "national security, sovereignty and territorial integrity," which have together formed the stock-in-trade of the Turkish state's rhetoric on the Kurdish question and its militarized implications.[9] These references are replaced with grander concepts such as "truth," "impartiality," and "credibility"—qualities of the coverage itself rather than the issue being covered. Where the series uses verbal narration, it does so mainly to enhance those qualities to which the series lays claim. This is evident in the following phrases the host utters periodically: "none of what is happening right now is fictional," "whatever we experience is what we are relaying to you," "we are bearing witness on your behalf," and "you are witnessing a moment right now." All in all, *Bear Witness* is a show in which image prevails over word, epitomizing the age of televisual sensationalism that prioritizes videography over speech in order to stir up public emotion while also purporting to give viewers direct access to on-the-ground reality.[10]

In its attempts at abstaining from deep-seated conventions of state-endorsed discourse, how does the show rely on images in comparison with use of words? Consider the following three-minute scene about halfway through episode 7, in which the film crew is caught up in a skirmish in Mêrdîn (Mardin, in Turkish). As militants and counterinsurgency personnel begin to exchange gunfire, the host merely relays the chain of events without qualifying them or naming the actors involved:

> Right now, as far as I can see, there's a response. And, right now, a bomb exploded. Right now, right now, yes, right now a skirmish has started—yes, yes, yes, yes, right now, just when we're also there. We are right there, right now, yes. Right now, there's a response. Yes, right now we're in the middle of the skirmish. . . . Yes, yes, yes, yes, what you're seeing, what you're witnessing right now is a spontaneous event. . . . Yes, right now you're seeing all that's happening.

> You're seeing right now. Contact has been established on all points. Contact has been established. If you want to grasp the events and see the difference, there you go, either you'll come here and live through it, or no one will speak. . . . Right now it's impossible for you to even hear my voice. Yes, with what's happening right now, it's impossible for you to hear my voice.

The host utters these words over footage consisting of handheld follow shots of himself, static shots obtained at ground level from behind the law enforcement convoy (figure 3.1), dashcam recordings of the spatial context obtained from law enforcement cameras but not acknowledged as such, and aerial videography as seen from the control desk. The vantage point that viewers are offered is therefore thoroughly that of the law enforcement units. Where the insurgents are shown, they are seen from a bird's-eye view throughout the entire series. The way verbal discourse gives way to image making as the main medium of narration in *Bear Witness* aims to enhance the viewer's emotional identification with counterinsurgency personnel—an aim videography is known to be particularly potent in achieving by prioritizing the senses over cognition.[11]

Such portrayal of counterinsurgency is also noteworthy for its spatial implications. It demonstrates that *Bear Witness*'s primary spatial interest lies in a certain interiority as experienced, ostensibly, by state forces. This interest is evident not only in the series' use of aerial footage as seen from the control desk (figure 3.2) and street-level footage filmed from inside combat vehicles (figure 3.3), but also in the type of settings where counterinsurgency personnel are interviewed: the interiors of armored security vehicles and headquarters (figure 3.4). As this footage is broadcast to TV screens in interior spaces across the country, where it is meant to be viewed, viewers' sensorial identification with the experience of interiority that structures the series' vantage point and with the state security forces personnel is enhanced.

The series seeks to further bolster viewers' identification with counterinsurgency personnel by using interviews with them designed in both content and form for this purpose. Interviewees share their problems, including personal ones, such as the difficulties of working "in the region," evidenced, according to one officer, by the high incidence of resignations and divorces. Professional problems are also exposed, as when the same officer remarks that "we are way, way behind other public servants in terms of social security and other types of security" or that "everyone's life just gets worse by the day." In an interview with the police chief of Şırnak's Cizre district in his

FIGURE 3.1. A still from *Bear Witness* featuring a skirmish scene that mimics citizen journalism by combining handheld camera footage and near-ground-level filming.

FIGURE 3.2. A still from *Bear Witness* featuring aerial views as seen from the control desk.

FIGURE 3.3. A still from *Bear Witness* featuring streetscapes as seen from inside counterinsurgency vehicles.

FIGURE 3.4. A still from *Bear Witness* featuring face-blurred members of law enforcement interviewed primarily in the interiors of counterinsurgency vehicles and headquarters.

office, the show's host draws attention to bullet holes in the walls to suggest that there is no part of town that is unaffected by the skirmishes. Follow shots during operations are coupled with the host's remarks that urban warfare is laden with professional difficulties for the forces in that it renders civilians and insurgents indistinguishable from one another. In episodes filmed before early December 2015, when curfews became standard practice, the camera occasionally happens upon children or the elderly during raids and patrols. In such moments, editing slows down, and the usual acid techno underscoring music gives way to a strings-based elegiac piece. "On the one hand, people continue to live," comments the host, "and on the other, is a group that makes life miserable. It's not so easy to tell one from the other. . . . the most difficult job on earth." Importantly, whereas counterinsurgency personnel have their faces blurred out for anonymity but are interviewed in depth, civilians' identities are visually exposed, but their voices are virtually never heard—lest the militants disagree with the civilians' remarks and track them down, suggests the host. That the blurring out of faces obstructs vision stimulates the rest of the senses to enhance the sensuousness of the viewers' identification with the counterinsurgency forces.[12]

An emphasis on interiority characterizes the series even when the camera is out on the streets. Combat scenes draw heavily on footage from handheld cameras that follow counterinsurgency units through winding streets, labyrinthine alleyways, and narrow staircases, turning abruptly in cases of skirmish to walls and paving or shooting from below eye level. During the skirmish in which the crew gets caught up, the host says the following about the government-declared curfews designed to undergird the counterinsurgency campaign:

> Right now, we are in the middle of a neighborhood. The fact is that people could have been here. If the curfew had not been declared and people had not left this area, they would be experiencing this, right? I cannot imagine, believe you me. You know, I'm used to these sounds. But I do not want to imagine what children go through when they find themselves in the middle of such sounds. Believe you me, I do not want to imagine it.

While emotionally manipulating the viewer by conjuring the image of children cowering in the midst of gunfire, the host's comments nonetheless testify to what the curfews actually entail in practice. Translated literally, the official Turkish-language term for curfew glosses as "ban on going out on the street" (*sokağa çıkma yasağı*). But as the host's reference to people's flight from "this area" implies, the mid-2010s curfews across northern Kurdistan meant the de facto wholesale evacuation of curfew-affected areas, rather than just an obligation to stay at home. This resulted in the sealing-off of entire neighborhoods from the outside world. *Bear Witness* offers ample visual evidence of this: the host follows counterinsurgency personnel into the kitchens and living rooms of abandoned homes. Set in a district of Amed, episode 1 navigates such domestic spaces with the host reporting thus:

> Instead of staying put amid the violence, people have deserted their homes. Where we are currently is inside one of those hastily abandoned houses. As you can see, people had to run leaving pots and pans as they are. . . . A year ago, this was a house full of all sorts of joy. They were going to work and to school in peace, going about their daily lives.

As these words are being uttered, law enforcement units are shown entering a home the intended way—using doorways and staircases rather than via overtly destructive means—and inhabiting as temporary shelter what used to be someone's living room (figure 3.5). The spatiality of showing counterinsurgency personnel entering these domestic spaces courteously to then become trapped in them is such that they replace civilians as the domestically besieged, heightening their vulnerability in the viewers' eyes.

The way *Bear Witness* engages spatial interiority serves two aims: to forge intimacy between viewers and law enforcement units and to prompt the viewer to share the counterinsurgency officers' purported sense of entrapment.[13] Exclusive to counterinsurgency personnel, up close and personal conversations portray them as no different from the ordinary citizen, frail and precarious rather than mighty and invincible, while the blurring of their faces enhances the sensuousness of this portrayal, which carries over into scenes of combat, raid, and patrol. When counterinsurgency personnel are not interviewed inside their vehicles and headquarters, they are portrayed as socioculturally respectful of the homes' now physically violated integrity. They seem to replace the civilians, who remain voiceless and appear in flashes, if they are not altogether missing from the picture portrayed. The sense of vulnerability and beleaguerment the series mobilizes is furthered by the immediacy and ubiquity of the medium itself. Telecommunication's ever-accelerating transmission of events to increasingly more distant and effortless viewers makes the movement of each event seem

FIGURE 3.5. A still from *Bear Witness* featuring law enforcement units in what used to be someone's living room.

much faster than it really is, creating in the viewer the delusion that the event is rushing toward the audience, similar to the way passengers inside an accelerating vehicle perceive the slower-moving or static objects outside as rushing toward them.[14]

In *Bear Witness*, there is also a temporal counterpart to the instrumentalization of spatiality. The series uses time as well as space to position the state as largely uninvolved in the fighting being shown. Time is used most especially in those scenes that do explicitly refer to the state and its presence in the settings where filming takes place. The state's presence is referenced in relation to the "before and after" of the counterinsurgency rather than to the present moment. This bookending of the present as portrayed in the show's combat scenes implies that the state is only involved here as the driver of essential economic and infrastructural development and that events in the region have regrettably brought its role as such to a halt. As a result, the present historical moment in which war takes place is treated as a lamentable diversion from the state's temporal imaginary of the country's steady linear progress on the path to increased prosperity. Consider a sequence from episode 3 where, as aerial views of Amed's historic center Suriçi appear on the screen, the host recalls that until just weeks ago, tens of renovation projects were being pursued here in conjunction with the district's new UNESCO World Heritage Site status. That this status was obtained through the efforts of Amed's Kurdish-run municipality is not mentioned. The idea that the war is lamentable because it has interrupted construction-led economic development marks scenes set in both historic areas and ordinary neighborhoods. With the exception of sites of destruction, buildings under construction where work has come to a halt due to the war are the most frequently featured building type in *Bear Witness*. The theme of development also permeates the host's speculations about the aftermath of the fighting. Ditches dug by PKK-affiliated groups are presented as severe damage to urban infrastructure, followed by direct references to "the state" as the actor that will undertake the necessary repair work as soon as the fighting is over.[15] The immediate shift to slow-motion editing and elegiac background music whenever the camera comes across children or the elderly in inhabited areas is also used in scenes set in neighborhoods under curfew, where the host encounters damaged shops and stores. In one such scene, the camera enters a ground-level office through its broken windows (figure 3.6) as the host elaborates.

> This, after all, is a business. . . . The fact is that the people living here are seriously affected by all that's happening. There will be financial compensation—all costs are covered by the state. But the reality is that there's a type of cost that can't possibly be compensated: the psychological one.

Such scenes position the state more as an organization that undertakes economic and infrastructural development both before and after war than as a warring party—that is, a party culpable for the damage inflicted.[16]

The abstraction of the state as a sociopolitically detached driver of development is so integral to *Bear Witness*'s account of the operations that it is pursued at the expense of contradicting some of Turkey's best-known official policies on the region. Consider, once again, episode 7 set in Mardin's Nusaybin district (Nisêbîn, in Kurdish) just across the border from Qamishli in Syria, a predominantly Kurdish-inhabited town then controlled by pro-Assad forces. Following the scene in which the film crew is caught up in a skirmish, the host contrasts the situation in Nusaybin with that in Qamishli:

> Across the border is Qamishli. When not a single shot is being fired over there, I have nothing to say to those who inflict this situation upon my country. . . . Take my word for it: unless this society raises a collective voice against those who are trying to turn this country into Syria, there will be no peace or joy.

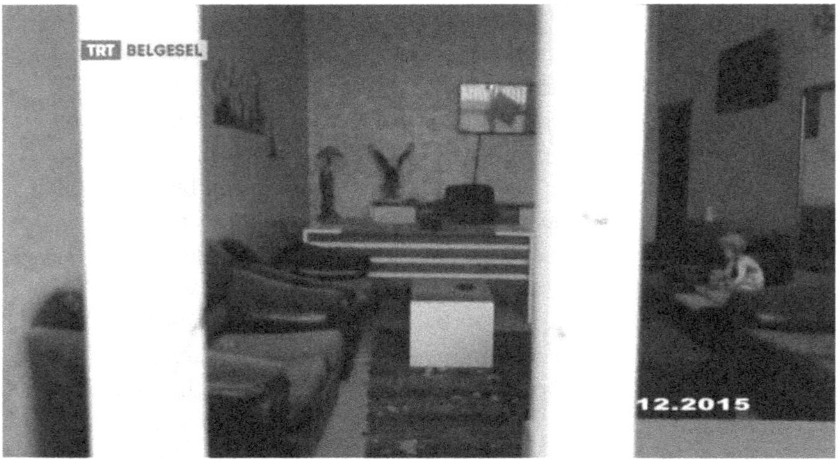

FIGURE 3.6. A still from *Bear Witness* featuring a close-up of what used to be an office space in Mardin's Nusaybin district.

Such is the series' effort to detach the state from the present historical moment of the war that the host draws a parallel between the state and the Assad regime by yearning for the kind of order that he points out as having been established across the border, when Turkey's official position on the Syrian war is in fact one of opposition to Assad.[17] *Bear Witness*'s approach to both the times and the spaces of war is designed to position the state as a neutral humanitarian actor whose involvement pertains to before and after the war, rather than an actor inextricably entangled in various armed conflicts on either side of the Turkey-Syria border.[18] If this positioning hinges on a portrayal of the counterinsurgency forces as ordinary individuals relatable in the precarious and beleaguered existence they inhabit, the more sinister flip side to this compassion-worthy relatability involves another set of contemporaneous images that circulated on social media and were purportedly taken by the counterinsurgents themselves.

VISUAL PARAMILITARIZATION ON AND THROUGH SOCIAL MEDIA

As one of the country's longest-standing industrial powerhouses, the city of İzmit in northwestern Turkey is a national demographic microcosm, having drawn scores of domestic migrants from all its regions (including my own parents). It is March 2016, and I am chatting with Osman (a pseudonym), a sixteen-year-old I have known since the day he was born. Osman's parents are service sector workers and moved here from the eastern Black Sea region a couple of years before his birth. He has seen no government other than Erdoğan's AKP and no parliamentary opposition other than the CHP, the Republican People's Party (*Cumhuriyet Halk Partisi*)—parties that have been in these roles since 2002. Like many in his generation, Osman associates both parties with the status quo, one of the reasons he was enthused over the Gezi protests of summer 2013. Although Osman did not go out on the street to participate in what ended up being one of the largest protest movements in Turkey's history, he followed closely on social media the protesters' witty slogans and creative interventions. Among them, the most popular was "Where are you, my love? I'm here [*burdayım*], my love," repurposed (from a Turkish pop song) by LGBTQ+ activists, who figured significantly in the Gezi protests. Slogans such as these, their materialization in the form of banners and graffiti, and their circulation on social media were central to the events of summer 2013 as they rendered the protests aesthetically and politically novel and helped them transcend deep-seated ideological camps in Turkey. Social media figured particularly prominently in this aspect of the protests. Wanting to keep up with the protesters was the reason many millennials, including Osman, created Twitter accounts in the first place. But social media's prominence in the protests also led the authorities to sweepingly demonize it, with Erdoğan repeatedly calling it "the worst menace to society" and endorsing its restriction.[19]

Now, just two and a half years after Gezi, Osman is showing me on his smartphone a series of topical images entirely different from those of summer 2013, and yet also somewhat reminiscent of them. What brought us to this point was my question about Osman's prospects as the final years of high school were approaching. I asked what he would like to study and then do for living. Osman said he wanted to be a member of the armed forces, but, failing that, at least join the special (i.e., counterinsurgency) police force. Taken aback, I asked him why. His grades were good, he was enrolled in a medical vocational high school, and he could prepare to apply for a relevant degree program to become a full-fledged healthcare professional—a prospect endorsed by his parents. "Aren't you aware of what's been happening? Perhaps you're not, as you live abroad. Let me show you," Osman says, and begins scrolling through a widely followed Instagram account named after a counterinsurgency unit. "See? It's almost as if they're abandoned out there on their own, taking care of themselves," he exclaims. "If you and I don't join the struggle, if we don't fight, sooner or later this fire will engulf us all," Osman says. "Even state officials don't care. If it wasn't for these posts, we wouldn't know what's really going on in there." Among the pictures he swiftly scrolls through is one where a man in a balaclava and military attire is posed against a wall graffitied with "Where are you my love? I'm in Sur [*Sur'dayım*], my love," "Sur" being shorthand for Amed's historic center and one of the districts worst affected by the counterinsurgency campaign.

This photograph, which features an exact duplicate of a well-known slogan from the Gezi protests except for replacement of the letter *b* in *burdayım* ("I'm here") with the letter *s* for *Sur'dayım*, meaning "I'm in Sur," is among tens of images circulated on social media accounts with hashtags named after various counterinsurgency units that purported to show armed personnel in war-torn Kurdish towns and cities. Upon being shared thousands of times on social media, the images also found their way into the picture galleries of various online newspapers, forums, and wiki sites, including those not directly supportive of the war or even vocally opposed to it.[20] Existing analyses of these images and their social media circulation, if few and far between, focus on their gendered—that is, misogynist—character. Nazan Üstündağ rightly situates this character within a recent history:

> Since the emergence of the Kurdish armed struggle in Turkey in the late 1970s, one of the most important fields where the battle between the Turkish state and the Kurdish resistance is most violently, intensely, and affectively waged has been the visual. While the Turkish state tried desperately to control what can be seen and not seen, by whom, in which frame and in what pose in regard to Kurds and the violence they faced, the Kurdish resistance struggled to transgress the frames of the state and its instituted regime of visibility. As Kurds created their own publications, news sites, and information channels, and as image making became democratized through digital technology, they also started to produce their own autonomous frames and poses.[21]

Üstündağ focuses the politics of the kind of images Osman was so engrossed in on their authors while ascribing an inherent democratization to the mediums and technologies through which they are produced and disseminated. This focus on authors is echoed in the other major text on these images, where Beja Protner conceptualizes their content as "perpetrator graffiti."[22] Protner goes further by also attending to the recipients of the images: through conversations with "university students or graduates, actively or ideologically involved in the Kurdish movement in Istanbul," Protner deduces that both those who "oppose" and those who "admire" the content of the images interact with it.[23] This interaction, moreover, occurs with varying intentions. Some reshare the photographs "to expose the excess of violence" by state forces and "to trigger political rage that leads to mobilization against the violence," while others refrain from doing so as they are "against the circulation of dead bodies or of any kind of war images."[24]

Yet the visual politics at work in these social media images may operate in ways irreducible to allegiances as clearly predetermined as those that figure in Üstündağ's and Protner's analyses. The sort of demographic exemplified by Osman is a case in point: youth who sympathetically consumed protester-authored images during the Gezi protests but then, in less than three years' time, became an approving consumer of images of counterinsurgency violence. My intention here is neither to draw a straight line from Gezi to the mid-2010s war nor to homogenize supporters of these two episodes as identical. While today the Gezi protests are retrospectively (and conveniently) often labeled as antigovernment, the highly varied political stances the AKP government then symbolized in the eyes of protesters are often glossed over. To name one such stance, the summer of 2013 was a time when sympathizers of various Turkish nationalist movements were vocally opposed to the Erdoğan administration and to its policies, especially to the unofficial peace process then underway with the Kurdish political movement. Many supported and some even joined the Gezi protests with this sort of opposition in mind.[25] That visual politics is not wholly shaped by preexisting and relatively clear-cut allegiances merits consideration due to much more recent developments than Gezi, including those that occurred just weeks before the mid-2010s war. Several voting intention polls ahead of the June 2015 general election—the first election to cost the AKP its parliamentary majority—showed that a striking 5 to 7 percent of those polled were oscillating between the pro-Kurdish party, HDP, and the right-wing Turkish nationalist party, MHP (Nationalist Movement Party). Many of the MHP supporters were first-time voters—teenagers a couple of years older than Osman—whose political inclinations were influenced more by media and communications than by historical ideological fault lines, except that they, like him and for reasons similar to his, saw both the AKP and the CHP as two sides of the same status quo.[26]

Given these context-specific reasons for approaching social media's visual politics as deriving from the circulation of images rather than simply from trenchant allegiances that preexist it, I turn to Adi Kuntsman and Rebecca Stein's work on "digital militarism" in Israel-Palestine. When images of state violence circulate on social media, Kuntsman and Stein argue, "Israel's occupation extends into the most private Israeli spaces and times, the most mundane networking contexts, zones of internet activity typically deemed beyond the purview of Israel's military projects."[27] Inviting ordinary citizens' investment in the visual field of state violence through "structures of *feeling*," digital militarism "renders the Israeli occupation at once palpable and out of reach, both visible and invisible."[28] Put differently, digital militarism both makes state violence "instantly available" and "minimalizes" its intensity, "normalizing it through the veneer of the social media everyday" and obscuring the real-world impact it makes on its victims.[29] Because politics is never reducible to ideology, Kuntsman and Stein propose that such tensions are all the more reason for subjecting the images that are the stuff of digital militarism to critical political analysis, rather than shunning them for fear of spreading their authors' ideologies.[30]

The images purporting to show counterinsurgency personnel in war-torn Kurdish towns and cities appropriated textual and visual elements and means of dissemination associated with the then-recent nonviolent Gezi protests demonized by the authorities. Following Kuntsman and Stein's reference to "structures of feeling," it is possible to identify four feelings that were the subject of this appropriation: playfulness, passionate love, solidarity, and ephemerality. The first, playfulness, manifested in graffiti that likened the war to a game (in many cases, a video game), echoing precedents from Gezi that had compared the protests to popular video games such as *Call of Duty* (figure 3.7). The second feeling, passionate love, a particularly distressing distortion of its antipatriarchal counterparts at Gezi, manifested—alongside the slogan "Where are you, my love? I'm in Sur, my love"—in variants of the phrase "Love is in the air," purportedly graffitied in places ravaged by war and accompanied by the relevant place-name.[31] The third feeling, solidarity, manifested in Scotch-taped donations annotated with handwritten letters ostensibly penned by counterinsurgency forces apologizing for having had to take food supplies from homes or violate their integrity, which mimicked precedents at Gezi, including a donation wall for dry foods and other essentials (figure 3.8). The fourth and final feeling is ephemerality. Already inherent in the medium of graffiti itself, ephemerality was used for propping up an antiestablishmentarian image, particularly through informal memorialization. Photographs portraying streets renamed informally to honor counterinsurgents killed in action, which obliviated the fact that renaming urban spaces after fallen personnel has long been an official tradition of the Turkish state, appropriated a practice popularized by the then-recent Gezi protests as a way of commemorating protesters killed by the police.

FIGURE 3.7. Images circulated on social media. The graffiti translates as follows (counterclockwise from top left): "If Nusaybin [a Kurdish town affected by the counterinsurgency campaign] is a videogame, we have plenty of tokens"; "We were playing nicely. You died too quickly"; "If you're going to be offended, we'd better not play." The top right image is from the Gezi Park protests.

The ways these images appropriated from Gezi their textual elements (slogans), visual spirit (graffitied, handwritten, makeshift), and means of dissemination (social media) facilitated a kind of sensorial investment in the state's campaign. Yet this campaign was geared specifically toward audiences whose allegiances were not as clear-cut as those considered by Üstündağ and Protner. The investment the images facilitated hinged on the counterinsurgency forces' being aesthetically associated with antiestablishmentarian dissidence rather than with official state power. Here, the war was portrayed as though it took place between two insurgent forces—militants and vigilantes—rather than between one militant force and the state. This helped the authorities secure a certain freedom from culpability vis-à-vis the likelihood of legal investigations into war crimes. Indeed,

FIGURE 3.8. Top: donation wall set up at Gezi Park during the protests. Bottom: examples of images circulated on social media purporting to document charitable solidarity by counterinsurgency forces.

when images of the sort discussed in this section first surfaced in late 2015, the Minister of Internal Affairs announced that he would launch an internal investigation to find those responsible for graffitiing people's homes, all the while shunning the question of other war crimes, such as the killing of civilians or maltreatment of combatants.[32] When images of a guerrilla's dead body being dragged behind a vehicle by counterinsurgency forces appeared on social media, the then prime minister, Ahmet Davutoğlu, promised to find those responsible for photographing the incident and disseminating the photographs, not those responsible for the act itself.[33] In short, if Kuntsman and Stein's "digital militarism" entails a banalization of violence that facilitates ordinary individuals' identification with its author—that is the state—the examples here merit a two-way reconceptualization of the second term in the authors' coinage: militarism. In the context of mid-2010s Turkey, these images indicated a *para*militari*zation*: a bidirectional process where the state detaches itself from the violence it wages and where audiences sensorially engrossed in images featuring the conveyors of this violence disidentify with the state.

EXPOSING THE EXTRACTIVISM OF HYPERVISIBLE WAR

The TV series *Bear Witness* and the circulation and consumption of social media images associated with the counterinsurgency forces discussed in this chapter were integral to bolstering the state's campaign in mid-2010s northern Kurdistan. They were integral not simply by building on impassioned allegiances that preexisted the fighting—for instance, by demoralizing or infuriating pro-Kurdish individuals and emboldening Turkish nationalists. Their innovation was to advertise the campaign to new audiences relatively more ambivalent in their political attachment. *Bear Witness* accomplished this by portraying the counterinsurgency forces as vigilantes whose precarious existence nevertheless did not prevent them from carrying out their work in a manner respectful of the settings where war was taking place. In this way, the series positioned the state as a neutral humanitarian actor involved not in the war itself but only in the postwar processes of repair and recovery, akin to a disaster relief organization. Indeed, the law that the state used in the wake of the counterinsurgency campaign for expropriating and reconstructing 80 percent of Amed's historic district is called the Disaster Act, which dates from 2012 and aims to better prepare Turkey for natural disasters.[34] This refashioning of the state as repairer rather than belligerent was reinforced by the social media images that portrayed counterinsurgency personnel as vigilantes. But, differently from *Bear Witness*, they drew aesthetically on the then-recent Gezi protests to take the state's dissociation from war to a new extreme. These images mobilized medium-specific feelings associated publicly with the Gezi protests to position the counterinsurgency forces as antiestablishmentarian actors.[35]

A compelling challenge to this positioning surfaced in 2016 when hundreds of social media users liked and reshared Kurdish journalist and feminist activist Zehra Doğan's digital watercolor that was based on a photograph of the counterinsurgency forces taken just days earlier. The photograph, which is a bird's-eye view of the forces leaving Nusaybin on June 4 after the end of an eighty-two-day counterinsurgency campaign, captures a town in ruins but also one draped in Turkish flags. Turkish establishment media had circulated the photograph widely the morning after, with multiple newspapers using it to announce that "Nusaybin has been cleansed."[36] Doğan reproduces the photograph in a darker shade by using digital watercolor to repurpose the digitality of the original's medium of circulation and expose what its barrenness hides: the havoc wreaked on lives, which the dripping, the bleeding, and the haze characteristic of watercolors help highlight. There is also a marked difference in content: added to the counterinsurgency forces' vehicles is heavy construction and extraction equipment (figure 3.9). She adds gigantic backhoes and dump beds to the vehicles, making them resemble monstrous excavators and earthmovers and therefore highlighting counterinsurgency's inextricability from extractive industries. Moreover, Doğan's choice of photograph and her decision to alter its content only minimally draw attention to visuality's centrality to what this chapter has termed *humanitarian extractivisms*. Following "terrorist propaganda" charges she faced in December 2016 for her social media posts, including the Nusaybin drawing, which led her to spend nearly three years in jail, Doğan's defense was to argue, "I did not do this, they did."[37] If these words recall Pablo Picasso's reputed answer to a Gestapo officer inquiring about his *Guernica*, Doğan's case differs from his in one respect: her answer points not only at the armed forces but also at the visual mediation arm of the war machine. She based her drawing on this particular photograph, Doğan has explained, because it was the one that establishment newspapers chose for their headlines celebrating Nusaybin's "cleansing."[38] Her drawing, then, unmasked the antiestablishmentarian garb of the counterinsurgency by exposing its links with extractivism as a force that involves both conventional extractive industries and new ones such as visual culture.

Another work that challenges the aesthetics of humanitarian extractivisms discussed in this chapter is *Silence* (2018) by Cengiz Tekin, the artist whose earlier practice was discussed at length in chapter 2. Its challenge to war's hypervisibility involves breaking with the visual medium altogether and centering sound instead. The work intersperses the sounds of eight of the weapons used in Amed's historic district during the counterinsurgency campaign with brief technical information about them: where, when, and by whom each weapon was invented; how much it weighs; how many rounds it can fire per minute; and how long its range is. A dispassionate, expert voice narrates this information in Kurdish, while white-on-black intertitles (the only visual component of the work) translate it into English.[39] *Silence*'s challenge to hypervisibility is not only as a counterinsurgency-related question but also as an artistic one, especially in the context of a legalistically inflected turn in 2010s contemporary art. The decade saw increasing numbers of artists dealing with state violence frame their practice in testimonial and evidentiary terms. As mentioned in this book's introductory chapter (see the section "Extractivism, War, and Visual Ecologies in a Statusless Colony"), the premise of this artistic framework was that, in a time of unprecedentedly democratized access to and use of the latest visual technologies, art dealing with violence could do more than just contest the universality

FIGURE 3.9. Zehra Doğan's *Nusaybin*, digital watercolor (reproduced with the artist's permission).

of truths produced by the powerful. It could now beat the powerful at their own game by producing the truths that make the most sense—that are epistemically and sensorially most convincing.

This artistic turn was relevant to 2010s northern Kurdistan not only because they both involved violence but also because the region at this time became the subject of artworks with evidentiary or testimonial claims. Take internationally award-winning Turkish auteur Özcan Alper's twelve-minute-long film *Among the Ruins* (2018)—an animation based on one hundred social media images of the state's counterinsurgency campaign in Amed's historic center.[40] The film is effectively a requiem narrated entirely in Kurdish and uses Kurdistan's minstrelsy tradition, *dengbêj*, extensively to accomplish what the director has called "bearing witness" to the loss of lives and livelihoods.[41] Such elegiac use of the Kurdish language and singing tradition is not unproblematic. Historically, *dengbêj* singers have never been lamenters only; they are bards who sing tales of love, war, and resistance as well as pain and suffering.[42] But, in Alper's film, their practice is reduced to one of mourning. If *Among the Ruins* testifies to loss through an animation based on images circulated widely on social media, another contemporaneous work relies on them for producing evidence and solving a political crime. This work is Forensic Architecture's twenty-seven-minute-long video *The Killing of Tahir Elçi*, which investigates the incident that titles it: the death of Amed's bar association president in the early days of the counterinsurgency.[43] This was a hypervisible death; it occurred in broad daylight and in front of cameras as Elçi was speaking to the press in Amed's historic district and a nearby police chase of two militants happened upon the gathering. The video extracts sonic and visual data from the images that have rendered Elçi's death hypervisible to make the case that the lethal bullet was fired by a police officer and not by a militant. Prepared in both English and Turkish but without a Kurdish version, the video bears the hallmarks of Forensic Architecture's standard practice: narration that adopts an expert tone and a montage that surgically slows down, speeds up, and zooms in on or out of images, including quite graphic ones.[44] While the video uses visual realist formal principles that are legible to state institutions and legal systems, it has been presented not only to the prosecutors in charge of the court case but also in numerous artistic spaces where Forensic Architecture has shown work.[45]

The critical import of Cengiz Tekin's *Silence* becomes clear when viewed vis-à-vis these two examples that brought the legalistically inflected artistic turn of the 2010s to bear on northern Kurdistan. It indicates that art's preoccupation with meeting the powerful on their own ground might risk reaffirming the aesthetic principles at work in war's hypervisibility: seeing suffices for believing, voices of victims and survivors are only useful for mourning or as raw data, and aesthetic practice is significant to political violence simply as a tool for solving it or sensitizing audiences to its humanitarian exceptionality. In breaking with war's hypervisibility and treating Kurdish voices as experts with the agency to historicize violence anew, *Silence* raises questions about the aesthetic partitions that slip under the radar when artists rush to unlock the evidentiary and testimonial potential of their images. Such questions include who the evidence-producing experts versus raw-data-providing witnesses are; what language the evidence or the testimony is delivered in (e.g., Kurdish versus English or Turkish, and the technical language of experts versus emotionally charged survivor testimony); what artistic testimony or evidence might do to escape the sensory orbit of the visual resolutions and rhythms of war's hypervisibilities; and what histories other than the split second of weapons being fired or individual victims' suffering might be woven into the evidence and the testimonies artists produce.[46]

In an age where the production and circulation of images are presumed to have become instantaneous and "democratized," as Üstündağ puts it, state propaganda no longer hinges solely on the qualitative effort to control the narrative. As this chapter has argued, control increasingly turns on *quantitative* and *formal* domination. It quantitatively dominates the platforms where war is made hypervisible (hence the crackdown on widely circulated images like Doğan's digital watercolor that threaten precisely this quantitative domination). State propaganda also achieves domination through form insofar as artistic production dealing with war oscillates between a visual realism required by courts of law and a humanitarian exceptionalism oriented exclusively toward mourning (the oscillation that Tekin's work *Silence* breaks with). Images shot from the vantage point of state forces numerically proliferate across social and conventional media and the art world, often unaccompanied by official discourse and at times even in purported spite of it. The faster and more varied the proliferation is, the easier it becomes for audiences of various ideological persuasions (or none at all) to concur that hypervisibility suffices to resolve questions of responsibility, accountability, and authority—to make sense of violence in line with extractivist aesthetics.[47] Images circulated in the mid-2010s through *Bear Witness* and on social media furthered extractivism in at least two ways. Treating northern Kurdistan as a perpetually victimized and underdeveloped region and rebranding the state as a neutral repairer and developer by way of the extractivist industry of construction, these images hid the state's hand in creating the victimhood and the need for development in the first place. They also reduced northern Kurdistan to a source mineable for "raw" (discourse-free and visceral) visual material whose value, as per extractivism's overall framing, derives from its circulatable quantity. The strength of Doğan's drawing is precisely to expose the extractivism underpinning the visual ecologies formed by and formative of these images. The critical purchase of Tekin's work is that these visual ecologies implicate contemporary art as well as social media and the mainstream press. The next chapter discusses a case of visual production that testifies to war in northern Kurdistan through a relation that is fundamentally different from reducing this region to a mineable resource—a relation that I term *nonextractivist*.

4

TESTIFYING TO SURVIVAL ENVIRONMENTALLY AND NONEXTRACTIVIST AESTHETICS

ON OCTOBER 18, 2020, TURKEY'S minister for environment and forestry, Veysel Eroğlu, tweeted his own take on the "how it started, how it's going" meme. The meme had just recently begun trending in a pandemic-afflicted Twittersphere searching for hope by disseminating stories of success and achievement. Eroğlu's tweet appended the trending memetic phrase with two recent aerial views of the Tigris riverbank from Cizîr, a town located on Turkey's border with Syria, only about forty kilometers northwest of where the two countries' borders meet Iraq's (figure 4.1). The minister was boasting about a government project that embanked the Tigris in Cizîr: on the left was the riverbank before the project and on the right what it had become in the space of only a year. Launched in the wake of the counterinsurgency campaign of 2015–2016, the embankment is one of several infrastructural projects the government implemented in Cizîr, an epicenter of the war. Upon completion of the project in summer 2018, pro-government news agencies published the following text online, alongside images of the sort tweeted by the minister:

> Hitherto associated with terrorism, Cizre . . . now has a beautiful coast thanks to a project that has rehabilitated the Tigris River. . . . along a stretch passing through the district's center. . . .

> This 16-kilometer stretch, where sand quarries have deformed the riverbed . . . has now been turned into a viewing terrace. . . . First, the dumping grounds either side of the bridge in central Cizre were cleared. . . . Recreation areas were created . . . where citizens can comfortably go for a walk and some respite. . . . 250,000 cubic meters of excavation-pile rocks were used in the enrockment. 850,000 cubic meters of dump was cleared. . . . The entire district of Cizre has now been cleaned up . . . and given a spectacular appearance. . . . Aerial images taken before and after the works evidence the difference.[1]

The recreational centerpiece of the embanked area is a park built to replace one of the dumping grounds complained about in the news extract above. In its vicinity is a group of neighborhoods that witnessed some of the recent counterinsurgency's most violent episodes: the former dumping ground contained much of the rubble from houses demolished as part of the state's campaign. Human rights observers visiting Cizîr in the campaign's aftermath reported seeing body parts in the rubble dumped at this very location.[2]

The extractivist valuation of the colonized and the racialized strictly in quantifiably measurable terms, which characterized the "Swallow Sensibility" story discussed in chapter 1, reverberates here in the emphasis on cubic meters of dump cleared or stones used for embanking the river. So, too, do the references to viewing terraces and aerial views echo the visualities that often manifest this extractivist aesthetics of quantifiable measurability. The claim that the embankment project repaired the environmental damage done by sand quarries and dumping grounds recalls the mid-2010s visual discourses and practices evident in *Bear Witness* and the pro-counterinsurgency social media images discussed in the previous chapter. All of them position the state as a nonaligned humanitarian repairer and never as a party to the processes that necessitate repair. Like the work of Cengiz Tekin, a male artist from Kurdistan, the work I discuss here by a woman artist from western Turkey, belit sağ, involves a visual practice that, in my view, challenges this extractivist gaze. Based in Amsterdam since 2009, sağ is a videographer and visual artist with a background in video-activist collectives based out of Turkey's capital, Ankara, and its largest city, Istanbul. Discussing the work of someone with sağ's profile introduces a new set of questions around positionality and its role in imagining nonextractivist aesthetics.

In late September and early October 2015, following her first visit to the town in May 2015, sağ filmed a body of visual realist work in Cizîr's Nur neighborhood. The Nur neighborhood is significant here not only because

FIGURE 4.1. Screenshot of Veysel Eroğlu's tweet dated October 18, 2020.

it was one of Cizîr's neighborhoods worst affected by the counterinsurgency campaign but also because much of the embankment built recently along the town's Tigris riverbank, including the dumping ground turned recreational park, lies within it. The period between May and October 2015 was when the state's informal peace talks with the PKK collapsed and gave way to full-blown war. This rapid paradigm shift is reflected in the reasons sağ traveled to Cizîr on two occasions bookending the period. On her first trip, sağ joined a group of activist-artists to run workshops with children in Cizîr on the theme of peace. The trip was organized by a charity called Gündem Çocuk (Children On the Agenda), which campaigns for children's rights in Turkey. The workshops yielded radio programs and video documentaries produced by and with Cizîr's children where they reflected on peace in the context of the informal talks between the state authorities and the PKK. On her last trip, sağ joined Barış İçin Kadın Girişimi (Women's Initiative for Peace) activists who had traveled from across western Turkey to Cizîr and nearby Kurdish towns as a show of solidarity with their residents in the wake of the first counterinsurgency siege (September 4–12, 2015). "Witnessing" was prominent among the activist group's avowed motivations for the trip and manifested in taking several camerapersons with them to Cizîr, among them, sağ.[3] The group pooled the footage they filmed during the trip and made it accessible to wider activist, artist, and journalist circles wanting to create awareness of the war. They also edited it into a YouTube documentary of their own.[4] The footage that came out of sağ's handheld camera made its way into six of her films ranging between three and forty-one minutes in duration.

In this chapter I take seriously the claim to witnessing that figured prominently in the motivations of the activists with whom sağ traveled to Cizîr and which also informs the way sağ approaches her medium: "Video is both a document and a witness."[5] I discuss sağ's six visual realist films on Cizîr as a particular type of testimony that has critical potential vis-à-vis the extractivist aesthetics problematized in this book—the ways extractivism *makes* sense, literally, by engaging the senses and sensibilities. Drawing on recent conceptualizations of witnessing and bearing witness, especially as conceived by visual theorists, I develop the concept of "testimony as environment" to unpack the critical potential of sağ's work. Recent scholarship on art's role in the politics of testimony has tended to foreground the uses to which relevant artistic works are put, ranging from survivors' pursuit of resubjectivation to rights defenders' quest for justice in courts. In foregrounding these uses, the tendency has been to place on the back burner the artifacts that art creates and the politics of the artistic decisions that produce them. Yet the imperative to challenge extractivist aesthetics requires revisiting this tendency, an imperative that informs my conceptualization of "testimony as environment" in this chapter. I argue that sağ's work is nonextractivist because it displays an environmental sensibility that both grasps the spatially homogenizing character of the violence she explores and, by foregrounding relationality and positionality, avoids reproducing this homogenization.

THE IMPORTANCE OF FRAMES AND FRAMING TO TESTIMONY

Central to the particular significance of the body of work that sağ filmed in Cizîr and that informs my concept of "testimony as environment" is a preoccupation with the photographic act of framing and the artifact resulting from it: the frame. Already-existing frames figure prominently in this body of work and not solely for the epistemic purchase they facilitate on violence and its environmental implications. They also figure as cause for reflection on the role of images and image production in political violence and its environmental implications, helping reflect in particular on its patriarchal character. Each occasion that took sağ to Cizîr focused on constituents

FIGURE 4.2. Stills from belit sağ's films made in Cizîr: clockwise from top left: *Sept.–Oct. 2015, Cizre*; *My Camera Seems to Recognize People*; *Nurcan*; *In Front of the Yellow House* (reproduced with the artist's permission).

historically marginalized by patriarchy: women and children. This focus characterizes the spaces and subjects foregrounded in her films. The protagonists are almost exclusively women and children, who offer their testimonies on the violence waged by counterinsurgency forces. Most filming locations are domestic or near-domestic spaces, such as the forecourts of houses where homemakers and their children spend time throughout the day together with their peers, free from the presence and gaze of men (figure 4.2). Such spaces remain the departure point even when the camera follows protagonists to other locations such as streets, squares, or homes other than their own.

The counterinsurgency campaign of 2015–2016 had a markedly gendered character. The spatial policy central to the campaign was, officially, curfews and thus a ban on going outdoors. But what the authorities effectively sought was to oblige residents to leave their homes and hometowns or risk becoming a target. This was made plain from day one as homes became among the foremost targets of shelling and raids by counterinsurgency forces. The gendered character that was physically evident in the violation of domestic space also reverberated in the symbolism deployed by the state. "We will penetrate their nests" (*inlerine gireceğiz*) was a prominent idiom with which leading government representatives boasted about the counterinsurgency campaign.[6] Social media accounts set up in support of counterinsurgency forces circulated slogans—including those graffitied on walls of homes violated by shelling and raids—that spoke of the campaign as a sexual assault and that accused the insurgents of cowardice for dressing as women so as to evade surveillance.[7]

sağ's films implicate photography in these gendered intrusions of violence into domestic space with a particular focus on the photographic frame. The most significant case in point is *Sept.-Oct. 2015, Cizre* (2015, 14'50"), where sağ is hosted by residents in their homes.[8] The film opens with a shot of an immaculate living room complete with a fan blowing a light breeze. The room is unpopulated, decorated minimally, and dominated by pastel colors, which makes the large-screen LCD television placed against one of its walls stand out as would a framed painting. Everything seems perfectly serene except the news breaking on the screen (figure 4.3): a violent assault on pro-Kurdish peace activists in Turkey's capital, Ankara (the October 10 bomb attack that killed 109 and wounded more than 500 activists). As the film proceeds, subjects scrolling through their smartphones to show-and-tell with images documenting the recent campaign develops into a prominent motif. Bright images of bullet casings, large families sheltering in disproportionately sized rooms, homes damaged or destroyed by shelling and raids stand out against the domestic spaces in which they are shown (figure 4.4). In other show-and-tell scenes, sağ follows subjects as they turn toward architectural openings onto outdoor spaces with significantly brighter light conditions. One might typically expect that such tracking shots transitioning from indoors to outdoors would offer spatial and visual liberation from the presumed constraints of domesticity. But the subjects' narration of the landscapes seen from their windows and balconies belies this expectation. A homemaker takes sağ to the topmost floor of her house, talking her through the surrounding landscape amply viewable from this vantage point (figure 4.5). The landmarks she points out are sniper posts and buildings targeted by shelling. In another scene, children take sağ to the window of a ground-floor room to tell her how scared they are to go to school due to a streetscape they describe as a minefield (figure 4.6). Whether framed through architecture or screens, landscapes of violence intrude on domesticity even when no fighting is taking place.

The past three decades have seen growing critique of videography that documents political violence and its aftermath as first mass media and then the internet have led footage of this kind to circulate ever more widely and rapidly. The critique's focus has largely been the assumption that the proliferation of such footage is sufficient on its own for prompting awareness or action against violence. For critics, not only is this proliferation insufficient for prompting audiences to organized action; it often also risks

FIGURE 4.3. Still from belit sağ's film *Sept.–Oct. 2015, Cizre* (reproduced with the artist's permission).

FIGURE 4.4. Still from belit sağ's film *Sept.–Oct. 2015, Cizre* (reproduced with the artist's permission).

desensitizing them.[9] Either way, violence-themed videography is considered implicated in the perpetuation of the very violence it documents. But this line of critique has itself been problematized for tending toward the opposite extreme: for assuming that violence-themed videography, almost independently of its content, is categorically limited in its political effects.

FIGURE 4.5. Still from belit sağ's film *Sept.-Oct. 2015, Cizre* (reproduced with the artist's permission).

FIGURE 4.6. Still from belit sağ's film *Sept.-Oct. 2015, Cizre* (reproduced with the artist's permission).

In response, scholars have proposed "rawness" of footage and "banality" of what it portrays as characteristics of content that complicates pessimism about violence-themed videography's political effects on audiences.[10] This critical response has therefore highlighted the presumed quality of the situations being documented (e.g., banality) or the forms this documentation takes (e.g., rawness).

The significance of sağ's work in Cizîr escapes these two lines of critique even as it confirms the first's emphasis on how images of suffering are implicated in the perpetuation of violence and the second's attention to the specificities of content. Indeed, sağ's films are aesthetically and politically significant precisely because much of their content is dedicated to addressing head-on the implication of images of suffering in the perpetuation of violence. But their significance in this respect is also irreducible to the situational or formal qualities of what the films portray. This significance also derives from the ways sağ problematizes methodological mainstays of visual realist image production, specifically, the practice of framing and the artifact it yields: the frame. Unpacking this point requires dwelling on the criticism that images of violence are implicated in the very phenomenon they document. This criticism resonates markedly with a much older critical tradition that has amply made a similar point about still images, or what one may call photography proper.[11] But acknowledgment of this critical resonance is often absent from the works cited and discussed by critics of violence-themed videography. In noting this absence, my intention is not to police other scholars' practices of citation and theorization but rather to justify my own: I propose to turn to critical photography scholarship for contemplating, together with sağ, the problem of videography's implication in the violence it portrays, in a manner that differs from existing contemplations. If critique of violence-themed photography's presumed political effects on audiences resonates markedly with that of similarly themed videographies, then how one responds to violence-themed videography stands to benefit from how others have responded to violence-themed photography.

Ariella Azoulay has offered one of the best-known rebuttals to the critical tradition that limits its horizon to pointing out photography's implication in the proliferation of the violence being photographed. Writing on photographs of state violence, Azoulay notes that periodically since the 1980s, successive waves of critics have cropped up to discover with astonishment that the meaning of a photograph is produced not only by the photographer or the photography critic but also by laypeople: those who look at and use it.[12] The reason this discovery reappears time and again, she argues, is that critics overlook the civilian or public potential that has characterized the medium of photography since its inception. Whereas predominant understandings of photography fixate on the photograph that is photographed by a photographer using a camera, Azoulay proposes to understand it as an "encounter."[13] Collective in nature, this encounter features the photographer as but one actor, the taking of a photograph as but one action, and the photograph as but one artifactual trace among multiple others. For this reason, the aesthetics-as-politics of photography will never lend itself to the complete control of photographers, even though they have long been presumed to be photographic proprietors and experts par excellence. What is more, because the quality of photography's collective encounter applies not only to past contexts in which photographs were taken but also to various present-day contexts in which they are shown and circulated, photography critics and scholars (as well as the photographers themselves) are denied full control over photography's meanings and functions.[14] If the "imperial scopic regime of the shutter" equates "what was there" when a photograph was taken to "what made it into the *frame* as a legible object," then this equation can be undone only through collective work involving experts and nonexperts alike rather than uncovering supposedly "intrinsic" meanings of photographs through expert critique.[15]

Azoulay's emphasis on photography's openness to various uses and interpretations reverberates across the palpable ways sağ's work in Cizîr indexes images' already-existing yet divergent uses among, and effects on, the residents. Photographs of devastated buildings and survivors stored on smartphones help the residents historicize the counterinsurgency, at times by directly referencing visuality's indispensability to defiance as well as to the violence. *Sept.–Oct. 2015, Cizre* features a resident who, as she shows the camera footage of tanks she was able to film from inside a moving car, recounts the backlash she and her fellow townspeople faced from the counterinsurgency forces in attempting to document the military equipment poured down on the town. War-afflicted landscapes glimpsed through architectural openings infringe on domestic space, enabling violence to continually remind the residents of itself even in their everyday lives. If footage of the bomb attack in Ankara that opens the film serves as a similar reminder, the final scene features the residents' response to it: we are told that the public will shortly gather outside to protest the attack. Part of this gathering is then captured in a separate film, *The Day White Flags Turned into Black in Cizre* (2015, 7'32"), which chronicles women coming out of their homes to join the protest.[16] Such sequences confirm Azoulay's insight that, for better or for worse, there is no single meaning or function that inheres in an image of violence, much less one that is wholly determined by its producers or expert interpreters.

But the question remains as to how a visual practitioner like sağ, who, after all, has no chance of completely disavowing her expertise due to her being a professional artist, might address this insight through and within her own practice. This is where her own acts of framing come into play. In asking this question and exploring it through a focus on framing, I take my cue from Judith Butler's thoughts on photographs of US soldiers torturing Iraqi prisoners at Abu Ghraib. "In framing reality," suggests Butler, "the photograph has already determined what will count within the frame and this act of delimitation is surely interpretive."[17] Butler continues:

> Unless, of course, the mandatory framing becomes part of the story; unless there is a way to photograph the frame itself. At that point, the photograph that yields its frame to interpretation thereby opens up to critical scrutiny the restrictions on interpreting reality. It exposes and thematizes the mechanism of restriction, and constitutes a disobedient act of seeing. The point is not to engage in hyper-reflexivity, but to consider what forms of social and state power are "embedded" in the frame, including state and military regulatory regimes. Rarely does this operation of mandatory and dramaturgical "framing" become part of what is seen, much less of what is told. But when it does, we are led to interpret the interpretation that has been imposed upon us, developing our analysis into a social critique of regulatory and censorious power.[18]

Certainly, sağ's work in Cizîr uses its own framing opportunities to facilitate precisely the task of "interpreting the interpretation" Butler invokes. But it also interweaves such "reflexivity" with an altogether different task of considering "social and state power" to the point where these two tasks become much less disentangled from each other than they are for Butler.

TESTIFYING TO VIOLENCE BY ACCOUNTING FOR FRAMING'S CENTRALITY TO TESTIMONY

There are two sensorial—that is to say, mostly but not exclusively visual—elements whose relation to sağ's camera is foregrounded in the films time and again to implicate the camera in the power relations that underpin the violence it documents: the specific technologies of framing found in Cizîr and the broader norms involved in their use. To begin unpacking the point about technologies of framing, consider *The Day White Flags Turned into Black in Cizre*. The film is one long take, where the camera follows women from forecourts of houses through narrow streets onto a square-type open space where they gather for the protest against the Ankara bomb attack. Early in the film, when the tracking shot goes past the barricades and the ditches mounted by Kurdish youth to proclaim the autonomy of their neighborhoods, the audio suddenly disappears for about a minute due to reasons that remain unidentified by sağ (figure 4.7). The penultimate scene in *Sept.–Oct. 2015, Cizre* shows a woman going out onto her topmost-floor balcony to map her testimony onto the landscape. She points to the cultural center on the hill opposite, built by the town's pro-Kurdish mayor a decade before, explaining how the counterinsurgency forces occupied it during the campaign and used its commanding position to shell the neighborhood.[19] At this point, a military helicopter begins to hover over the landscape. "See, its door is open. It can drop something any time," says the resident, prompting sağ to turn her camera toward the helicopter. The camera repeatedly fails to focus on the helicopter, and sağ verbalizes her puzzlement at every turn (figure 4.8). The opposite of this failure looms large in *My Camera Seems to Recognize People* (2015, 3'23"), a film that opens with footage sağ filmed during a memorial service for the victims of the counterinsurgency campaign. Constituting a third of the film, this opening scene is a continuous take that slowly slides past a row of victims' framed headshots, with the camera effortlessly autofocusing on each victim, and sağ this time being astonished by the effortlessness (figure 4.9). In these scenes, then, sağ's camera frames its own implication in the sensorial framing technologies that already exist in Cizîr and are inflected by or used in the war.

A second set of scenes indexes the sensorial norms informed by and formative of these technologies. *My Camera Seems to Recognize People* closes with a scene filmed in an everyday setting with children playing on the street in the presence of homemakers, where a little girl lifts her shirt to show the camera a bruise just above her waist. The scene begins in slow motion, overlain with sağ's voice saying that the "girl recognized my camera." As the footage transitions into normal speed and diegetic sound, sağ asks what caused the bruise, and one of the homemakers responds that the girl fell as she was running away from shelling. Noticing that the girl remains in a photographic pose with her shirt lifted and continues to show her bruise far longer than is needed for the taking of a photograph, the homemakers instruct her to stop posing, as her bodily testimony will already have been captured on camera (figure 4.10). *In Front of the Yellow House* (2015, 20'43") features a boy who also poses for the camera but, this time, nonstop (i.e., almost throughout the entire film) in the background as others give their testimonies (figure 4.11).[20] In *Nurcan* (2015, 41'35"), where sağ's camera follows a woman resident of Cizîr whose name titles the film, the protagonist takes the filmmaker through buildings and streets devastated by raids and shelling, offering her testimony in situ (figure 4.12).[21] As Nurcan

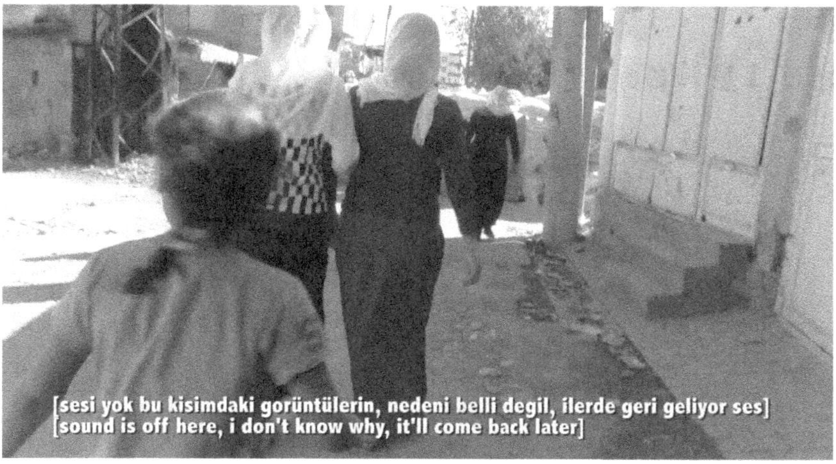

FIGURE 4.7. Still from belit sağ's film *The Day White Flags Turned to Black in Cizre* (reproduced with the artist's permission).

FIGURE 4.8. Still from belit sağ's film *Sept.–Oct. 2015, Cizre* (reproduced with the artist's permission).

shows to the camera damaged water tanks, demolished buildings, and the like, she repeatedly asks sağ to check that what she is presenting is captured within the filmmaker's frame. Therefore, this second group of scenes shows not only what is presented to or posed for the camera but also the residents' insistence on presenting things to or posing for it. In so doing, the scenes highlight the sensorial norms that condition what sorts of testimony are

FIGURE 4.9. Still from belit sağ's film *My Camera Seems to Recognize People* (reproduced with the artist's permission).

FIGURE 4.10. Still from belit sağ's film *My Camera Seems to Recognize People* (reproduced with the artist's permission).

granted or denied epistemic legitimacy—norms that heavily depend on the predominant notion of photography as the framing of an instant.

The dynamics between reflexivity and power at work here are more complicated than in Butler. As her camera becomes implicated in the unevenly distributed abilities and inabilities to focus or record and in the residents' familiarity with an epistemic regime that imposes the burden of tangible

FIGURE 4.11. Still from belit sağ's film *In Front of the Yellow House* (reproduced with the artist's permission).

FIGURE 4.12. Still from belit sağ's film *Nurcan* (reproduced with the artist's permission).

proof on survivors, it is reflexivity that situates sağ within the power relations her work addresses. Crucially, this is not the kind of reflexivity that monopolizes critique to become a source of power in its own right—the kind that validates Butler's caution against hyper-reflexivity. The second set of scenes discussed above, where acts of posing figure prominently, is especially significant in this regard. The politics of the pose has long been central to the imbrications of violence and visuality. Discussing Troubles-era Northern Ireland, Allen Feldman considers the pose to enact a patriarchal politics that has historically combined "the militarized gaze and the realist gaze . . . with the male gaze."[22] Posing for the camera, regardless of one's gender, is associated with femininity. Contrarily, the militarized-male gaze, which manifests in the various instructions and impositions operating outside of the frame to ensure the pose, is established as the neutral eye on the real world rather than the specifically positioned and violent gaze that it actually is. That sağ's films situate acts of posing—in particular, posing by patriarchy's historical others: women, children—in the events that surround them means being reflexive about her own camera's inevitable entanglement in the patriarchal politics of the pose and the gaze. That the reason these events figure so prominently in the films is not always the cameraperson's own will or not entirely under her control leads this reflexivity to avoid reproducing patriarchal politics at the level of critique. Whether by insisting on posing for the camera or deeming this unnecessary, whether by showing violence's remains to the camera or making sure that sağ has captured them, patriarchy's others find in these films a platform for demonstrating their critical agency. Not only are they portrayed as aware of the continuum between guns and cameras—aware that cameras' long-standing penchant for what is scarred by guns is what brings many to settings like Cizîr in the first place.[23] These residents are also portrayed as capable of deciding what to make of this continuum, even as this decision varies from one moment to another.

It is worth continuing to think with Butler about this portrayal, and specifically with the philosopher's speculation on the critical potential of "photographing the frame," or of a kind of image that promotes reflection on its own methodological conventions. Further into the same discussion referenced above, where Butler speculates on this potential, the philosopher emphasizes that the camera is not just an imaging device but also an element "situated spatially in the field of vision" that is "the technological precondition of an image" or "the scene" in which it is taken.[24] When a photograph becomes the subject of "public debate," this "scene" expands to encompass the full range of social scenes in which it is circulated, used, and interpreted.[25] The scenes from sağ's films exemplify this expansion from Butler's first, originary type of scene to the second, social one as they often point out both the social and the material-spatial situatedness of the camera and of photography in general. But they also overlap Butler's two types of scenes by framing what the photographic subjects make of photography's methodological conventions. Where recent scholarship considers a socio-spatial overlap of this sort, it does so through examples that make the act of photography practically accessible to communities long marginalized by violent injustices and objectified by predominant visualities. These examples often involve such communities' taking hold of the camera. Several sequences from sağ's films feature a takeover of this sort but with implications for the politics of visual realist image production and its relationship to extractivism, which differ from those explored by scholars interested in interweaving the two scenes typologized by Butler.

SURVIVORS FRAMING THEIR OWN TESTIMONIES

The scenes scattered throughout the first half of *Sept.-Oct. 2015, Cizre,* where residents show sağ's camera the images of war stored on their smartphones, are interspersed with sequences where the camera travels from hand to hand through domestic spaces. The implication is that the camera does so less because sağ gives it to the residents than because they gradually claim it from her. A couple of scenes early in the film show a tranquil living room with camerawork that is noticeably shakier than in other scenes showing similar locations, and feature a voice inquiring into the workings of the camera. In a third scene, the camerawork becomes even shakier: the camera swirls around with close-ups of hands and faces accompanied by voices of children playing. A fourth scene shows sağ herself being filmed and interviewed about what she has seen and learned in Cizîr. As sağ begins to share her thoughts and feelings, she asks for the TV to be turned down. The interviewer approves by saying "TV—you disappear!" Following a couple of intervening scenes, the sequence where sağ is interviewed returns, with the interviewer suggesting it is now the filmmaker's turn to talk, as the residents have already spoken plenty. sağ answers questions about whether she has ever experienced anything of the sort of violence seen in Cizîr. The filmmaker responds negatively, saying that she "never lived in Kurdistan." The next sequence shows Nurcan, one of sağ's main interlocutors throughout her time in Cizîr, filming herself exiting domestic space and going out in the dark, leaving the filmmaker behind at the doorstep. sağ gradually shrinks into the background as she reminds Nurcan to check that the camera is still recording. Nurcan tells sağ not to worry and instructs her to "disappear," using the same expression she had used for the TV. The sequence becomes a minute-long continuous shot depicting children pausing their nighttime street play to gather around the camera and comment on the political context. The scene retrospectively helps put a face and a name to the voice that inquired about how to work the camera and interviewed sağ in the scenes where the filmmaker did not have the camera. Nurcan, as viewers find out thanks to the opening credits, also "has the camera" throughout *The Day White Flags Turned into Black in Cizre*, the single-shot film that chronicles the protest against the Ankara bomb attack.

How might the photographic subjects' taking hold of the camera overlap with the two kinds of settings Butler discusses, the first being where an image is produced and the second where it is circulated, used, and interpreted? As the gesture central to this question—the handover of the camera—has come to figure prominently in recent violence-themed videography, it has also attracted increasing commentary. Consider Ruthie Ginsburg's discussion of the Israeli human rights organization B'Tselem's Camera Project, a prominent object of analysis in the wider body of relevant contemporary scholarship.[26] The project distributes "video cameras to Palestinians in the West Bank and Gaza Strip so that they can document rights abuses."[27] Focusing on the project's women participants, Ginsburg observes that they consistently film from inside their homes the rights abuses occurring outside. For her, this act renders the home "a site for anti-colonial engagement" by addressing "public concerns" from a spatially situated "gendered position" rooted in "the private sphere."[28] Another object of analysis that has figured equally prominently in recent scholarship of relevance is Dutch contemporary artist Renzo Martens's film *Episode III: Enjoy Poverty* (2008). The film presents itself as a documentary chronicling a five-year project by the artist where he trains local photographers in the Democratic Republic of the Congo so that they can profit from what foreign artists and photojournalists have long monetized: the poverty and violence their country has suffered. As Martens familiarizes the Congolese photographers with the formal conventions of predominant visualities of suffering and with the markets through which they circulate, international journalists and humanitarian workers operating in the country, including the artist himself, remain in the film's spotlight. Like the Camera Project, *Enjoy Poverty* has been celebrated for subverting artistic, journalistic, and humanitarian conventions of addressing non-Western suffering. It has been praised for subverting the victimization and unequal power relations these conventions tend to cause by continuously spotlighting the sufferers and concealing the methods and motivations of the artists, journalists, and aid workers or organizations.[29] However, both projects have also become subjected to criticism for reproducing the hierarchy that characterizes extractivist aesthetics and that reduces the colonized and the racialized to sources of raw material or manual labor, while privileging colonizers and whiteness as the provider of marketable products or intellectual labor.[30]

Rethinking this commentary in light of sağ's films helps nuance both the problem of extractivism that critics have pointed out and the political potential proclaimed by favorable commentators. For these critics, political potential tends to flow directly from spatiality: either from one's gendered spatial situatedness or from what, following Feldman, may be termed one's "scopic" situatedness—who gets to be behind the camera as opposed to being in front of it.[31] But if there is any critical potential in the sequences from sağ's films where the camera travels from hand to hand, it is not constituted solely through spatial positionality. Spatial situatedness undoubtedly plays a central role in these scenes and does so in ways that resonate with the focus on gendered and scopic spatial hierarchies. Those among whom the camera travels are patriarchy's archetypal others—women and children—and it is not insignificant that they get to film as well as be filmed. But arguably more significant than this borrowing of the camera is the fact of whose actions lead scopic places to be swapped: the residents' rather than the filmmaker's. This contrasts with such cases as the projects by B'Tselem and Martens. Even as it may be celebrated for its inherent political potential, the agency that informs and is amplified by the scopic reversal at work in sağ's films both draws on and avoids perpetuating gendered spatial situatedness. The residents take hold of the camera to shoot in the filmmaker's absence, on the streets and in the dark, as well as to film and interview her. Going out to film by leaving the filmmaker behind altogether annuls, rather than merely reverses, scopic and gendered spatial hierarchies. Its power is constituted in not simply controlling the camera as such but rather being in the presence of fellow residents also othered by patriarchy: children playing outdoors at night and women attending a protest. Platforming photographic subjects' views and uses of photography's methodological conventions, then, becomes a question of whether the platform is demanded by them or granted to them and whether the agency it promises is only self-referential or requires relationality instead: being with and among others similarly excluded from scopic and gendered spatial hierarchies.

These questions interweave social critique and material practice—two foci that are allocated to separate types of scenes in Butler's typology. They indicate that the practice of photography is itself a platform of social critique and that image circulation, interpretation, and use have their own materialities requiring critical reconsideration. Reconsidered in this way, the problem with cases such as B'Tselem and Martens is not that footage is sourced from Palestinians or the Congolese but that the uses communities may make of it is reduced to a single type of use defined by solutionism and pragmatism in line with long-standing legal and financial orders:

documentation or evidence production in B'Tselem's case and monetization in Martens's. This is the reductionism that, I argue, sağ's work escapes. To rephrase this argument in a way that speaks to the existing criticisms of violence-themed videography, which center images' effects on audiences, sağ positions (and films) photographic subjects as such an audience.

TESTIMONY AS ENVIRONMENT (AS BOTH DOCUMENT AND MONUMENT)

I have thus far explored three ways in which sağ's work is preoccupied with the photographic act of framing and the device of the frame and what it does with them in relation to violence's witnesses among whom filming was conducted. First, frames have proliferated in Cizîr as a prominent device through which violence is experienced and interpreted—a prominent testimony device. Second, much of sağ's work is dedicated to acknowledging this already-existing prominence by framing the frames used in testifying to violence. Third, the work positions the witnesses of violence as capable of framing frames as such and of doing so in both a scopic and hermeneutic sense of the verb *to frame*. These three ways in which framing and testifying relate to one another inform my concept of *testimony as environment*. Testimony is irreducible to witnessing, irreducible to the act of an individual with a discrete subject position testifying to a spatiotemporally isolable occurrence. Testimony also involves bearing witness, the gradual and ever-continuous formation of subjectivity by way of addressing alterity and receiving a response from it.[32] Testimony, then, concerns not only how violence unfolded or who was responsible for it but also whose sociopolitical agency it incapacitated and how this incapacitation might be reversed. In short, testimony is about ethics as well as epistemics.

Recently there has been a surge of material- and visual-cultural interest in the idea that environments and even the earth itself might be considered witnesses to political violence.[33] Critical of the post-Holocaust paradigm of testimony and its premise that knowledge of past violence is per definition subjective and never wholly attainable, this surge of interest has been useful in revitalizing the ideal of a universally resonant, collectively experienceable, and publicly defendable truth about violent histories. Its sociopolitical horizon, however, has remained confined to the production of such a truth—and therefore to an epistemics authorized by predominant institutions of knowledge production such as the court, the museum, and the university. Where testimony has been considered for its ethical implications, critique has often done so by problematizing Eurocentric humanisms' exclusion of that which is nonhuman or inarticulable in terms of vision and reason—two faculties these humanisms have tended to privilege.[34] Meanwhile, critique has risked reproducing the very exclusion it has claimed to problematize due to the implication that vision and reason are the prerogative of cultural critics and practitioners who inevitably continue to engage these faculties even when problematizing them. The question of how violence's survivors subjected to the same exclusion might themselves respond to it has remained sidelined. This is the question that sağ's work encounters in Cizîr.

Historian Marc Nichanian's conceptualization of testimony in relation to the Armenian genocide resonates with the encounter that characterizes sağ's work. He questions the same post-Holocaust paradigm of testimony problematized by proponents of treating the environment or the earth as a witness. However, unlike them, Nichanian's problem is not that the post-Holocaust paradigm surrendered the ideal of a singular and documentable truth by settling for individualized and fragmented truths but that it subjected survivor testimony to the principle of documentability as per the epistemic logic of the modern archive.[35] For Nichanian, in addition to hindering survivors' capability to come to terms with the embodied impact of the violence, charging survivor testimony itself with the burden of proof perpetuated the unequal power dynamics resulting from genocide. Nichanian terms this approach "testimony as document" and counterposes to it what he calls "testimony as monument": survivor testimony that approaches truth as a question irreducible to realism. "Testimony as monument" centers figuration, imagination, and interpretation rather than factuality, immediacy, and authenticity.

I invoke Nichanian's work here for context-specific as well as conceptual reasons. Cizîr had a significant Armenian population prior to the genocide—an estimated total of 4,300 and thus considerably higher than that of its environs.[36] Genocide arrived in the town with the men being arrested, taken to the town's outskirts, "stripped of their belongings and murdered," and their bodies being "dumped downstream in the Tigris" to avoid causing panic among their families.[37] Two days later, the families were liquidated. "Most women were raped, shot dead, and thrown" in the Tigris, with "the decaying corpses" causing such "pollution" that "the population of Mosul," about 170 kilometers downstream of Cizîr, "was forbidden to drink from the river for a month."[38] This is an environmental legacy of the genocide evident in colloquial landform names still used in northern Kurdistan such as "Armenian's Pit," "Bloody Cave," and "Massacre Stream."[39] The only survivors in Cizîr were women and children abducted by local notables and tribal leaders, mainly for forced labor and sexual servitude.[40] During the recent counterinsurgency campaign, the state forces' intimidatory broadcasts from speakers were recorded to have addressed Cizîr's residents as "all of you Armenians" and "Armenian offspring."[41]

When reconsidered in light of the town's genocidal history, the survivor testimonies featured in sağ's films not only resonate with Nichanian's "testimony as monument" but also indicate that it may not necessarily require overriding what he calls "testimony as document." Particularly worth reconsidering in this light is sağ's attention to the frames that already exist in Cizîr and that help violence intrude on the everyday environments the residents inhabit. Since its historical inception, imperial and state nationalism has used visuality to naturalize itself. Landscape architecture, painting, and photography have configured and represented the environment to this nationalist effect through an optics of framing.[42] If sağ's films in Cizîr acknowledge and repurpose the significance of frames beyond the documentation-versus-figuration binarism, they do so by pointing up the fact that documentation and figuration have in fact always been inseparable in nationalism's self-naturalization in Cizîr and its environs. Marking this inseparability is the regional historiette of the Armenian genocide. By pursuing unprovability through invisibility, the perpetrators and deniers of genocide have in effect inscribed Armenianness for the genocidal gaze into nearly the entirety of the region's population. Over time, this inscription has become a geographic one written into the landscape and the ways locals inhabit it, turning the documentability of violence—the kind of violence that sustains a nation-state founded upon genocide—into a lived reality for the region's residents who have continued to survive that violence.

The kind of realism underpinning Nichanian's "testimony as document" already permeates Cizîr as the hallmark of a violence that interweaves coloniality and visuality before any testimonial use anyone may ascribe to it.[43] Coloniality is known to have featured documentarized frames of violence prominently as instruments for extending realism's influence into the present and imposing it on the bodies of the colonized and the environments they inhabit, including quotidian and domestic ones.[44] The way sağ's films feature the residents' insistence on testifying "documentarily" à la Nichanian is aimed less at relaying their account of the violence realistically than at indexing the realism that already exists in their lives and that inscribes violence into the environments they inhabit. The films foreground the residents' various and often mutually conflicting attitudes toward the documentarian approach to testimony, even as they engage it. In a context where the unresolvedness of historical episodes of racial violence enables new ones and blurs the distinction between victims and survivors of the past and those of today, what Nichanian calls "testimony as monument" and "testimony as document" operate interdependently. Specifically, "testimony as monument" involves a reflexive "testimony as document" where survivors upon whom realism is imposed use it as an imaginative and figurative modality whether by subjecting it to continual reinterpretation or by meeting its veracity claims with sheer indifference. Survivors' agency therefore lies in the license to approach both these modalities of testimony with some critical distance and to capitalize on whatever each modality might offer to their recovery of a sense of control over their own lives and life stories.

NONEXTRACTIVIST AESTHETICS THROUGH SELF-REFLECTION ON THE EXTRACTIVIST GAZE

The final quarter of *In Front of the Yellow House* features children singing as they are surrounded by homemakers spending leisurely time together on a doorstep. One of them is the boy who lurks in the background throughout the film, incessantly posing as if for a photograph. He raps a song whose lyrics begin in Kurdish and end in Turkish. The lyrics effectively offer a sonic map of Kurdistan, naming its mountains and its officially unrecognized capital and regions. The song culminates in an homage to PKK leader Abdullah Öcalan and a reference to the "imperative to join the guerrilla." Speaking from behind the camera, sağ asks the boy where he heard the song and is told that it is his own. The homemakers then invite a girl whose singing they say is renowned. The boy makes space for her. sağ remarks that the doorstep has become a "*sahne*," the Turkish-language word for both "stage" and "scene." The girl replaces the boy and starts singing a requiem for the Kurdish fighters who died in Kobanê—for the Kurds, an epicenter of the Syrian war and their quest for autonomy (its capture by ISIS in late 2014 caused street protests in northern Kurdistan as Erdoğan expressed his indifference to the event).[45] Other girls soon join her, crystallizing the song's anthemic character. The overt geopolitical import of these two songs is paralleled by no other sequence in sağ's films; most dialogues simply relay survivors' experiences during the counterinsurgency campaign, while overtly political discourse figures only in sporadic references to generic ideals like "peace" and cessation of "suffering."

In the Cizîr sağ portrays, the realism that characterizes documentarian testimony becomes available for testifying to violence monumentally by virtue of its environmental quality. Inspired by Nichanian's two modalities of testimony but also compelled by sağ's films to reconcile them, I term the survivor testimony her work presents *testimony as environment*. The term works against the grain of recent formulations of the environment or the earth as a witness to violence. These formulations either remain oriented toward documentability or rush to denounce Eurocentric-humanist vision and reason without questioning how such Eurocentrisms continue to implicate even the most avowedly non-Eurocentric scholar and artist insofar as these scholars and artists operate within the current global knowledge economy. Testimony as environment is dedicated neither to figuration nor to documentation alone but to relation: the power relations within which survivors claim agency by insisting that both figurative and documentational modalities remain at their disposal in the face of disparate and ever-changing norms that ascribe political, ethical, or epistemic potency to one modality or the other. Testimony as environment reveals the ways this claim to agency is articulated from and addressed to specific positionalities inflected by unequal power relations, rather than aiming for and speaking to power in general. But it also reveals how the specificity of these positionalities does not mean they are fixed in time and space. Indeed, this unfixity is part of the reason testimony as environment merits recognition for its environmental quality. At times, sağ's being a woman activist who has recently worked with children in Cizîr allows for positional overlaps with the residents, which materialize in the cohabitation of domestic space and quotidian time. At other times, her being from the west of Turkey or a professional visual practitioner aligns her with power, an alignment that manifests especially in what residents do to and with her camera. Her work's challenge to the extractivist gaze involves not replacing this gaze but acknowledging one's own implication in it and using that acknowledgment as room for continual action and rearticulation of positionalities and relations rather than for defeatism and fixation.

This chapter's exploration of extractivism as a question that implicates visual production has worked from recent and ongoing war to arrive at a history of genocidal violence that is more than a century old. The next chapter pushes this exploration further by discussing a series of artworks contemporaneous with sağ's films in Cizîr that also bear the imprint of this history but do so by entangling art in extractivism materially rather than only formally.

5

HAUNTING AS ECOLOGY AND COUNTEREXTRACTIVIST AESTHETICS

THE 2015 OUTBREAK OF FULL-BLOWN war in northern Kurdistan involved a mode of violence that was overt and embodied. The half decade preceding it had seen violence's "structural" and "slow" workings become a prominent theme in the country's political and cultural mainstream.[1] Events surrounding the Gezi Park protests, which erupted in Istanbul against a government-endorsed speculative development project threatening one of the few remaining green spaces in central Istanbul and then spread across Turkey, had made unprecedentedly visible the slow violence of an economic model reliant on extractivist industries like construction. The violent histories that have structured modern Turkey as we know it were thrust into the mainstream as the government began in the late 2000s and early 2010s to engage with calls to "confront the past"—meaning past episodes of state violence—in the context of a neoliberal democratization initiative propelled by EU membership talks.[2] The first half of 2015 had witnessed both these processes reach a zenith. Much of the political dissidence emanating from the Gezi protests had fed into the pro-Kurdish party HDP's campaign ahead of the June 7 general election, leading to their unprecedented victory with the third-largest share of parliamentary seats.[3] April 24 that year had witnessed the centenary of the Armenian genocide—Turkey's founding episode of state violence—and thousands, including survivors' descendants traveling from different parts of the world, had gathered in the country's foremost public space, Taksim Square in Istanbul, to commemorate the victims.[4] The growing mainstream interest in the slow and structural workings of violence was observable in the art world, too, most famously in the 14th Istanbul Biennial, Turkey's largest contemporary art event. Themed "Saltwater"—in its curator's words, "the water of our tears"—and launched as war broke out in northern Kurdistan, the biennial's curatorial framework both engaged questions around "the catastrophes of the Anthropocene" and directly referenced "the brutal cleansing of" Armenians "associated with the year 1915" as an "unresolved" history that would be "interwoven into the texture of the whole exhibition."[5]

What happens when images of direct and embodied violence burst in on the center of a national contemporary art context preoccupied with violence's structural and slow workings? What critical responses might arise from such a context, and how might they inform existing approaches to extractivism's aesthetics? In this chapter, I explore these questions as hauntological ones. I think with two examples of artistic practice from western Turkey: *Meteors* (2017), an experimental film by Gürcan Keltek that revolves around the recent war in northern Kurdistan, and *In the Rivers of the North of the Future* (2014–2017), a series of watercolors and a video portraying them by contemporary artist İz Öztat that address water extractivism across Turkey. Both works merit a hauntological approach not only because they include verbal references to haunting but also because they imbricate—if not always intentionally—war and the genocide materially. They do so in line with what I term *counterextractivist aesthetics*, as the artists appropriate extractivism's abstracting techniques to expose extractivist violence. Here, the structural and environmental violence that had become a prominent artistic theme in Turkey in the lead-up to the mid-2010s war haunts the ways this war is encountered through its images, and vice versa. The filmmakers activate this bilateral ghostliness by minimizing chromatics to the effect of foregrounding materiality, which opens to debate the preoccupation with absence/presence that characterizes much hauntology scholarship. While operating to a distinct political effect in each work, this formal technique shifts the site of haunting from individuals, objects, or places to the relations between and among them, or to "ecologies" in a Batesonian-Guattarian sense. This shift toward ecology in turn brings relationality and the collective work of making, unmaking, and remaking relations to the fore as the site within which to act upon the histories constituting the stuff of haunting.

GENOCIDE HAUNTING WAR, OR SHADOWS OF TREASURE HUNTING

I begin with *Meteors*, an eighty-one-minute-long film named after its penultimate section—one of a total of six. Keltek's film interweaves two types of footage. The first is found footage of events surrounding the mid-2010s war in northern Kurdistan, which the filmmaker sourced online as he was following the war at home in western Turkey. The second type of footage is material Keltek himself filmed, including landscapes he had shot during his previous visits to the region and new scenes he staged for this film. In the filmmaker's own words:

> I had become sick with a hospital virus and was housebound. While sitting at home, I began to watch Periscope broadcasts from southeastern Anatolia—especially from Sur, Cizre, and Diyarbakır. My main aim was to find out what was happening there. But watching these broadcasts for such a long time, I realized something: you would see static shots for, say, 45 minutes, but then an incredible moment would transpire and that is in fact what cinema is. I began stumbling on these incredible moments and recorded some of them.[6]

Meteors is rendered entirely in black and white. While this ameliorates the visual discrepancies resulting from the multiplicity of footage sources, it is more than just a pragmatic fix. Divesting from color helps Keltek engage the critical potential of other formal aspects of film, such as exposure, focus, and resolution—an engagement that manifests in his repeated stretching of footage to its material limits by zooming inward, enlarging, or defocusing (figure 5.1). The critical potential at work here concerns an invitation to reflect on the violent events being portrayed, on images' role in them, and on visuality's historical centrality to colonialist and nation-statist violence at large as questions of a strictly material nature.

The opening section sets the tone for this invitation. Titled "Hunters," it comprises scenes of mountain-goat hunting. The species being hunted is famously endemic to the mountains of northern Kurdistan and distinguishable by the males' curled horns, which are larger than their head. Following the 1980s and 1990s, when these mountains were premier settings of guerrilla war and counterinsurgency, informal peace talks in the 2000s and the accompanying deceleration of violence encouraged hunters to take to the mountains, pushing the goats toward extinction. Growing public criticism

FIGURE 5.1. Stills from Gürcan Keltek's film *Meteors* (reproduced with the artist's permission).

of this development led the central government to begin to regulate hunting activity in the name of conservation, which effectively legalized it. As of the 2020s, hunting permits are still being issued, especially to foreign agencies marketing this activity as an upmarket touristic product to North European and North American customers.[7] "Hunters" teems with footage that zooms in to and out from the mountains and scans them for the goats, resembling what a hunter would have done with a rifle scope—a resemblance aided by achromatization (figure 5.2). This first section orients the film's use of black and white toward highlighting the inextricable links between violence and visuality and considering landscape as their product. Indeed, "Landscape" was the theme of the annual film festival in London dedicated to "the cinema of the real," where I first watched *Meteors* in 2018.[8] In the postscreening Q and A, Keltek said that, coupled with achromatization, focusing on the landscape "protected" the film from "embroilment in current politics" and rendered it "universal" in tone.

The film's intended universalism relies significantly on Keltek's attention to the supernatural—a force that has long been influential on notions and experiences of landscape in many parts of the world. The section that titles the film, "Meteors," is especially marked by this attention. It revolves around a meteorite shower that took place on September 2, 2015, in northern Kurdistan just as war was reaccelerating. The section begins with extreme long shots of the skies, filmed by local residents and journalists from a Russian

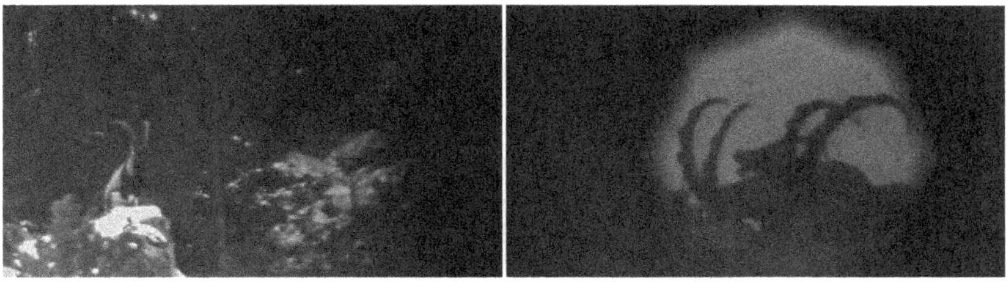

FIGURE 5.2. Stills from Gürcan Keltek's film *Meteors* (reproduced with the artist's permission).

news agency who were there to follow the war in neighboring Syria (figure 5.3). They happen upon the meteors but assume the noise and the lights are from military activity. The sequence then turns to footage and interviews filmed by journalists who visited the village of Sarıçiçek in Bingöl Province (Çewlîg, in Kurdish), about 140 kilometers north of Amed, where the meteorites fell in the hundreds (figure 5.4). Villagers explain how they initially did not make much of the celestial event as they mistook it for war and so went to sleep. But upon realizing its true nature, they began scanning the fields for meteorites using precious metal detectors. Meanwhile, researchers from the local university arrive at the scene and, noticing the scientific importance of the event, inform astronomers from universities in western Turkey. These astronomers, in turn, contact their European and North American counterparts, including those from NASA, and travel together with the latter to the village, where they buy meteorite samples from the villagers to take away to their labs.[9] "Meteors" thus chronicles a celestial event that brings war informally and temporarily to a halt as the authorities facilitate a transactional process by granting outsiders access to a region otherwise subjected to increasing militarization and blockades. If the event's extraterrestrial character already renders it frameable as supernatural, this possibility is further consolidated in the film's following and final section. Titled "Mount Nemrut," the section comprises dramatic golden-hour shots of the ancient, giant deity statues for which this mountain in northern Kurdistan, located 160 kilometers west of Amed, is world-renowned (figure 5.5).

During my interview with Keltek, he acknowledged that the film's closing section is intended to enhance the supernaturalism of the penultimate "Meteors." In fact, supernaturalism also permeates the section immediately preceding "Meteors." Titled "Disintegration," this section features footage Keltek obtained from the archives of the Women's Initiative for Peace

FIGURES 5.3–5.5. Stills from Gürcan Keltek's film *Meteors* (reproduced with the artist's permission).

activists who, as discussed in the previous chapter with a focus on belit sağ, traveled from western Turkey to northern Kurdistan in the wake of the first episode of counterinsurgency siege of the region in 2015 (some of the footage used in "Disintegration" is identical to that featured in belit sağ's film *Sept.–Oct. 2015*—used here, sağ wishes to note, despite her disapproval [personal communication, February 2, 2025]). Documenting the siege's aftermath, the footage occasionally sees residents speak of a "bad spell" (*büyü*, in Turkish) cast and a "curse" (*ax*, in Kurdish, also meaning "soil" and "country," as expounded in the next chapter) put on the region. When I asked Keltek about these remarks, he said that unlike what he does in the final two sections, where *Meteors* thematically orients toward the supernatural, such an orientation was not his intention here. But I suggest that they, too, merit consideration in relation to the supernaturalism the director intentionally mobilizes later on in the film to universalize his treatment of the subject matter. These intermittent references to a "curse" and a "bad spell" serve, if unintentionally, to convey the context-specific reasons why the supernatural is a relevant thematic to mobilize in the first place. They oblige us to ground in particularity the universality that the director and others might associate with supernaturalism. The "bad spell" and "curse" invoked here are the residue of a violent history—the genocide against Armenians and Assyrian Syriacs that marked the late Ottoman Empire's transition into modern Turkey in northern Kurdistan. This residue is most extensively documented in Adnan Çelik and Namık Kemal Dinç's oral history book, whose title translates as "The century-old curse" and which chronicles the ways inhabitants of the region around Amed remember the genocide.[10] The inhabitants believe that the victims and survivors "cursed" not just the specific individuals who perpetrated, aided, or profited from genocide but the region in its entirety with profoundly material and spatial implications. For these inhabitants, the curse resides in local sites associated with the genocide (e.g., sites of massacre, kidnapping, and confiscated property) and manifests in environmental disasters that affect large parts of their region.[11]

The flip side to this disquieting supernaturalism is the activity of treasure hunting, which has become widespread in the region as documented by recent ethnographies. Writing about 2010s Mêrdîn (Mardin, in Turkish), located ninety kilometers southeast of Amed, Zerrin Özlem Biner documents narratives about jinn—supernatural creatures believed to dwell in haunted places—that circulate among inhabitants and users of properties confiscated in the genocide's wake. These narratives proliferate especially among individuals who dig for treasures the victims are rumored to have buried under their abandoned and confiscated stone houses. Biner discusses how treasure hunters often dig where they see or hear of signs associated with jinn presence, considering them as proof of the existence of treasures being haunted by their previous owners.[12] Taking seriously the marked visual character of the constant interplay between obscuration and discovery that characterizes treasure hunting, Alice von Bieberstein conceptualizes it as a "shadow" activity. She writes about mid-2010s Mûş, a city located two hundred kilometers northeast of Amed and one hundred kilometers east of the village that was the scene of the meteorite shower. Treasure hunters here rely on "ocular extensions such as the gold-detector" while also often operating "in the dark of the night" to evade "the surveilling eye of the state": digging for treasure is subject to bespoke search permits that treasure hunters find both bureaucratically onerous and financially unfavorable, with a 50 percent tax rate levied on any profits gained.[13] These recent ethnographies of treasure hunting in northern Kurdistan help make sense of why the residents of Sarıçiçek—the epicenter of the celestial event that titles Keltek's *Meteors*—were already in possession of the metal detectors they speak of in the film as they recount their meteorite search efforts. Prior to genocide, Sarıçiçek was an Armenian village named Darbasan. Online treasure hunters' forums have featured accounts of villagers caught up in the meteorite rain while treasure hunting with their metal detectors.[14] In *Meteors*, then, war is haunted more by genocide than it is by the celestial universe.

What might genocide's haunting of war—and doing so *visually*—mean for the politics of extractivism, which this book associates with coloniality? Since Jacques Derrida's and Avery Gordon's foundational works on hauntology, haunting has received growing attention in critical scholarship on the politics of coloniality in the Middle East.[15] A most recent and generative case in point is Nivi Manchanda and Sara Salem's discussion of violence and resistance in Egypt and Afghanistan. Inspired by Derrida's and Gordon's hauntologies, Manchanda and Salem challenge the ways scholars of "the Middle East" tend to premise empirical evidence on "presence" rather than "absence" and to pit "the present" (i.e., postcoloniality) against "the past" (i.e., coloniality) and "knowledge" against "feeling."[16] They challenge these tendencies by tracing recent developments in Afghanistan and Egypt to absences resulting from colonial legal infrastructures and from the postcolonial nationalization of the Suez Canal, respectively. This move centers "capitalism and imperialism as global structures that condition Middle Eastern politics."[17] Focusing one's understanding of "the Middle East" on such structural forces by attending to their "ghosts, invisibilities and intangible effects" also works to unsettle "empiricist approaches, such as the transition paradigm, and instead calls for a more radical approach to theory-making."[18]

A hauntology such as Manchanda and Salem's is useful for my discussion because it complicates the reduction of coloniality to colonies proper being in evidence. Moreover, the way they focus hauntology on infrastructures resonates with my theorization of extractivism through aesthetics: as a material politics of coloniality that makes sense literally—materially—by making sense of the earth and making it available to the senses. That said, I also wish to dwell further than they do on the visually and corporeally charged invocations of absence versus presence, invisibility versus visibility, and intangibility versus tangibility that frequently recur in their analysis, as is the case in much hauntological scholarship.[19] These invocations indicate a hauntology focused squarely on recovering what is rendered absent, invisible, or intangible through that which is present, visible, or tangible. Problematizing this focus, Martha Lincoln and Bruce Lincoln have critiqued new hauntological scholarship for its empirical imprecision.[20] Calling for a "critical hauntology," they have distinguished between "primary haunting"—haunting that has direct bodily (including psychic) implications such as specific individuals being haunted by ghosts proper—and "secondary haunting"—the kind of sociopolitical, cultural, and ethically charged but corporeally anonymous ghostliness that marks much hauntology scholarship.[21] For the Lincolns, unless hauntology scholarship acknowledges this distinction, it remains self-contradictory: it avows ghostliness's empirical significance and yet "denies ghosts ontologic status and recodes the unquiet dead as persisting in texts, memory, and uneasy silences rather than spirit."[22] Building on the Lincolns' distinction, Douglas Hollan has argued that the specificities characterizing different types of haunting require scholars to turn away from the "haunter end of the ghost/haunter–haunted relationship" to "the haunted" end: the "highly contingent and variable" relationalities which determine the haunted's "transferential flow of awareness and unawareness of ghosts."[23] He has theorized these relationalities as an "*ecology* of haunting" in Gregory Bateson's sense of the term: "a host of interconnecting and mutually sensitive feedback systems."[24]

Hollan's Batesonian conceptualization of haunting as dependent upon ecologies is necessary but insufficient for understanding the visual-ecological way genocide haunts war in Keltek's *Meteors*. Whether to universalize the situations the filmmaker portrays or to formally synthesize footage he has sourced from multiple sources, or even to accomplish both, Keltek has mobilized materiality. Coupling achromatization with a focus on landscapes, he has mobilized both the film's own materiality and that of the situations it portrays. Loosening them from the specific war in which they occurred has served to spotlight, if inadvertently, the long-standing relationalities that constitute ecology in the Batesonian sense and that condition the ways these situations are experienced, responded to, documented, and portrayed, including by the film itself. Recall the "curse" and the "bad spell," which residents consider cast upon "here," or the treasure-hunting infrastructure (i.e., the metal detectors and the treasure hunters) already in place, which is then repurposed for the meteorite search. Recall, too, the multiscalar (i.e., both local and international) relationalities interconnecting those who valuate, buy, and sell meteorites—activities exempted from the counterinsurgency siege laid over the region's towns and cities.[25] In such instances, genocide haunts war not ecologically *tout court* but *as* ecology itself. This haunting is graspable neither by prioritizing haunted individuals and their bodily experience over haunters nor by centering haunters as individuals who—having long been absent, invisible, or intangible—are recovered at long last by hauntologists. If anything, it calls into question the focus on individuals that is shared by these otherwise contrasting approaches to haunting.

Haunting as ecology operates somewhat akin to the legal and physical infrastructures that orient Manchanda and Salem's hauntology—like them, ecology is a structural force. But, by the same token, haunting as ecology is not addressable by recovering or experiencing that which has been absented. What is at stake in haunting as ecology is not absence and presence in and of themselves but rather the sociopolitical relationalities that condition the very production and distribution of absence and presence. *Meteors* throws these relationalities—this ecology—into sharp relief as the primary site of haunting due to Keltek's urge to avoid probing the boundaries of the "presentable"—the showable and the sayable—around the time of the film's production. The filmmaker has spoken to me of "the difficulty of producing work on ongoing developments" being "one reason why we did not show the film in Turkey"; of recent "Kafkaesque" laws that give those who document war firsthand a free pass but penalize those who use material produced by firsthand war documentarians to write or create work about war zones from a distance; of identifying not as "an activist filmmaker" but strictly as "a film director"; of "know[ing] the limits and the ambit of this" identification.[26] The urge to circumvent the structural dynamics invoked here by Keltek has led him to use a technique that has ended up conveying a history it was not meant to convey. The technique has mobilized materiality to the unintended effect of unearthing the historical event that has structured these dynamics and that has turned the landscapes portrayed in *Meteors* into "an extractive zone."[27] Because it is the film's mobilization of materiality that has led to this unintentional unearthing, the production and perpetuation of northern Kurdistan as an extractive zone figure in *Meteors* as a question that embroils the filmic medium even as the work itself is not neatly categorizable as extractivist or antiextractivist.[28]

WAR HAUNTING GENOCIDE, OR WATERY ECOLOGIES OF VIOLENCE

I turn now to a body of work another artist based in western Turkey, İz Öztat, produced near-simultaneously with the recent counterinsurgency campaign in northern Kurdistan. The work centers on her watercolor series titled *In the Rivers of the North of the Future* (2014–2017) but also involves three other works she authored or coauthored during the same period and in close conversation with the watercolors: the installation *Sculpture for Rainwater Harvest* (2014), the video *Recounting Nightmares to Running Water* (2015), and a second installation, *Who Carries the Water | Will Flow Free* (2015; with Fatma Belkıs). I discuss this body of work alongside Keltek's *Meteors* not only because they both mobilize materiality to render genocide the stuff of what I term *haunting as ecology* but also because Öztat's practice introduces a different angle to this ecohauntology. Her work, I suggest, indicates a hauntology operating in a temporal direction opposite to that of *Meteors*. Unlike Keltek's film, which takes war as its starting point but then ends up being haunted by genocide, Öztat works from genocide to then encounter war—the coloniality that the counterinsurgency campaign crystallized. This difference has important implications for the politics of haunting as ecology, especially with respect to the temporalities that characterize this haunting and the collective work required for transforming the systemic injustices that underpin it.

The process behind the watercolors of *In the Rivers of the North of the Future* originated in Öztat's 2014 installation *Sculpture for Rainwater Harvest* (figure 5.6). The installation was placed in Şişhane Park in Istanbul's Beyoğlu district, just minutes away from Gezi Park and Taksim Square, where the popular, ecologically motivated, and nonviolent protest movement of 2013 had erupted. The two sites are historically interconnected: until the early twentieth century, the site of today's Şişhane Park was part of a network of cemeteries whose centerpiece was the area around what is now Gezi Park. This historical fact was popularized during the 2013 protests when the fact of Gezi Park having been built (in the early 1940s) on an Armenian cemetery received wide media coverage. The Istanbulite Armenian activist group known as Nor Zartonk, who participated in the protests, developed the slogan "You took away our cemetery, but you will not be able to take away our park!"[29] As for Şişhane cemetery, while this was not a burial ground for non-Muslims, the surrounding area hosted a high concentration of non-Muslim residents and shops—until, that is, their subjection to early-twentieth-century processes of violent nation-state-making, which culminated here in the pogrom of September 6–7, 1955, against them.[30] This social upheaval was preceded by an environmental one. Şişhane cemetery began to disappear in the late nineteenth century when Eurocentric landscapist notions of the environment as a picturesque view to be enjoyed (rather than a place to be inhabited) combined with developmentalism to give the site its current spatial and topographical contours. Debris from the

FIGURE 5.6. Installation view of İz Öztat's *Sculpture for Rainwater Harvest* (photograph dated October 28, 2014; courtesy of the artist).

nearby construction site of a subway funicular line was brought here and used in landscaping the area in line with the Orientalist quest for unspoiled panoramas of Istanbul's historic peninsula. Alongside Şişhane Park, consequences of this landscaping included numerous newly built hotels, residences, and painting studios catering mainly to a Western clientele.[31] And then, in the 2010s, Şişhane Park itself became the subject of yet another landscaping revamp, with an exhibition titled *The Moving Museum* being held in 2014 to mark the occasion. Öztat's installation was commissioned for this exhibition. For forty-seven days, she took over four-fifths of a square meter of the park for her rainwater-harvesting structures, which collected eighty-two liters of rainwater.

Soon after she deinstalled the installation, Öztat began having nightmares about the histories she had encountered during her research. As a way of processing the nightmares, she decided to make watercolor paintings using the water she had harvested in Şişhane. This led to the more than two dozen watercolors that today compose *In the Rivers of the North of the Future*. The watercolors are both chromatically and formally minimalist, consisting of abstract brushstrokes in three colors only. "I limited

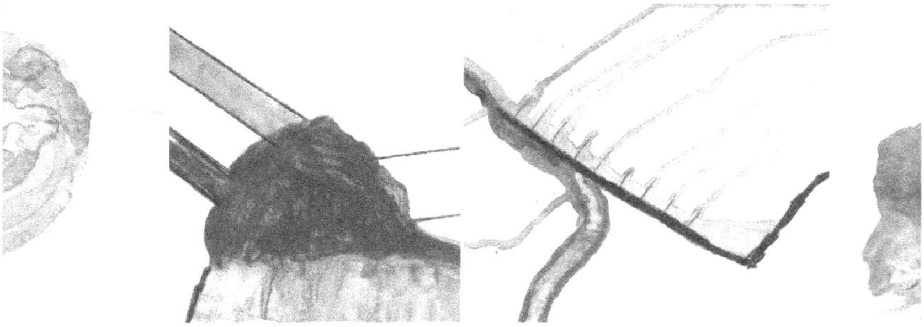

FIGURE 5.7. Stills from İz Öztat's video *Recounting Nightmares to Running Water* (reproduced with the artist's permission).

my color scale to blue, black, and red," Öztat has explained. "Black lines try to control flow and bring it into line, blue currents spring from red sources," all "abstract expressions of the ideas I had while reading" about water extractivism.[32] She then used the first batch of these watercolors to produce the nine-minute video *Recounting Nightmares to Running Water* (figure 5.7), titled after a tradition associated with Armenian folklore for preventing nightmares from coming true by telling them to running water and having them wash away.[33] In the video, the camera scrolls through the watercolors lined up next to one another as Öztat's stream-of-consciousness voice-over reflects on the nightmares. Much of her reflection is dedicated to interweaving Turkey's histories of violent nation-state-making with the destruction caused by widespread damming of its rivers for hydropower plants. "From the nightmares I laid in water, I pluck catastrophes,"[34] says Öztat, invoking the word *catastrophe*'s inextricable associations in this context with genocide, as well as its better-known sense of environmental disaster: "Their burdens vary. Some weigh as much as a ghost." As evidenced by these sentences and others throughout the video—for example, "The ghosts of dried rivers haunt urban citizens"—the work features haunting as a key way of bringing histories of Turkish nationalist violence to bear upon recent and ongoing environmental destruction.[35]

How might Öztat's work help us to better grasp what I term *haunting as ecology*—its visual-cultural relevance to extractivist politics? It is worth addressing this question first by taking seriously the two halves that together constitute the compound word *watercolor*—the name of the technique used by the artist. Both water and color have come to figure prominently in recent decolonial visual culture scholarship. Artistic practice has been considered potent for exposing water extractivism, for recovering relationships to water that coloniality has sought to suppress, and even for visually hindering extractive infrastructures by making geography invisible to them or by making it visible in ways radically different from and illegible to extractivist ones.[36] If Öztat's work also intervenes in the imbrications of visuality and water extractivism, it does so less in terms of visibility and invisibility than by engaging materiality. In incorporating water as a material in her work, she emphasizes the ways artistic practice is embroiled in extractivist histories even as it may seek to challenge them. In this sense, Öztat engages water as others have engaged color. "Color is a colonial subject," and recent scholarship has highlighted its centrality to exoticization of colonized places, exploitation of their lands, and appropriation of their knowledges.[37] Awareness of this centrality has inspired artistic researchers to recover—both materially and historiographically—Indigenous dyes extracted, industrialized, and appropriated by colonizers.[38] While Öztat's use of water in her watercolors resembles such artistic responses to color's embroilment in the racial violence of colonialism, it also differs from them. The difference is that she responds to this embroilment not as though it were a pragmatic question that artistic practice can resolve by recovering violently seized or suppressed knowledges but rather as the stuff of a ghostliness that implicates artistic practice and is thus irresolvable by artworks.

Water taken as a target of extractivism informs Öztat's engagement with the ghostliness at work here as a force that implicates artistic practice, because watery ecologies, like the visual ones in which art operates, are at once expansively relational and sociospatially specific. Note that her exploration of riverine extractivism—rivers being a prominent focus in much critical practice and scholarship on extractive politics—materially originates in rainwater she harvested herself. This extraction-evoking technique serves not only to highlight art's implication in the problem it explores but also to remind us of water's irreducibility to rivers—this reducibility being a major extractivist principle. As Dilip da Cunha has demonstrated, the concept of *river* is a colonial invention that has sought to discipline wetness by incarcerating it into a line with a source and a singular course, thus severing the inextricable entwinement between land and water.[39] Öztat seems to suggest that the context with which her work deals is one where turning to wetness instead of rivers does not resolve but instead exacerbates haunting. The suggestion recalls the way historian Talin Suciyan has spoken of the Armenian genocide's legacy in Turkey. According to her, while most critics of this legacy have settled for "using the state's archives to criticize the state's language," such an approach is bound to fall short as genocide denial is a "foundational paradigm."[40] Denial, Suciyan shows, is a state policy that originated contemporaneously with genocide itself and has since structured all areas of life from language and culture to law and economics, constituting a "habitus."[41] Her notion of genocide denial as habitus mirrors the way I speak of it in this chapter as the stuff of ecology; Suciyan says it operates "like the water we drink, the air we breathe, the seas we swim in."[42] To extract water from the atmosphere at a site central to Istanbul's visually charged histories of organized violence and dispossession, as Öztat does, is to engage them as the stuff of just such a habitus and ecology.

What critical potential might such an engagement bring forth? The question resonates with Christina Sharpe's discussion of "the wake" of slavery in the United States, which, reminiscently of Suciyan's conceptualization of genocide denial as an atmospheric and hydrospheric phenomenon, conceptualizes "antiblackness as total climate" or "atmosphere."[43] Whereas dominant US historiographies often portray slavery "as a singular event even as it changed over time and even as its duration expands into supposed emancipation and beyond," for Sharpe,

> slavery was not singular; it was, rather, a singularity—a weather event or phenomenon likely to occur around a particular time, or date, or set of circumstances. . . . In what I am calling the weather, antiblackness is pervasive as climate. The weather necessitates changeability and improvisation; it is the atmospheric condition of time and place; it produces new ecologies. *Ecology: the branch of biology that deals with the relations of organisms to one another and to their physical surroundings; the political movement that seeks to protect the environment, especially from pollution.* . . . But the shipped, the held, and those in the wake also produce out of the weather their own ecologies.[44]

Such new ecologies are what Öztat set out to explore in *Who Carries the Water*, an installation that immediately followed on from her first batch of watercolors and the video that featured them. As part of her collaboration with the contemporary artist Fatma Belkıs, the installation's research phase saw the pair travel to various parts of Turkey where dam construction projects for run-of-the-river hydropower plants had sparked grassroots resistance. Among all the places they visited, the one that left the most indelible imprint on Öztat was Dêrsim, a historical province situated in the northernmost tip of Mesopotamia (about two hundred kilometers north of Amed).[45] Following the genocide of 1915–1916 that wreaked havoc across Dêrsim's Armenian villages, its predominantly Alevi population became the target of a genocidal campaign in 1937–1938 that the state carried out in the name of counterinsurgency.[46] Öztat and Belkıs's visit to the region coincided with an Armenian genocide centennial commemoration held there by a group of activists hailing from Dêrsim and identifying as descendants of genocide survivors (mainly women) adopted or abducted, or both, by non-Armenian families.[47] The commemoration was held in the countryside at a cliff infamous for having witnessed a massacre during the genocide—not far from the valleys now targeted by extractivist dam construction. Connections between 1915–1916, 1937–1938, and 2010s extractivism were thrown into sharper relief on another occasion during Öztat and Belkıs's Dêrsim visit: the reinauguration of a grave located on the shores of a new hydropower plant dam reservoir (figure 5.8). Rebuilt semiclandestinely by activists in the form of a tomb, the grave belongs to Armenak Bakırciyan, an Armenian and a leading member of the 1970s guerrilla organization TİKKO (Türkiye İşçi ve Köylü Kurtuluş Ordusu; literally, Workers' and Peasants' Liberation Army of Turkey), who was killed in 1980. TİKKO was founded in 1972 on the anniversary of the Armenian genocide, much of its membership hailed from Dêrsim, and its activities also centered on this region, leading

FIGURE 5.8. Inauguration of Armenak Bakırciyan's relocated grave site in Dêrsim (photograph courtesy of İz Öztat).

some to interpret its insurgency as retribution for 1915–1916 as well as 1937–1938.[48]

In acquainting themselves with how traditions of Armenian survivorship, revolutionary militancy, and contemporary eco-activism were imbricated with one another in Dêrsim, Öztat and Belkıs encountered not only verbal and textual material, such as beliefs and stories about land and water, but also material and visual techniques. Mimeography, a low-cost document-reproduction technology popular among 1970s revolutionary militants, was one such technique. Upon returning to Istanbul, Öztat and Belkıs contacted veteran revolutionaries there and learned of a disused mimeograph. They had it repaired and used it for producing leaflets that became part of their *Who Carries the Water* installation (figure 5.9). The leaflets present "a fictional dialogue" featuring "human and nonhuman elements" such as River, Ghost, Artist, and Academic.[49] The lines in this dialogue come from sources Öztat and Belkıs encountered during their research and are interspersed with texts the pair penned themselves.[50] Alongside chronicling environmental harm, these texts imply epistemic and artistic representation's complicity in it. They are rich with allusions to scholarly concepts thingifying life, bucolic representations overriding complex local traditions, theorists setting up power plants on schools of thought, and villagers emphasizing that their village is their home and not metaphor or scenery, as artists and academics would have it. In this way, Öztat and Belkıs interweave the various ecologies featured in their work, including artistic, scholarly, activist, statist, and natural ones.

Simultaneously with *Who Carries the Water* meeting audiences for the first time as part of the 14th Istanbul Biennial, war intensified in northern Kurdistan. In late 2015, Öztat returned to producing the watercolors as a way of coping with having to witness war from a distance. In late December, she joined a group of activists known as I'm Marching to Peace, who traveled from southwestern Turkey to Amed to witness the war firsthand and show solidarity. Five of their members were arrested. An article Öztat wrote to reflect on the trip, illustrated with one of the watercolors, speaks repeatedly of being haunted by ghosts of catastrophes and frequently cites the Ottoman Armenian woman writer Zabel Yesayan's 1911 book on a massacre in southern Turkey that was the prelude to the genocide.[51] When I asked Öztat what led her to take part in the trip, she referred me back to the process behind *Who Carries the Water*. The process meant that places now targeted by the counterinsurgency campaign "were no longer unfamiliar places; they are places where you have made friends and you want to be able to look into their eyes when all this ends."[52] As war raged into 2016, the artist

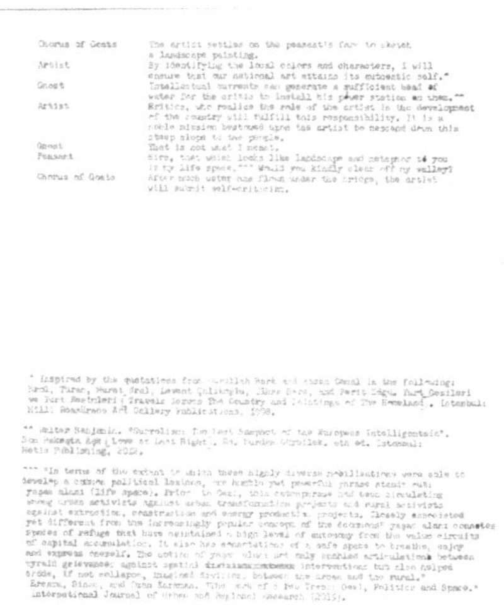

Chorus of Goats	The artist settles on the peasant's farm to sketch a landscape painting.
Artist	By identifying the local colors and characters, I will ensure that our national art attains its authentic self.*
Ghost	Intellectual currents can generate a sufficient head of water for the critic to install his power station on them.**
Artist	Critics, who realize the role of the artist in the development of the country will fulfill this responsibility. It is a noble mission bestowed upon the artist to descend down this steep slope to the people.
Ghost	That is not what I meant.
Peasant	Sirs, that which looks like landscape and metaphor to you is my life space.*** Would you kindly clear off my valley?
Chorus of Goats	After much water has flown under the bridge, the artist will submit self-criticism.

* Inspired by the quotations from [illegible] and [illegible] in the following: [illegible], Turan, Murat Ural, Levent Çalıkoğlu, [illegible], and Ferit Edgü. Yurt Gezileri ve Yurt Resimleri (Travels Across The Country and Paintings of The Homeland). Istanbul: Milli Reasürans Art Gallery Publications, 1998.

** Walter Benjamin. "Surrealism: The Last Snapshot of the European Intelligentsia". Son Bakışta Aşk (Love at Last Sight). Ed. Nurdan Gürbilek. 6th ed. Istanbul: Metis Publishing, 2012.

*** "In terms of the extent to which these highly diverse mobilizations were able to develop a common political lexicon, one humble yet powerful phrase stands out: yaşam alanı (life space). Prior to Gezi, this catchphrase had been circulating among urban activists against urban transformation projects and rural activists against extraction, construction and energy production projects. Closely associated yet different from the increasingly popular concept of the 'commons' yaşam alanı connotes spaces of refuge that have maintained a high level of autonomy from the value circuits of capital accumulation. It also has connotations of a safe space to breathe, enjoy and express oneself. The notion of yaşam alanı not only enabled articulations between myriad grievances against spatial interventions but also helped erode, if not collapse, imagined divisions between the urban and the rural." Erensü, Sinan, and Ozan Karaman. "The Work of a Few Trees: Gezi, Politics and Space." International Journal of Urban and Regional Research (2015).

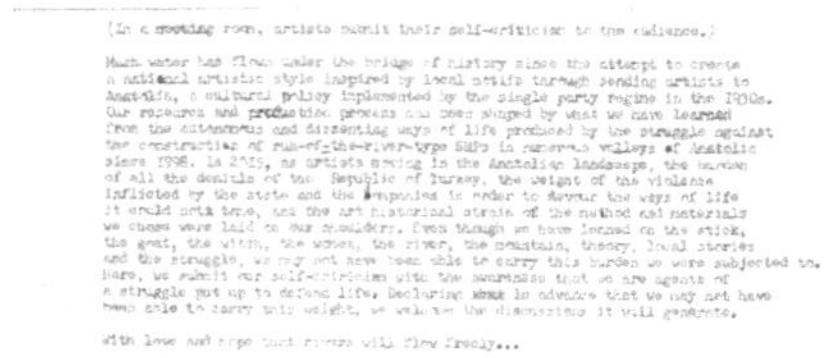

(In a meeting room, artists submit their self-criticism to the audience.)

Much water has flown under the bridge of history since the attempt to create a national artistic style inspired by local motifs through sending artists to Anatolia, a cultural policy implemented by the single party regime in the 1930s. Our research and production process has been shaped by what we have learned from the autonomous and dissenting ways of life produced by the struggle against the construction of run-of-the-river-type HEPs in numerous valleys of Anatolia since 1998. In 2015, as artists moving in the Anatolian landscape, the burden of all the denials of the Republic of Turkey, the weight of the violence inflicted by the state and the companies in order to devour the ways of life it could not tame, and the art historical strain of the method and materials we chose were laid on our shoulders. Even though we have leaned on the stick, the goat, the witch, the women, the river, the mountain, theory, local stories and the struggle, we may not have been able to carry this burden we were subjected to. Here, we submit our self-criticism with the awareness that we are agents of a struggle put up to defend life. Declaring in advance that we may not have been able to carry this weight, we welcome the discussions it will generate.

With love and hope that rivers will flow freely...

FIGURE 5.9. Top: Pages 13 and 17 of the mimeographed leaflets. Bottom: Installation view of İz Oztat and Fatma Belkıs's work *Who Carries the Water | Will Flow Free* (2015; wood-printed, naturally dyed muslin) as photographed by Kayhan Kaygusuz during the exhibition *Yield Events* held in 2024 at Bayetav Sanat, İzmir (courtesy of the artists).

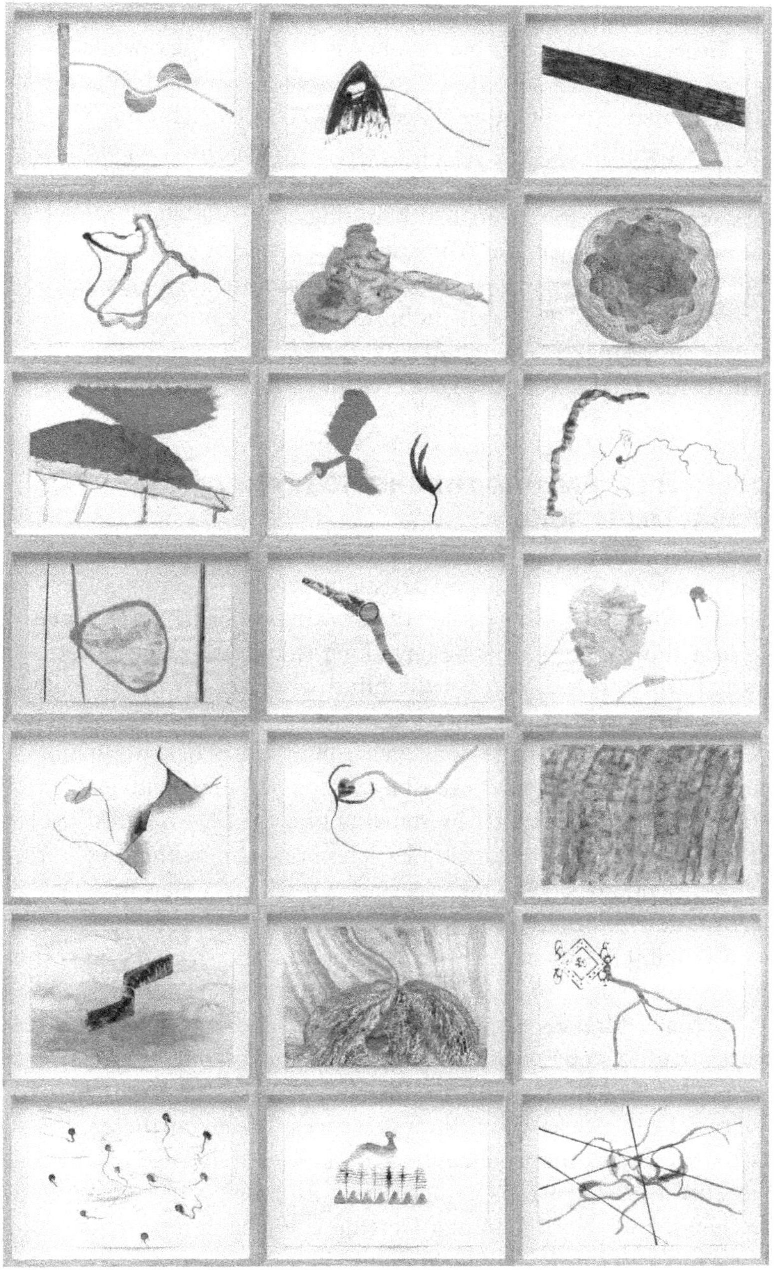

FIGURE 5.10. Watercolors from İz Öztat's *In the Rivers of the North of the Future* series (courtesy of the artist).

continued to make the watercolors, and they eventually became the series *In the Rivers of the North of the Future* (figure 5.10). Meanwhile, together with her coconspirator Belkıs (alongside Özgür Atlagan and Nihan Somay), Öztat instituted a cooperative called BAÇOY-KOOP (Basma, Çoğaltma, Yayma Kooperatifi; literally: Print, Copy, Distribution Cooperative) dedicated to using mimeography for collective and independent publishing. Öztat's response to the ecological hauntings that she encountered while researching *Who Carries the Water*, and to those that confronted her later during the war in northern Kurdistan, has therefore been oriented toward collectivizing, organizing, and mobilizing—an orientation which artistically manifested in the production techniques and methods she used rather than in formal characteristics of the artworks.

COUNTEREXTRACTING THE GHOSTS THAT STRUCTURE VISUAL MEDIATION

In this chapter, I have discussed artistic practices whose mobilization of materiality throws into sharp relief the workings of haunting as ecology. As anti-racist thought and struggle have long shown us, racial injustices are not simply the result of ideas in the mind. They are organized materially, including through environments and landscapes, and so, too, must be the work of grasping and challenging racial injustices. Focusing haunting as ecology on the two art practices I have discussed here contributes to this fundamental insight not only by showing that the materialities at work in racial injustices and their ongoing legacies are co-constituted by both that which is absent, invisible, intangible and that which is present, visible, tangible. My contribution is also that these absences/presences, (in)visibilities, and (in)tangibilities must be taken seriously for their visual and corporeal undertones. As a field of practice whose mainstay is corporeality and visuality, art that addresses extractivism-afflicted landscapes and particularly artworks that do so by prioritizing materiality over content are instructive for situating extractivist politics in the absences engendered by long histories of racial violence as well as their presences. Taken together, Keltek's and Öztat's work shows that ecohauntologies of racial violence involve multiple visually mediated arenas, ranging from militancy and activism to petty trade, news, and the arts. When Derrida coined the term *hauntology* in 1994, he spoke of "media tele-technology" in terms resonant with how I use *aesthetics* in this book, writing that it "assures and determines the spacing of public space, the very possibility of the res publica and the phenomenality of the political" and, as such, "itself is neither living nor dead, present nor absent: it spectralizes."[53] This chapter has indicated that the characteristics Derrida attributed to the news media characterize all realms of marketized visual mediation, including art, and that this media tele-technology does not simply spectralize; it is in fact haunted by ghosts of its own.

In *Meteors*, genocide's ghosts haunt the mediation of counterinsurgency-era northern Kurdistan by revealing, if unintentionally, that the ecologies that became palpable here at this historical juncture in fact stretched back to absences inflicted by genocide. In Öztat's body of work, there are glimpses of ecologies that not only result from but also challenge ghostliness.[54] Here, war haunts the mediation of genocide by permeating artistic expressions initially envisaged to help process ghosts of the past, and by engendering new forms of organizing. Considering these two examples of practice together requires rethinking the temporality of haunting in relation to extractivism. Temporality is a question that, compared to spatiality, has remained underexplored in hauntology scholarship. An important exception is the work of Mark Fisher. Writing against the grain of those who conflate haunting with "the *no longer*" of avowedly progressive past sociopolitical projects and therefore with nostalgia and melancholy, Fisher instead theorized haunting as involving "the *not yet* of the futures that popular modernism trained us to expect, but which never materialized"—as "spectres of lost futures."[55] That foregrounding materiality in one's exploration of nation-founding violence may lead contemporary war to haunt the mediation of past genocide—just as it may cause the genocide to haunt the war—introduces the "always already" to Fisher's dyad of the "no longer" and the "not yet." If avowedly progressive sociopolitical projects throughout modernity have always already extracted from racialized populations and lands, then the ecologies haunted by their lost futures may well engender nonextractivist pathways. And in geographical and sectoral contexts that remain totally—climatically—structured by both past genocidal violence and present-day genocide denial, a grounded manner in which to start following these pathways may well involve counterextractivist aesthetics: turning the abstracting and absenting techniques that are the hallmark of extractivism against it rather than chasing new ones in a rush to break with extractivist abstractions and to make absences present.

In her book *In the Wake*, Christina Sharpe immediately follows her conceptualization of slavery as having engendered "ecologies" by saying that "the shipped, the held, and those in the wake also produce out of the weather their own ecologies. When the only certainty is the weather that produces a pervasive climate of antiblackness, what must we know in order to move through these environments in which the push is always toward Black death?"[56] In the final chapter, I consider Sharpe's question of "what must we know?" through an example of visual ecologies developed in Amed in the wake of the mid-2010s counterinsurgency campaign. That this example involved me in ways far more direct than those discussed in the previous chapters allows me to include myself in the "we" Sharpe references. That I inhabited this "we" primarily as a producer of academic knowledge prompts me to complement her question of "what must we know?" with the questions of "how" and "with whom must we know?"

MOVEMENT IN AND WITH ASHEN COUNTRY, OR TOWARD NONEXTRACTIVIST SCHOLARSHIP

THIS BOOK BEGAN WITH THE premise that if contemporary extractivism remains inextricable from sites of conventional extraction (e.g., mines, dams, coalpits, oil wells, etc.), it also operates irreducibly to them. The environmental violence taking place at sites of conventional extraction operates interdependently with other forces along the violence-culture continuum, ranging from the overtly violent and ostensibly anti-cultural (i.e., counterinsurgency) to the seemingly nonviolent and reputably highbrow (i.e., contemporary art). Grasping this interdependence requires approaching coloniality's relationship to extractivism as much more than simply a historical backdrop to processes now unfolding on a planetary scale. In northern Kurdistan—in the words of some of my collaborators, a "statusless colony"—the violence of extractivism is ongoing as an embodied and emplaced phenomenon. It is emplaced and embodied because it relies on the constant unmaking and remaking of the landscape and because it mobilizes the senses and sensibilities corporeally to obfuscate questions of responsibility and culpability and to foreclose the agency of collective political work carried out against it. The agency extractivism assigns to the colonized instead is an individualistic (whether heroized or villainized) one valuated in the quantifiably measurable terms of a marketable and minable resource. As this book has argued, critique of extractivism would fall short if it is exclusively understood as a socially and physically destructive enterprise. Much of extractivism today is about moving the senses and sensibilities (especially environmental and humanitarian ones), but doing so in line with a metrics that has long oriented extraction's geophysical movement of earth. As such, extractivism is about earthmoving—moving of and through earth—as per my context-specific rendition of *hafriyatçılık*, the Turkish word for the line of work that involves excavation and transport of soil, rubble, and debris.

Context-specificity has figured in this book not only as a feature of the extractivist movement involved in hafriyatçılık, or earthmoving. It has also figured as a feature of survival, critique, objection, and defiance through the word *ax*. Recall from the previous chapter that this is the word that Kurds use to mean "soil" and "country" as well as to talk about "curses" or "bad spells," including those believed to have been inherited from genocide against the region's non-Muslims and especially Armenians. The same word is also the foremost exclamation of mourning and lamentation in the Armenian language—particularly with respect to the genocide.[1] The Kurdish expression *axîn kişandin* means to pull, move from one place to another, weigh or carry *ax*—both in the geophysical sense and in the corporeal one of sighing mournfully as one works through loss. As such, *ax* best conveys not only that the politics of racial violence is a geological and environmental politics but also that communities obliged to live in and with its landscapes rely on and borrow from each other's cultures of survival, critique, objection, and defiance to make sense of this violence *otherwise*. To communicate in the English language the practices that engage this obligation, I have come to settle for *ax*'s etymological relative *ash*. If movement *of* and *through* earth is what extractivism does, its survivors, critics, objectors, and defiers move *in* and *with* ashen country. The collective work involved in this movement, then, is nameable as *ashwork*.

The context-specificity of the insights captured in these words is not intended for regional specialism. Rather, it is meant to resonate with relevant developments across today's warming and warring world. This is a world where extractive enterprise continues to intensify simultaneously with environmental harm's increasing visibility in mainstream consciousness and visual culture's consolidation as an extractivist industry unto itself. These simultaneous processes, which are palpably ongoing in northern Kurdistan and which therefore make it especially relevant to thinking about the rest of the world, imbue the question of extractivism with new complexity. The complexity is that what is at stake in extractivism is no longer its visibility or invisibility but, as this book has demonstrated through and through, what kinds of agency these various visibilities and invisibilities facilitate or hinder. Shifting away from the two extremes of heroic solutionism versus villainous complicity, the book has focused agency instead on relationality between differentially positioned subjects—subjects unevenly affected by and implicated in extractivism. The objective in so doing has been to recognize their opportunities for reciprocity and self-reflexive collaboration. To be sure, subjects unevenly affected by and implicated in extractivism include scholars like me who write about and theorize it. I therefore wish to return to the question I introduced just before I embarked on the book's core chapters. What might approaching extractivism as a question that implicates scholarship's own methodologies and epistemologies mean for theory's relation to ashwork?

THEORIZING AS REQUIRED BY ASHWORK

A growing number of scholars across the social sciences and the humanities today consider extractivism as a force that shapes their own positionalities vis-à-vis those of their nonacademic interlocutors: "The systemic extraction of raw commodities from (formerly) colonized countries finds its analog in academics' piratic practices of 'raw' data extraction for processing into refined intellectual property, to be published at prices which exclude the original contributing 'knowers.'"[2] "Academic extractivism" abstracts knowledge from the sociopolitical contexts within which it is produced, an abstraction that relies on a distinction between "theory . . . as a lens through which to view the world" and "practice" as the world itself, as "the realm of the practitioner."[3] Extractivist research methods, then, relate to "practitioner" interlocutors not as sociopolitical actors but only as resources of data to be mined and taken away to universities (often to those based in the Global North), where critical analysis, theorization, and dissemination turn data into valuable (commodified) knowledge. Recent self-reflexive responses to academic extractivism propose to abolish the dyad of "theory" (knowledge "refined" through critical analysis) versus "practice" ("raw" data to be analyzed) by involving interlocutors as equal partners in the entire research process from design to dissemination and by using both academic privilege and knowledge to empower marginalized communities.[4]

The process behind this book has in many ways resonated with these critical responses to academic extractivism. It began with me traveling to northern Kurdistan not for research in the conventional sense but for volunteer work coordinating an informal academy program on behalf of a local institution: a free-of-charge summer school on urban political ecology organized in 2019 by the local branch of the Chamber of Architects. The summer school's main venue was Loading, an independent artist-run space itself founded during the fallout from the recent counterinsurgency campaign. Loading's founders, Cengiz Tekin and Erkan Özgen, are members of the city's first generation of contemporary artists, both towering figures and mentors to many of their younger counterparts. Tekin and Özgen founded Loading in 2017 when, as part of the post-2016 purges, the central government suspended them from their day jobs as art teachers in the national education system (together with hundreds of others deemed to be PKK sympathizers). The pair rented a flat where they and other cultural producers experiencing a predicament like theirs could weather the storm collectively and productively. Loading began then as a coworking space, events venue, kitchen, archive, and library open to all, and even as its cofounders were eventually reinstated to their day jobs, it has continued to operate as such.

When we met during the summer school, Tekin and Özgen asked if I would volunteer to translate from English into Turkish parts of an edited volume on Loading they were then preparing. Having translated these pieces, I volunteered to translate parts of Özgen's portfolio into English. The pair's appreciation of this work upon positive feedback from their contacts in the Anglophone art world led them to invite me as their inaugural resident in the summer and early fall of 2019. Although the resident profile they had initially had in mind involved artists, "no problem," said Tekin and Özgen, "we'll call it an artist/researcher residency" to include someone like me who is a researcher but not an artist. The residency saw me coordinate four workshops on ecology (three in collaboration with Amed-based women from relevant professions, including Dicle Beştaş, who soon afterward became Loading's program coordinator). I also wrote the proposal for a workshop series that I then coordinated in 2020–2021. Participation in these workshops was free of charge and was geared toward emerging artists and researchers from Amed and its environs. In certain respects, then, the process that eventually birthed this book resonated with the principles of social empowerment and equal partnership of interlocutors that critics of academic extractivism have advocated: it saw me partner with Loading—a partnership that has since continued—and adopt their commitment to empowering those on the margins of the institutional art world.

But the research process also threw up situations that complicate the tendency of academic extractivism's scholarly critics to consider the object of their critique resolvable by abolishing the dyad of theory and practice.

When preparing to begin my researcher residency at Loading, I was keen to disavow the positionality of a critical analyst and theorist due to my familiarity with the critiques of academic extractivism highlighted above. I made every effort to position myself as a practitioner (my practice being teaching and writing), hence my work in delivering the various workshops and translations for Loading and for the local branch of the Chamber of Architects. But I was soon confronted with expectations that repositioned me as a producer of critical analysis and theory. During the summer school organized by the local branch of the Chamber of Architects, an activist-architect involved in the coordination, with whom I would later coauthor a book chapter for an edited volume, picked up on my intermittent references to UK-based developments relevant to the politics of ecology.[5] He asked me if I could dedicate more of my teaching to such developments from across the world and then relate them back to the context of Turkey and Kurdistan, effectively describing one of theory's main purposes. Indeed, Loading's cofounders had appreciated my translations not because they were word-for-word copies of the originals in a different language but because they were "makeovers" in a sense reminiscent of Walter Benjamin's notion of translation as the transmission of "inessential" and "emotional" content rather than only the reproduction of meaning.[6]

These exchanges were only the first signs of my being repositioned as a theorist. Loading's cofounders repeatedly said, "We're confident about our practice, we've got a bit of a theory deficiency" (pratiğimize güvenimiz tam, teori konusunda biraz eksiğiz). While they had full faith in their home city's artistic capacities, they felt it could benefit from the input of theorists capable of criticism that is innovative, that does their work justice, and that would be legible to art critics and institutions worldwide. Making Loading's work legible to wider sets of actors was often an acutely practical question due to needing funding to sustain it as a space open to all. Loading's funders to date had not welcomed proposals that were theoretically framed but had imposed such frameworks on it instead—frameworks that often contrasted sharply with the cofounders' own ideas regarding what makes their work significant. Having come across a new funding call during my residency, Tekin and Özgen asked if I could write the proposal for it by creating a theoretical framework that would translate Loading's work for an audience familiar with the latest artistic and cultural developments relevant to the politics of ecology, leading to the workshop series we coordinated in 2020–2021 (online due to the COVID-19 pandemic).

Such instances indicate that retaining the theory-versus-practice dyad might in fact be conducive rather than inimical to social empowerment and equal partnership of interlocutors. What might this conduciveness mean for the ways we grasp and challenge academic extractivism? Worth revisiting here is the fundamental problem of abstracting knowledge from its sociopolitical contexts that, as mentioned above, characterizes academic extractivism according to its critics. Interlocutors develop ideas and practices not simply because they are novel but primarily because they are socially and politically useful—because they matter to the political claims and the social formations that bring communities together and that, in colonialism-afflicted contexts, are fundamentally about the community's sovereignty over its own life.[7] Even scholarship that celebrates the ideas and the practices of the marginalized might become entangled in extractivism if it erases the political claims and the social formations as part of which those ideas and practices are developed.[8]

My point is that visual culture is a discrete realm for communities to organize sociopolitically for regaining sovereignty over their own lives, and its appraisal as such must center not on *individuals* (be they academics or their nonacademic interlocutors) but on *institutions* (understood in the broadest sense possible as social formations that organize and are organized around political claims). Loading is testament that such institutions already exist in relevant contexts.[9] Seen in this light, then, the question of addressing academic extractivism becomes less about abolishing the theory-versus-practice dyad (or, for that matter, altogether collapsing the positionalities of the academic theorist and the nonacademic practitioner). Insofar as this dyad remains a practical reality of the institutional lives that involve the same interlocutors whom academic researchers wish to empower and partner with, its abolition is useful only as a collectively approachable horizon rather than as a task achievable by individual scholars. If anything, treating it as an individual task may even create a new imposition on interlocutors that is unhelpful for tackling the challenges facing them. The question is instead about letting the interlocutors take the lead in deciding whatever academic skills, including theorization, may benefit the institutions they already have in place.[10]

ASHWORK ESCAPING ACADEMIZED THEORY

Recognizing the usefulness of the theory-versus-practice dyad does not mean that it cannot be rethought. The process behind this book also has implications for such rethinking. Consider the workshop series that Loading invited me to coordinate in 2020–2021, where my role included providing the theoretical framework at the proposal stage. Titled "Photography's Violent Ecology," the series proposed to "reconsider photography's increasingly prominent role in the recent violence that Amed and the surrounding region have witnessed." Instead of "taking at face value the promise of documenting violence truthfully that photographs are often ascribed in such contexts," the series aimed "to foster a critical and self-reflexive practice that attends to the techniques, gazes, perspectives and circulation mechanisms involved in photography."[11] Hailing from Amed and its environs, the participants all had a long-standing commitment to documenting relevant sites and events in the region.

Indeed, several of the workshop participants developed new works during the series by revisiting material they had produced long before it. Among them is Sedat Akdoğan's video trilogy *About Dry Land and Soft Clouds*. It repurposes photographs Akdoğan took in the late 2000s and early 2010s, the period widely associated with a peace process in northern Kurdistan. Each composed of a minute-long loop, the videos index the multilayered and ongoing histories of violence that have imbricated nation-statism with coloniality to turn northern Kurdistan into a site of extractivism. One video, for example, reuses a photograph of kids playing around a pit in an abandoned building in Amed's historic center of Suriçi (figure 6.1). Due to the all-out war that erupted only half a decade after Akdoğan took the photograph and that killed tens of youth in just such buildings, this scene of kids' play is now rendered uncanny. Collaged into the pit is a different photograph: one of a mountain, a landscape that is as beautiful as it is an unmistakable symbol of insurgency in this context where "going to the mountain" is a euphemism for joining the guerrillas.[12]

In addition to interlinking these different spaces involved in the ever-protracted war and the constituents that have moved between them, Akdoğan's collage invokes treasure hunting. Suriçi and other historic districts in the region witnessed a boom in treasure hunting following the recent counterinsurgency campaign. Treasure hunters have included security personnel operating behind security fencing mounted by the authorities during the fighting and then kept in place for several years on grounds that the area needed protection against just such looting activity.[13] As news of Suriçi's historic buildings—like the one shown in Akdoğan's 2009 photograph—being dug up for treasure failed to create any outrage in Turkey, another incident of treasure hunting made the headlines. The so-called Bottomless Tarn in the Black Sea highlands, whose widely circulated photographs of water reflections Akdoğan's collage invokes, was dug up by treasure hunters with an official permit, to the extent that it dried up entirely. In

FIGURE 6.1. Still from Sedat Akdoğan's video trilogy *About Dry Land and Soft Clouds* (reproduced with the artist's permission).

lamenting the destruction of the tarn, mainstream Turkish media pointed to the handful of individuals who dug it up for treasure and those who issued their permit: the "ignorance" of a few had destroyed a rare natural beauty.[14] The histories referenced in this media coverage remained limited to the volcanic tarn's twelve-thousand-year-old geologic history; the Later Roman Empire, whose rumored treasures the hunters had referenced in their permit application; and the space of a few recent days in which the dig had taken place. What the media omitted was the fact that the very village hosting the tarn was, until the transition from the Ottoman Empire to the Republic of Turkey, home to Greek-speaking non-Muslim populations and that treasure hunters have long raided the area due precisely to this history.[15] Akdoğan's collage speaks to this omission. It intersects older histories of non-Muslim dispossession with more recent ones of war. It moreover traces the ongoing injustices arising from this intersection in the glaring difference between the outrage with which the Bottomless Tarn case has been received in Turkey while events in Suriçi have largely been ignored.

Another work produced during "Photography's Violent Ecology" is Pınar Süer Alpkaya's video *Hidden* (figure 6.2). The video revolves around an abandoned hamlet located right in the middle of the first two dams built on the Tigris. The hamlet is part of a larger, formerly Armenian village called Hretan which, following the genocide, was settled by Muslim Kurds and renamed as Kırkpınar. The village was evacuated during the 1990s state of emergency that accompanied the state's counterinsurgency campaign in northern Kurdistan. While the hamlet featured in Alpkaya's work is called Layeyayru in the local Kurdish dialect of Zazaki, its official Turkified name is Aşağı Saklı, which literally translates as "Lower Hidden"—hence the video's title. The audio track comprises villagers' testimonies about the impact of the dams on the village's ecosystem, climate, and agriculture. Overlain with this audio is silent footage of abandoned buildings and devastated flora and fauna. The scenes are not only from the hamlet itself but also from the living room of the artist's own home in central Amed, where printed stills of footage filmed on-site are hung. Close-ups of a decomposing pomegranate dominate these scenes. Long considered by Armenians as a symbol of postgenocide survival, the pomegranate has recently become appropriated by mainstream approaches to remembering this violent history. The 2016 exhibition "With the Intention of Pomegranate: Time to Remember Not to Forget" organized by the Turkish state, for example, romanticized the pregenocide past as one where Turks and Armenians coexisted peacefully, implying that the genocide was a necessary if unfortunate measure against Armenian insurgents provoked by the West to turn on their Turkish brethren.[16]

Hidden exposes the gendered links between genocide and war by deromanticizing and repoliticizing the pomegranate as a more-than-symbolic feature of material ecologies in today's northern Kurdistan. The testifying villagers, some of whom, we learn, are grandchildren of Armenian women abducted during the genocide, explain that the pomegranate trees are in a terrible state due to a nonnative pest commonly known as medfly. The pest only appeared here after the 2000s, when the two dams just upstream of the village went into operation and unprecedentedly humidified the upper Tigris's climate. The contemporary material ecologies within which the video situates the pomegranate involve photography, too: scenes show domestic walls adorned with stills of the pomegranate and its parasitic pest, taken from footage the artist filmed in the hamlet. That the stills are shown decorating this domestic and thus gendered setting implies Alpkaya's personal familiarity with and commitment to the sites portrayed, while also opening to debate the role of the medium of photography in rendering scenic the kind of violent histories that have shaped this village. *Hidden* throws extractivism into sharp relief for being as much about gendered racial violence as about dam-building and climate change, while also gesturing toward photography's implication in all of these extractivist processes.

Both *About Dry Land and Soft Clouds* and *Hidden* epitomize the ways in which the workshop participants' practice responded critically to the framing that I, as the theorist, was asked to develop at the outset. Instead of confining their exploration of violence to "recent" or "regional" episodes as

FIGURE 6.2. Still from Pınar Süer Alpkaya's video *Hidden* (reproduced with the artist's permission).

suggested in the framing text, the participants explored it across multiple spatial and temporal directions and scales while also working from their own embodied positionality within a gendered and racialized landscape. They used sites in northern Kurdistan to address not only anti-Kurdish violence but also obfuscation of the violent histories that have targeted non-Muslim communities both in this region and elsewhere, pointing to a relation of interdependence between the two. Workshop outputs such as the two I have discussed here also spoke back to the way my initial theoretical framing had problematized photography's documentary promise. Whether by referencing water-reflection photography or still-life photography, both Akdoğan and Alpkaya did embroil photography's documentary promise in the forces that sustain the interdependence between the violent injustices that have unfolded and continue to unfold in northern Kurdistan and elsewhere. Nevertheless, both also insisted on images taken long before the workshop series and with a view toward documentation, meaning they refused to altogether abandon photography's documentary promise and the visualities associated with it. This insistence did not diminish the works' critical potential but rather enhanced it by orienting the viewer toward the relations that unfold around and through photography, instead of just the photographs themselves and their formal conventionality or nonconventionality. That this book has endorsed just such an orientation through and through is indebted to the collaborations that brought it into existence, including "Photography's Violent Ecology."

ACADEMICS ADOPTING ASHWORK

As with most concepts that orient a theoretical framework, the concept of extractivism is open to criticism for homogenizing the various processes it helps theorize. Cultural studies scholars Imre Szeman and Jennifer Wenzel have recently penned a prime example of such criticism, pointing out two interdependent rationales. First, "extractivism . . . tends to flatten the ground, collapsing historical, geographical, and cultural distinctions that should be important to fully understanding the specific operations of extraction, including the ideologies and imaginaries that surround it at any given time and in any given space."[17] Such a "generalisation of extraction" then turns extractivism into "a process writ large, the name for any kind of taking out or drawing out—whether of iron ore and oil, value, work, data, or meaning, or indeed any other process that appears to fit the mould."[18] Szeman and Wenzel go on to argue that

> the presumption is that a dominant ideology is absorbed by every practice, by every aspect of a given configuration of power. Thus, once one starts reading for oil or looking for extractivism, one finds and names it everywhere—but on freshly flattened ground. And after such naming, then what? Out in the world, the digging continues. This is not to say that critical or pedagogical work has no effect, but to acknowledge that the site of its intervention is almost never the site of extraction.[19]

While echoing Szeman and Wenzel's wariness of an all too unspecific conceptualization of extractivism, the experiences I have discussed in this final chapter also indicate that critical or pedagogical intervention that is seemingly at a remove from sites of extraction is itself implicated in extractivism. This insight tops off a fundamental point made throughout the book: that visual cultural production in and on sites of extraction becomes conducive to nonextractivist imaginaries not simply by making extractivist damage and suffering visible but rather by refusing to let those with an avowed interest in intervening critically or pedagogically into extractivism off the hook. Ensuring conceptual and political specificity cannot involve a trade-off between using the concept of extractivism as an analytic device and preserving it for traditionally extractive industries like mining. The trade-off is invalidated by the fact that those using extractivism as an analytic are already implicated in extractivism as a material process due to the extractive industrialization of their own realms of professional ideational production, including academic research as well as artistic and cultural production.

The extractive industrialization of research is especially salient in today's Anglophone academe, where I have been based since early 2011. Here, the last two decades' withdrawal of state funding from the social sciences and the humanities has subjected researchers to performance metrics that valuate research as per the same quantifiable measurability and marketability characteristic of extractivism, impacting early-career and minoritized researchers especially negatively.[20] Moreover, sites of critical or pedagogical intervention across Anglophone academe are materially linked to those of extraction even when they do not spatially overlap with one another. This book's story is instructive in this respect, too. Most research and writing took place during a full-time fellowship that I was awarded in 2018 after more than half a decade of part-time teaching jobs. Called the Leverhulme Trust Early Career Fellowship, it is one of just three postdoctoral schemes available to UK-based scholars preferring to remain in the UK. The Leverhulme Trust was founded in 1925 upon the death of William Hesketh Lever (b. 1851, d. 1925), also known as Lord Leverhulme, whose will bequeathed for this purpose some of the shares he held in his company Lever Brothers, known as Unilever since its 1930 merger with Margarine Unie. Throughout the first half of the twentieth century, Lever Brothers developed and ran palm oil plantations in what is now the Democratic Republic of the Congo or DRC, then a Belgian colony, and in the Solomon Islands, then a British colony, collaborating directly with colonial administrations to coerce the colonized into abusive labor conditions and exploit their lands for materials used in soap production.[21]

In the first summer of the pandemic, as the Loading team and I were preparing to kick off the workshop series "Photography's Violent Ecology" from our homes, Britain (my home for a decade at the time) was witnessing a new phase of anticolonial and anti-racist protest simultaneously with the revival of Black Lives Matter in the US. The British protesters took inspiration from Rhodes Must Fall, the South African student movement of spring 2015 that succeeded in bringing down a statue of the late nineteenth-century colonial mining magnate and politician Cecil Rhodes on the University of Cape Town campus. On June 7, 2020, the British protesters toppled slave trader Edward Colston's (b. 1636, d. 1721) statue in Bristol, a former port city central to colonialism and the empire. The statue was toppled extemporaneously during a well-attended protest, dragged by the protesters to the harborside, and dumped into the water at a bridge named after Pero Jones, an enslaved man who spent the final decade and a half of his life in Bristol.

The courageous, spontaneous, and collective nature of the act inspired campaigns across the country against statues and place-names commemorating those with links to the empire's slavery-based economy, including Lord Leverhulme's statue in the port city of Wirral, pivotal to his soap empire.[22]

That summer, several British institutions active in the fields of arts, culture, and academic research released statements that acknowledged their colonial legacies and began setting up initiatives to account for them. The Leverhulme Trust was not among them. In response, a group of Leverhulme-funded researchers in the UK, including me, started an initiative to petition the Trust (confidentially, as a sign of our constructive intentions) to change course. The response we received emphasized the Trust's track record in funding research on racism, encouraging cooperation between universities in the UK and those in Africa, and supporting scholars based in African institutions. Absent was any critical reflection on Leverhulme's specific legacy, its implications for the present, or a road map for further action. We followed up by sending the Trust a second letter early in the new year, highlighting these absences. The response we received about a month later revealed that Leverhulme had just decided to fund an independent research initiative (overseen by a panel of scholars including one from our group) on William Lever's and the Lever Brothers' business operations in the DRC and the Solomon Islands. In May 2022, the Trust's website finally began to display acknowledgment of Leverhulme's colonial legacy, including a hyperlink to an initial scoping survey conducted by the new research initiative.[23]

This recent episode complements what my work in Amed has taught me regarding extractivism's contemporary workings across realms of professional ideational production. As argued throughout the book, the fact that colonialism remains an ongoing reality in parts of the world means that its relationship to extractive industries is not only as their historical backdrop. Rather, as an ongoing reality, colonialism requires the extractive industrialization of new realms, such as the realm of visual cultural production—and theorization—in and on northern Kurdistan of the 2010s. That said, colonialism does bear also as a historical force upon extractivism's continual threat to engulf professional ideational production within today's global capitalist system, where much of the wealth that now funds this production originates in colonial violence. If divesting from this system entirely is a complex task for the individual professional ideational producer, this book has argued that professional ideational production must come with a certain acknowledgment of its own limitations arising from this complexity. The distinction between individual artistic practice and activism proper that has suffused this book is a manifestation of that acknowledgment. Against the grain of much relevant scholarship, the book has conceptualized examples of artistic practice as only conducive to nonextractivist imaginaries rather than as capable on their own of transgressing or abrogating extractivism altogether. As the work of the individual professional artist must categorically prioritize the art world, appraising it in terms of its ability to undo extractivism by creating novel forms burdens artists unfairly with a role that at best overlooks their material obligations and at worst obscures the colonially grounded capitalist system in which most are entangled and which continually covets novelty. The Leverhulme Trust case is evidence that the same entanglement applies to the individual academic researcher. My response, informed by those with and among whom this book was researched and written, has been to partake in collectives that amplify the work of activism proper by intervening into whatever is within one's professional reach.

ACKNOWLEDGMENTS

I NEVER PLANNED TO WRITE this book. It was spoken into existence collectively—by numerous individuals and communities. The process started when I, having recently started a new research project on race and earthquake resilience in Turkey, received an invitation to coordinate a summer school in Amed on behalf of the city's professional organization for architects. I am grateful to Herdem Doğrul, who at the time was the architects' organization representative, and to Başka Bir Atölye (Gül Köksal, Asena Yıldırım, and Pelin Kaydan) and Efrîn Özyetiş, with whom I coordinated the summer school. It was during this summer school that I met Loading, the community whose contribution to this book's existence is unmatchable. I will be forever grateful to the cofounders Cengiz Tekin and Erkan Özgen, who invited me to be their inaugural artist/researcher in residence. The opportunity to sleep at Loading; to open and close it daily; to meet other artists through it; to edit and translate texts for it; to organize my own workshops under its aegis; to have intense and extensive conversations with Tekin, Özgen, and their wider communities; and to walk and drive with them in Amed and its environs are all experiences I am indebted to them for. I would like to thank Yasemin İmre, who was Loading's program coordinator in the lead-up to my residency. In late 2019, she handed this role over to Dicle Beştaş, to whom I am grateful for being a most unswerving coconspirator since I met her then. Alongside Beştaş, Evindar Tokur and Berivan Aslan were my two other collaborators in the workshops I initiated during my residency, and I am therefore indebted to them as well. I would like to also thank the following individuals (in no particular order), whom I met at the time in Amed and who have all contributed to my thinking in their own important way: Hakkı Kanat, Bawer Ulaş, Zeki Kanay, Selçuk Ertekin, Murat Biricik, Doğan Hatun, Samed Uçaman, Sevdet Acar, Rıdvan Kuday, Süleyman Kızıl, Derman Üngür, Halim Üngür, Sedat Akdoğan, Hüsamettin Bahçe, Lezgin Kani, Ferat Demiroğlu, Pınar Süer Alpkaya, Bişar İçli, Fatma Çelik, Rozelin Akgün, Leyla Keskin, Ateş Alpar, Aylin Kızıl, Bilge Işık, Gülistan Kenanoğlu, Ümit Alptekin, Canan Fidan, and Faruk Okuduci.

I would like to thank those who invited me to share with their artistic or academic communities my ideas in progress that are now featured in this book: Samuel Merrill and Anastasia Kavada (University of Westminster), Zeyno Pekünlü (Istanbul Biennial Production and Research Programme), Sibel Horada (SALT), Larissa Araz and Gizem Karakaş (Poşe), Merve Ünsal (Arter), Özlem Güçlü and Sibel Yardımcı (Mimar Sinan Fine Arts University), Marina Lathouri (Architectural Association School of Architecture), Senem Doyduk (Sakarya University), Didem Kılıçkıran (Kadir Has University), Sinan Erensü and Yaşar Adanalı (Center for Spatial Justice), Bahar Topçu and Hilal Şenel (Pera Museum), Esin Kömez and Aylin Alicanoğlu (Middle East Technical University), Hande Tekdemir (Boğaziçi University), Melis Gayretli and Aslı Tuncer Madge (Turkey's Chamber of Architects), Melis Oğuz Çevik (Medyascope), Deniz Gündoğan İbrişim (Açık Radyo), Başak Şenova, Margarethe Makovec and Anton Lederer (Rotor), Didem Yazıcı (Yapı Kredi Culture and Arts), Deniz Karabekiroğlu (Bilgi University), Martin Karcher (Kunstverein in Hamburg), Evren Uzer (Parsons School of Design, The New School), Maria Six-Hohenbalken (Austrian Academy of Sciences in Vienna), Andrea Muehlebach (University of Bremen), Katy Beinart (University of Brighton), Richard Difford (University of Westminster), Katrin Nahidi (University of Graz), Abdurrahman Gülbeyaz (Nagasaki University), Thomas Symeonidis (Eleonas Biennial in Athens), and Hakan Irmak (Mardin Biennial).

In situ work and writing were funded by a Leverhulme Trust Early Career Fellowship (2018–2022). The fellowship was based at the European Institute, London School of Economics and Political Science (LSE), which could not have been possible without Esra Özyürek. I am grateful to her for this life-changing opportunity and for becoming a most generous mentor ever since. I worked with the following individuals at academic events I organized during my LSE years, and I am indebted to each and every one of them for considering me as a conversation partner: Christine Okoth, Ignacio Acosta, Thandi Loewenson, Ishita Sharma, Rojda Tuğrul, K. Yoland, Alice Owen, Siti Maimunah, Margarida Mendes, Jacob Badcock, Kate Lewis Hood, Lara Fresko Madra, George Ygarza, Anousheh Kehar, Anna

Engelhardt and Sasha Shestakova, Andrew Barry, Nishat Awan, Mangalika de Silva, Helene Kazan, Philipp Sattler, Dubravka Sekulić and Milica Tomić, Oscar Pedraza and Hannah Meszaros Martin, Allen Feldman, Vahap Avşar, Merve Bedir, Zerrin Özlem Biner, Lindsay Bremner, Nerea Calvillo, Ryan Centner, Ayça Çubukçu, T. J. Demos, Başak Ertür, Tariq Jazeel, Gürcan Keltek, Alisa Lebow, İz Öztat, Peg Rawes, belit sağ, Serkan Taycan, Shela Sheikh, Austin Zeiderman, Fatma Gökçe and Florence Samuels, Grace Adeniyi-Ogunyankin, Melanie Dennis Unrau, and Tanzil Shafique.

The communities that generously accepted me during the process that birthed this book are not limited to those of artists and architects. Another such community consists of visual culture scholars. I am indebted to the editorial collective of the *Journal of Visual Culture*, who first gave me the opportunity to guest-edit a special issue on a theme related to this book and then invited me to join them. Manca Bajec deserves a special mention here as the editorial collective member who initiated this process. In 2020, the leading Turkish-language publisher, Everest, published my book of essays on Anthropocene art and architecture. For this opportunity, I am grateful to editors Cem İleri, Murat Çelik, and Saadet Özen. The book allowed me to give interlocutors and collaborators insight into my thoughts in progress and led further communities of artists and architects to engage with my work. Due not least to the generous interest these communities showed in the book, it ended up receiving a major literary award; I am grateful to all its readers and commentators.

I express my sincere gratitude to University of Texas Press editors Jim Burr and Mia Uribe Kozlovsky for their unwavering support and for placing the book with the most constructively critical and intellectually generous readers that an author can ever hope to have (thanks also to Bethany Mowry for contributing to this process). I will be forever indebted to the three anonymous readers for engaging with the book on its own terms and helping unlock its critical potential. Thank you very much to Theresa Truax-Gischler for her peerlessly meticulous and boundlessly patient editing work on the book as the first person ever to lay eyes on it. Many thanks to Carolyn at Sophia Editing for copyediting the book with such close attention and care, and to Robert Kimzey from the press for facilitating this process.

As ever, my deepest indebtedness and gratitude is to Sera Bal.

NOTES

Author's Note

1. Francis O'Connor, *Understanding Insurgency: Popular Support for the PKK in Turkey* (Cambridge: Cambridge University Press, 2021), 8.

2. Joanna Bocheńska, *Rediscovering Kurdistan's Cultures and Identities: The Call of the Cricket* (Berlin: Springer, 2018), 200–201.

3. For a comparable approach, see Özlem Belçim Galip, *Imagining Kurdistan: Identity, Culture and Society* (London: I. B. Tauris, 2015), 272.

4. Zeynep Kaya, *Mapping Kurdistan: Territory, Self-Determination and Nationalism* (Cambridge: Cambridge University Press, 2020), 6.

5. Dilar Dirik, *The Kurdish Women's Movement: History, Theory, Practice* (London: Pluto Press, 2021), 20.

6. Joost Jongerden, *The Settlement Issue in Turkey and the Kurds: An Analysis of Spatial Policies, Modernity, and War* (Leiden: Brill, 2007), 195–198.

7. Gözde Orhan, "How to Divide the 'Indivisible Unity'? Debates on the Division of Turkey into Geographical Regions in the Early Years of the Republic," *SİYASAL: Journal of Political Sciences*, no. 32 (2023): 101–115.

8. BİA News Desk, "DEM Party Commemorates Armenian Genocide Anniversary," *Bianet*, April 24, 2024, https://bianet.org/haber/dem-party-commemorates-armenian-genocide-anniversary-294595. By "pro-Kurdish," I mean a diverse range of political movements that, despite their internal differences, are united in the objective of advancing the rights and freedoms of Turkey's Kurds and all the other peoples of Kurdistan. Since the 1990s, these movements have coalesced into a succession of legal parties; when the Turkish state shuts one down on grounds of aiding and abetting terrorism, the pro-Kurdish political movement founds another. The party active during the period discussed in this book (the mid-2010s) was HDP, Halkların Demokratik Partisi, or Peoples' Democratic Party. HDP remains unsurpassed as the most popular pro-Kurdish party in modern Turkish history, thanks to a record vote share it received in a general election held just three months before the start of the state's counterinsurgency campaign in September 2015 (Cengiz Gunes, "The Rise of the Pro-Kurdish Democratic Movement in Turkey," in *Routledge Handbook on the Kurds*, ed. Michael Gunter [London: Routledge, 2018], 259–269). The latest iteration is the DEM (Peoples' Equality and Democracy) Party.

9. Turkish anticolonial sociologist and political prisoner İsmail Beşikçi articulated this point in 1990 when he spoke of Kurdistan's status being "less than colonial" or "even lower than that of a colony" (İsmail Beşikçi, *International Colony Kurdistan* [London: Parvana, 2004], 18, 53).

10. Zerrin Özlem Biner, *States of Dispossession: Violence and Precarious Coexistence in Southeast Turkey* (Philadelphia: University of Pennsylvania Press, 2020), 14–16.

11. Ercan Ayboğa, "Ecology Structures of the Kurdish Freedom Movement," in *Ecological Solidarity and the Kurdish Freedom Movement: Thought, Practice, Challenges, and Opportunities*, ed. Stephen E. Hunt (London: Rowman & Littlefield, 2021), 77–96.

12. Seda Altuğ, "The Syrian Uprising and Turkey's Ordeal with the Kurds," *Dialectical Anthropology*, no. 37 (2023): 123–130.

13. R. A. Judy, "The Mūthoi of Selahattin Demirtaş," *Comparative Literature Studies* 61, no. 1 (2024): 79.

14. Just months before this book went into production, local elections held in March 2024 once again saw pro-Kurdish party representatives emerge victorious in much of northern Kurdistan. Within days of the elections, the central government attempted to confiscate Wan (in Turkish: Van) Metropolitan Municipality, but the attempt was ultimately thwarted in court. In June 2024, the municipality of Colemêrg (in Turkish: Hakkâri) was confiscated by the central government, followed by a further six such confiscations in November of the same year.

Movement of and Through Earth, or Extractivism and Its Aesthetics

1. Ahmet Ün and Burak Emek, "Dicle Nehri'ne ıslah için ilk neşter vuruldu" [The first scalpel is wielded for rehabilitating the Tigris River], *DHA*, January 17, 2018, https://www.dha.com.tr/amp/gundem/dicle-nehrine-islah-icin-ilk-nester-vuruldu-1560523.

2. In 2016, the central government ousted democratically elected pro-Kurdish mayors—a position distinct from the other administrative authorities operative at the local level across Turkey, including governors appointed by the Ministry of Interior Affairs—and replaced them with the so-called watchpersons it appointed (Tuvan Gumrukcu and Ali Kucukgocmen, "Kurdish Mayors Replaced in Turkey in Crackdown on Criticism of Syria Assault," *Reuters*, October 18, 2019, reuters.com/article/us-syria-security-turkey-kurds/kurdish-mayors-replaced-in-turkey-in-crackdown-on-criticism-of-syria-assault-idUSKBN1WX1GP). In the 2019 local elections, the pro-Kurdish party's members rewon most municipalities across the region, to then be replaced yet again with centrally appointed bureaucrats. The 2024 local elections have resulted in a similar level of success for the pro-Kurdish party, but the central government's undemocratic response has so far been less rapid and assertive than in 2019 (as of December 2024, all but seven pro-Kurdish mayors remain in their seats).

3. Abdülkadir Konuksever, "Zeki Usta'ya kulak verin" [Lend an ear to Master Zeki], *Al Jazeera Turk*, March 28, 2016, https://www.aljazeera.com.tr/al-jazeera-ozel/zeki-ustaya-kulak-verin.

4. Eray Çaylı, *İklimin estetiği: Antroposen sanatı ve mimarlığı üzerine denemeler* [Climate aesthetics: Essays on Anthropocene art and architecture] (Istanbul: Everest, 2023 [2020]), 248–262. One antecedent instance where the word *hafriyatçılık* has been used for discussing extractivism is a brief essay by Turkish climate activist and political scientist Ömer Madra, albeit without the focus on the colonially driven racial dynamics and the aesthetic workings that characterizes my use. See Ömer Madra, "Anlatılan bizim hikâyemiz" [The story being told is ours], in *İklim değişikliğinde son gelişmeler: IPCC 2013 raporu* [Latest developments in climate change: IPCC 2013 report], ed. Murat Türkeş, Ömer Lütfi Şen, Levent Kurnaz, Ömer Madra, and Ümit Şahin (Istanbul: İstanbul Politikalar Merkezi, 2013), 27–33. I am grateful to Sinan Erensü for the reference.

5. Kathryn Yusoff, Elizabeth Grosz, Nigel Clark, Arun Saldanha, and Catherine Nash, "Geopower: A Panel on Elizabeth Grosz's *Chaos, Territory, Art: Deleuze and the Framing of the Earth*," *Environment and Planning D: Society and Space* 30, no. 6 (2012): 971–988; Kathryn Yusoff, "Politics of the Anthropocene: Formation of the Commons as a Geologic Process," *Antipode* 50, no. 1 (2018): 255–276; Tomas Frederiksen and Matthew Himley, "Tactics of Dispossession: Access, Power, and Subjectivity at the Extractive Frontier," *Transactions of the Institute of British Geographers* 45, no. 1 (2020): 50–64; Levi Gahman and Gabrielle Thongs, "Development Justice, a Proposal: Reckoning with Disaster, Catastrophe, and Climate Change in the Caribbean," *Transactions of the Institute of British Geographers* 45, no. 4 (2020): 763–778.

6. On extractivist representations in early nineteenth-century British colonialism, see Andreas Malm, *The Progress of This Storm: Nature and Society in a Warming World* (London: Verso, 2017), 19–20. On the spatialization of race, see Uli Linke, "Racializing Cities, Naturalizing Space: The Seductive Appeal of Iconicities of Dispossession," *Antipode* 46, no. 5 (2014): 1225. On more recent examples of visuality's centrality to extractivism, see Sylvain Guyot, "The Eco-Frontier Paradigm: Rethinking the Links Between Space, Nature and Politics," *Geopolitics* 16, no. 3 (2011): 682; Andrew Barry, *Material Politics: Disputes Along the Pipeline* (Oxford: Wiley-Blackwell, 2013), 116–136; Macarena Gómez-Barris, *The Extractive Zone: Social Ecologies and Decolonial Perspectives* (Durham, NC: Duke University Press, 2017), 5–7; John Childs, "Extraction in Four Dimensions: Time, Space, and the Emerging Geo(-)politics of Deep-Sea Mining," *Geopolitics* 25, no. 1 (2020): 189–213; Bruce Erickson, "Anthropocene Futures: Linking Colonialism and Environmentalism in an Age of Crisis," *Environment and Planning D: Society and Space* 38, no. 1 (2020): 113.

7. Joshua R. Eichen, "Cheapness and (Labor-)Power: The Role of Early Modern Brazilian Sugar Plantations in the Racializing Capitalocene," *Environment and Planning D: Society and Space* 38, no. 1 (2020): 35.

8. On quantification, see Yusoff et al., "Geopower," 635–652. On marketization as things, see Jonathan Rosa and Vanessa Díaz, "Raciontologies: Rethinking Anthropological Accounts of Institutional Racism and Enactments of White Supremacy in the United States," *American Anthropologist* 122, no. 1 (2020): 4. On the epistemic structure in question, see Andrew Baldwin and Bruce Erickson, "Introduction: Whiteness, Coloniality, and the Anthropocene," *Environment and Planning D: Society and Space* 38, no. 1 (2020): 6–7. In considering epistemic and semantic structures together here, I echo John Thornes's point about visuality's being important not only to human geography but also physical geography, as it relates both to "aesthetic subjectivity" and to "visualizing scientific objectivity" (John E. Thornes, "The Visual Turn and Geography," *Antipode* 36, no. 5 [2004]: 790).

9. See, for example, Daniela Soto Hernandez and Peter Newell, "Oro Blanco: Assembling Extractivism in the Lithium Triangle," *Journal of Peasant Studies* 49, no. 5 (2022): 945–968.

10. On extractivism's operations beyond colonies proper, see Childs, "Extraction in Four Dimensions," 201–202. On its operations in postcolonial geographies, see Gómez-Barris, *Extractive Zone*; Thea Riofrancos, "Extractivismo Unearthed: A Genealogy of a Radical Discourse," *Cultural Studies* 31, no. 2–3 (2017): 277–306; Gisela V. Rodriguez Fernandez, "Neo-Extractivism, the Bolivian State, and Indigenous Peasant Women's Struggles for Water in the Altiplano," *Human Geography* 13, no.

1 (2020): 27–39. On its quantifiability-based logics of valuation, see Fabiana Li, "Contesting Equivalences: Controversies over Water and Mining in Chile and Peru," in *The Social Life of Water*, ed. John Richard Wagner (New York: Berghahn, 2013), 18–35. Alongside these settings afflicted by direct European colonialism, China, as a new superpower, has recently become the subject of growing interest in extractivism scholarship, and so has the Middle East for exclusively oil-related reasons. See, for example, Childs, "Extraction in Four Dimensions," 190; Erik Post and Philippe Le Billon, "The 'Green War': Geopolitical Metabolism and Green Extractivisms," *Geopolitics* (2024), https://doi.org/10.1080/14650045.2024.2385411.

11. The village of Kıtılbıl referenced by Berivan's dad in his rehistoricization of the landscape is relevant in more ways than one to my point that not only destruction but also repair merits critical attention from those aiming to grasp and challenge extractivism. Kıtılbıl is not only where an extractivist riverbank and riverbed repair project was recently pursued but also where, in the wake of the Armenian genocide, the nascent Turkish republic strived to revert the damage done to environmentally charged industries such as agriculture, silk, and copper—industries that had long been spearheaded by Armenians. The 1920s saw the republican administration establish a "model farm" in Kıtılbıl "to revive the 5,000 acres of barren, 'abandoned' land" and salvage whatever agricultural know-how had managed to survive "to be emulated by local farmers and generate agrarian development" (Uğur Ümit Üngör and Mehmet Polatel, *Confiscation and Destruction: The Young Turk Seizure of Armenian Property* [London, Continuum: 2011], 156). In 2022, Amed's centrally appointed mayor renamed Kıtılbıl as the Fetih neighborhood. The word *fetih* means "conquest" in Turkish and is often used for referring to Ottoman capture of Byzantine lands, demonstrating yet another instance of the need to consider recent periods of war within long-standing histories of imperial nationalism. See Remzi Budancir, "Sur kayyımı tarihi Kıtılbil Mahallesi'nin ismini 'Fetih Mahallesi' olarak değiştirdi" [Sur watchperson changes Kıtılbil Neighborhood's name as 'Fetih Neighborhood'], *Artı Gerçek*, June 13, 2022, https://artigercek.com/guncel/sur-kayyimi-tarihi-kitilbil-mahallesi-nin-ismini-fetih-mahallesi-olarak-214726h.

12. TMMOB Diyarbakir Provincial Coordination Board, *2015–2016: TMMOB Destroyed Cities Report* (Ankara: Union of Chambers of Turkish Engineers and Architects, 2017); TMMOB Diyarbakır İl Koordinasyon Kurulu, "Sur raporu" [Sur report], *TMMOB Makina Mühendisleri Odası Diyarbakır Şubesi* [TMMOB Mechanical Engineers' Chamber Diyarbakır Branch], December 2, 2017, https://www.mmo.org.tr/sites/default/files/gonderi_dosya_ekleri/SUR%20RAPORU.pdf.

13. The union identified a total of seventeen such contraventions (TMMOB Diyarbakır İl Koordinasyon Kurulu, "Diyarbakır ili, Sur ilçesi koruma amaçlı uygulama imar planı değişikliği itiraz raporu" [Diyarbakır province Sur district conservation master plan implementation alteration objection report], *Diyarbakır Branch of the Chamber of Architects*, January 10, 2017, https://www.dimod.org.tr/haberler/diyarbakir-ili-sur-ilcesi-koruma-amacli-uygulama-imar-plani-degisikligi-itiraz-raporu-314). More than 22,000 residents were displaced, and 334 of the district's listed buildings were destroyed. See also Ömer Çelik and Mehmet Erol, "Sur, Surlulardan alındı" [Sur has been taken away from its residents], *Yeni Özgür Politika*, September 23, 2020, https://www.ozgurpolitika.com/haberi-sur-surlulardan-alindi-4964.

14. Eray Çaylı, "The Architecture of Dispossession, Disaster, and Emergency in Urban Turkey," in *The Routledge Handbook on Contemporary Turkey*, ed. Joost Jongerden (London: Routledge, 2022), 360–372.

15. In political and scholarly discourse, the notion of Kurdistan being a colony originates with modern Turkey's pro-Kurdish political movement, which, since its outset in the 1970s, has considered as colonizers both Turkey and the Allied powers that carved up Kurdistan during and after World War I (Jongerden, *Settlement Issue*, 54–57; Deniz Duruiz, "Tracing the Conceptual Genealogy of Kurdistan as International Colony," *Middle East Report*, no. 295 [2020], https://merip.org/2020/08/tracing-the-conceptual-genealogy-of-kurdistan-as-international-colony/). It also figured prominently in the official policies the founders and first administrations of the Republic of Turkey themselves devised and implemented in northern Kurdistan (Jongerden, *Settlement Issue*, 173–217), albeit never granting Kurdistan official colony status. See also Gullistan Yarkın, "İnkâr Edilen Hakikat: Sömürge Kuzey Kürdistan" [The truth that is denied: Colony northern Kurdistan], *Kürd Araştırmaları*, no. 1 (2019): 45–69.

16. Nik Heynen and Megan Ybarra, "On Abolition Ecologies and Making 'Freedom as a Place,'" *Antipode* 53, no. 1 (2021): 21–35.

17. These tendencies also characterize the burgeoning literature that discusses extractivism as a visual cultural question and especially as one that involves the field of contemporary art, where this book looks for nonextractivist pathways. Some in this literature have looked for challenges to extractivism in activist-artistic protest movements against the art world's financial and organizational embroilment in extractive industries due, for example, to the funding that art institutions receive from fossil fuel companies (Ashley Dawson, "The Work of Art in the Age of Extractivism," *World Art* 13, no. 2 [2023]: 221–244; Camille-Mary Sharp, "Oil-Sponsored Exhibitions and Canada's Extractive Politics of Cultural Production," *Imaginations* 13, no. 1 [2022]: 13–35). Others have looked to artworks or practices (especially by practitioners who straddle the worlds of art and activism) for ways out of the Eurocentric duality of humanity versus nature that is argued to underpin extractivist aesthetics (Paula Serafini, *Creating Worlds Otherwise: Art, Collective Action, and [Post]Extractivism* [Nashville, TN: Vanderbilt University Press, 2022]; Jens Andermann, *Entranced Earth: Art, Extractivism, and the End of Landscape* [Evanston, IL: Northwestern University Press, 2023]; Paula Serafini, "Art, Extractivism, and the Ontological Shift: Toward a [Post]Extractivist Aesthetics," *Theory, Culture and Society* [2024]: https://doi.org/10.1177/02632764241238330). And here extractivist aesthetics has tended to be understood largely (and differently from my understanding) as a negational and destructive force (Andermann, *Entranced Earth*, 17, and the special journal issue introduced by Mareike Winchell and Cymene Howe, "Unsettling Extractivism: Indigeneity, Race, and Disruptive Emplacements," *Journal of Latin American and Caribbean Anthropology* 29, no. 3 [2024]: 201–207).

18. On the environmental turn in political violence scholarship, see Arun Agrawal, *Environmentality: Technologies of Government and the Making of Subjects* (Durham, NC: Duke University Press, 2005); Stefania Barca, "Telling the Right Story: Environmental Violence and Liberation Narratives," *Environment and History* 20, no. 4 (2014): 535–546; Lawrence Buell, "Uses and Abuses of Environmental Memory," in *Contesting Environmental Imaginaries: Nature and Counternature in a Time of Global*

Change, ed. Steven Hartman (Leiden: Brill, 2017), 95–116; Rob Nixon, *Slow Violence and the Environmentalism of the Poor* (Cambridge, MA: Harvard University Press, 2011).

19. For a volume that presents a range of scholarship considerably representative of the diversity of this nascent field, see the edited volume introduced by Adam Bobbette and Amy Donovan, "Political Geology: An Introduction," in *Political Geology: Active Stratigraphies and the Making of Life*, ed. Adam Bobbette and Amy Donovan (London: Palgrave Macmillan, 2019), 1–36.

20. Paul J. Crutzen and Eugene F. Stoermer, "The 'Anthropocene,'" *Global Change Newsletter*, no. 41 (2000): 17–18.

21. Adam Bobbette and Amy Donovan, "Encountering the Earth: Political Geological Futures?," in *Political Geology: Active Stratigraphies and the Making of Life*, ed. Adam Bobbette and Amy Donovan (London: Palgrave Macmillan, 2019), 347–372; Adam Bobbette, *The Pulse of the Earth: Political Geology in Java* (Durham, NC: Duke University Press, 2023), 4, 8.

22. The premise of political geology is therefore not only "that the basis of politics is in geological resources such as fossil fuels, minerals, and sand and is ordered by their appropriation, processing and distribution" but also "that geology too emerges in and through political processes, as it is demarcated, framed, and becomes an object of knowledge" (Bobbette and Donovan, "Political Geology," 2–3). On race's centrality to geology's emergence through African enslavement and Indigenous dispossession in the Americas, see Kathryn Yusoff, *Geologic Life: Inhuman Intimacies and the Geophysics of Race* (Durham, NC: Duke University Press, 2024). On coloniality's and the plantation economy's centrality to the formation of the modern geological science of volcanology with a focus on Java, see Bobbette, *Pulse of the Earth*.

23. Bobbette and Donovan, "Political Geology," 1–2, 9–11, 13; Bobbette and Donovan, "Encountering the Earth," 352.

24. On drawings, see Bobbette and Donovan, "Political Geology," 7, 16–17. On maps, see Bobbette and Donovan, "Encountering the Earth," 361–363; Bobbette, *Pulse of the Earth*, 20–51.

25. Hannah Meszaros Martin, "Defoliating the World: Ecocide, Visual Evidence and 'Earthly Memory,'" *Third Text* 32, no. 2–3 (2018): 230–253; Shela Sheikh, "The Future of the Witness: Nature, Race and More-than-Human Environmental Publics," *Kronos* 44, no. 1 (2018): 145-162.

26. Eray Çaylı, "The Politics of Spatial Testimony: The Role of Space in Witnessing Martyrdom and Shame During and After a Widely Televised and Collectively Perpetrated Arson Attack in Turkey," *Space and Culture* 25, no. 4 (2022): 675–688.

27. Hagit Keysar, "A Spatial Testimony: The Politics of Do-It-Yourself Aerial Photography in East Jerusalem," *Environment and Planning D: Society and Space* 37, no. 3 (2019): 523–541; Laura Kurgan, "Conflict Urbanism, Aleppo: Mapping Urban Damage," *Architectural Design* 87, no. 1 (2017): 72–77; Susan Schuppli, "Dusting for Fingerprints and Tracking Digital Footprints," *Photographies* 6, no. 1 (2013): 159–167; Susan Schuppli, "Entering Evidence: Cross-Examining the Court Records of the ICTY," in *Forensis*, ed. Forensic Architecture (Berlin: Sternberg Press, 2014), 279–316; Jonas Staal, "Law of the State, Truth of Art: Two Case Studies of Art as Evidence," *On Curating*, no. 28 (2016): 14–23; Eyal Weizman, "Forensic Architecture: Only the Criminal Can Solve the Crime," *Radical Philosophy* 164, no. 9 (2010): 9–24; Eyal

Weizman, "Introduction: Forensis," in *Forensis*, ed. Forensic Architecture (Berlin: Sternberg Press, 2014), 9–32.

28. On critique that highlights the risk of reproducing the violence that has historically structured the conventions of dominant visual cultural paradigms, see Joshua Ewalt, "Mapping Injustice: The World Is Witness, Place-Framing, and the Politics of Viewing on Google Earth," *Communication, Culture and Critique* 4 (2011): 333–354; Allison Carruth and Robert P. Marzec, "Environmental Visualization in the Anthropocene: Technologies, Aesthetics, Ethics," *Public Culture* 26, no. 2 (2014): 205–211; T. J. Demos, *Against the Anthropocene: Visual Culture and Environment Today* (Berlin: Sternberg, 2017); Allen Feldman, *Archives of the Insensible: Of War, Photopolitics, and Dead Memory* (Chicago: Chicago University Press, 2015). For Nicholas Mirzoeff, violence has structured the entirety of "visuality" through histories of racial capitalism, imperialism, and colonialism (Nicholas Mirzoeff, *The Right to Look: A Counterhistory of Visuality* [Durham, NC: Duke University Press, 2011]). On the pitfalls of equating visibility with power, see Gil Z. Hochberg, *Visual Occupations: Violence and Visibility in a Conflict Zone* (Durham, NC: Duke University Press, 2015), 6–7. On critique that highlights the collective political labor required for engendering progressive social change, see Andrew Herscher, "From Target to Witness: Architecture, Satellite Surveillance, Human Rights," in *Architecture and Violence: Reception and Reproduction*, ed. Bechir Kenzari (Barcelona: Actar, 2011), 123–144; Andrew Herscher, "Surveillant Witnessing: Satellite Imagery and the Visual Politics of Human Rights," *Public Culture* 26, no. 3 (2014): 469–500; T. J. Demos, *Decolonizing Nature: Contemporary Art and the Politics of Ecology* (Berlin: Sternberg Press, 2016), 264–266.

29. Gregory Bateson, *Steps to an Ecology of the Mind: Collected Essays in Anthropology, Psychiatry, Evolution, and Epistemology* (Chicago: University of Chicago Press, 1972); Félix Guattari, *The Three Ecologies* (London: Athlone Press, 2000). This broad tradition also informs my repeated reference in the book to the *politics of ecology* rather than *political ecology*. Whereas political ecology is a specific field of study—one I do not directly engage here—the term *politics of ecology* indexes a wider set of relations involving "biophysical process and the nonhuman world" as well as human "knowledge," "expertise," and "material interests" (Matthew D. Turner, "Political Ecology II: Engagements with Ecology," *Progress in Human Geography* 40, no. 3 [2016]: 414–416).

30. See, for example, Sylvia Wynter, "Towards the Sociogenic Principle: Fanon, Identity, the Puzzle of Conscious Experience, and What It Is Like to Be 'Black,'" in *National Identities and Sociopolitical Changes in Latin America*, ed. Mercedes F. Durán-Cogan and Antonio Gómez-Moriana (New York: Routledge, 2001), 30–66; Jairus Victor Grove, *Savage Ecology: War and Geopolitics at the End of the World* (Durham, NC: Duke University Press, 2019); Cajetan Iheka, *Naturalizing Africa: Ecological Violence, Agency, and Postcolonial Resistance in African Literature* (Cambridge: Cambridge University Press, 2018); Whitney Mauer, "Unsettling Resilience: Colonial Ecological Violence, Indigenous Futurisms, and the Restoration of the Elwha River," *Rural Sociology* 86, no. 3 (2021): 611–634; Kyle Whyte, "Settler Colonialism, Ecology, and Environmental Injustice," *Environment and Society* 9, no. 1 (2018): 125–144; Jules Bacon, "Settler Colonialism as Eco-Social Structure and the Production of Colonial Ecological Violence," *Environmental Sociology* 5, no. 1 (2019): 59–69.

31. For comprehensive reviews, see Deborah Dixon, Harriet Hawkins, and Elizabeth Straughan, "Of Human Birds and Living Rocks: Remaking Aesthetics for Post-Human Worlds," *Dialogues in Human Geography* 2, no. 3 (2012): 249–270; Harriet Hawkins and Elizabeth Straughan, eds., *Geographical Aesthetics: Imagining Space, Staging Encounters* (Farnham: Ashgate, 2015).

32. Jacques Rancière, *The Politics of Aesthetics: The Distribution of the Sensible*, trans. Gabriel Rockhill (London: Continuum, 2004); Jacques Rancière, *Dissensus: On Politics and Aesthetics*, trans. Steven Corcoran (London: Continuum, 2010). Examples of relevant Rancièrian work in geography include Kanishka Goonewardena, "The Urban Sensorium: Space, Ideology and the Aestheticization of Politics," *Antipode* 37, no. 1 (2005): 46–71; Mustafa Dikeç, "Immigrants, Banlieues, and Dangerous Things: Ideology as an Aesthetic Affair," *Antipode* 45, no. 1 (2013): 23–42; Asher Ghertner, *Rule by Aesthetics: World-Class City Making in Delhi* (Oxford: Oxford University Press, 2015); Mustafa Dikeç, *Space, Politics and Aesthetics* (Edinburgh: Edinburgh University Press, 2016); Alan Ingram, "Art, Geopolitics and Metapolitics at Tate Galleries London," *Geopolitics* 22, no. 3 (2017): 719–739.

33. In making these two points, I echo Eric Goldfischer, "'Peek-A-Boo, We See You Too': Homelessness and Visuality in New York City," *Environment and Planning D: Society and Space* 36, no. 5 (2018): 835–836. See also Goldfischer's excellent review of visuality in geography: "Visuality," in *International Encyclopedia of Human Geography*, 2nd ed., vol. 1, ed. Audrey Kobayashi (Amsterdam: Elsevier, 2019), 175–179. The concept of "modernity/coloniality" I use here was coined by Aníbal Quijano and then developed by Walter Mignolo to express the ways coloniality constitutes modernity as opposed to simply deriving from it. It is a "shorter expression" for "the colonial matrix of power" that has been "constituted, managed, and transformed from . . . the sixteenth century to the present" (Walter Mignolo and Catherine E. Walsh, *On Decoloniality: Concepts, Analytics, Praxis* [Durham, NC: Duke University Press, 2018], 4).

34. Elaine Stratford and Colin Langridge, "Critical Artistic Interventions into the Geopolitical Spaces of Islands," *Social and Cultural Geography* 13, no. 7 (2012): 821–843; Ryan Jones, "Navigating Norman Creek: Engaging Art in Geographies of Plants and Urban Natures," *Cultural Geographies* 24, no. 3 (2017): 497–504.

35. Kathryn Yusoff, "Biopolitical Economies and the Political Aesthetics of Climate Change," *Theory, Culture and Society* 27, no. 2–3 (2010): 73–99; Kathryn Yusoff, "Aesthetics of Loss: Biodiversity, Banal Violence and Biotic Subjects," *Transactions of the Institute of British Geographers* 37, no. 4 (2012): 578–592.

36. Munira Khayyat, *A Landscape of War: Ecologies of Resistance and Survival in South Lebanon* (Oakland: University of California Press, 2022), 25.

37. Khayyat, *Landscape of War*, 11, 20.

38. Khayyat does acknowledge, in passing, "perspectival painting" as a capitalism- and imperialism-affiliated visual tradition that has shaped landscape discourse and practice, but without further engaging with it and its ongoing medium-specific legacies in the context she is writing about (Khayyat, *Landscape of War*, 29).

39. Salar Mameni, *Terracene: A Crude Aesthetics* (Durham, NC: Duke University Press, 2023), 7.

40. Numerous critics have problematized the same sweeping reference by arguing that climate change and environmental disasters, whether in their causes or in their effects, are in fact anything but homogeneously anthropic, and that racial capitalism

is the chief progenitor of this heterogeneity. On causes, see Baldwin and Erickson, "Introduction," 3–11; Eichen, "Cheapness and (Labor-)Power," 35–52; Timothy W. Luke, "Tracing Race, Ethnicity, and Civilization in the Anthropocene," *Environment and Planning D: Society and Space* 38, no. 1 (2020): 129–146. On effects, see Lindsey Dillon and Julie Sze, "Police Power and Particulate Matters: Environmental Justice and the Spatialities of In/Securities in US Cities," *English Language Notes* 54, no. 2 (2016): 13–23; Kathryn Yusoff, *A Billion Black Anthropocenes or None* (Minneapolis: University of Minnesota Press, 2018); Pavithra Vasudevan, "An Intimate Inventory of Race and Waste," *Antipode* 53, no. 3 (2021): 770–790.

41. Mameni, *Terracene*, 6.

42. For a passage where Mameni expounds the importance of senses and sensibilities to his approach, see Mameni, *Terracene*, 56. For passages where he writes in the colonial and decolonial terms of settler-colonialism and Indigeneity, see Mameni, *Terracene*, 4–5, 71.

43. Mameni's tendency to associate coloniality in the Middle East only with external powers becomes evident from the book's first pages onward, as he begins by pitting a (pre)Islamic creation story against modernity/coloniality as an exclusively Euro-American project (Mameni, *Terracene*, 5).

44. Such categorization becomes especially palpable when Mameni frames his arts-focused discussion as one that attends "to the residues of extractive and militarized cultures who come to be known as terrorists within the geopolitical order of the globe" (Mameni, *Terracene*, 10).

45. On life versus nonlife, see Elizabeth Povinelli, *Geontologies: A Requiem to Late Liberalism* (Durham, NC: Duke University Press, 2016).

46. Alexander G. Weheliye, *Habeas Viscus: Racializing Assemblages, Biopolitics, and Black Feminist Theories of the Human* (Durham, NC: Duke University Press, 2014), 2.

47. Kyla Schuller, *The Biopolitics of Feeling: Race, Sex, and Science in the Nineteenth Century* (Durham, NC: Duke University Press, 2017); Steve Hinchliffe, "Sensory Biopolitics: Knowing Birds and a Politics of Life," in *Humans, Animals and Biopolitics: The More-than-Human Condition*, ed. Kristin Asdal, Tone Druglitrø, and Steve Hinchliffe (London: Routledge, 2016), 152–170.

48. Alongside Weheliye, I also take my cue here from Ellen Armour's critique of Ariella Azoulay's civil contract of photography (Ellen Armour, "Decolonizing Spectatorship: Photography, Theology, and the New Media," in *Beyond Man: Race, Coloniality and the Philosophy of Religion*, ed. An Yountae and Eleanor Craig [Durham, NC: Duke University Press, 2021], 127–150). Azoulay's call for "getting rid of the distinction between the aesthetic and the political" has informed her conceptualization of photography's politics as the stuff of an inexpertly "civil gaze." Ariella Azoulay, "Getting Rid of the Distinction Between the Aesthetic and the Political," *Theory, Culture and Society* 27, no. 7–8 (2010): 239–262. Armour argues that "in evoking transcendence of self-interest in favor of universality, Azoulay seems to yoke the civil gaze to the very modern invention that her account of the camera's agency called into question, the (allegedly) self-sovereign subject" (Armour, "Decolonizing Spectatorship," 139).

49. Ussama Makdisi, "Ottoman Orientalism," *American Historical Review* 107, no. 3 (2002): 768–796.

50. According to the 1914 Ottoman census, 21 percent of the population in the province where today's Amed is located consisted of non-Muslims, and most were

Armenians. There is, however, cause to doubt the accuracy of these statistics (Jelle Verheij, "Diyarbekir and the Armenian Crisis of 1895," in *Social Relations in Ottoman Diyarbekir, 1870–1915*, ed. Joost Jongerden and Jelle Verheij [Leiden: Brill, 2012], 85–146). The actual number of non-Muslims was likely higher than the official census suggests, given the larger share of non-Muslims living in urban centers hosting mercantile populations, as was the case with Amed's historic district (Adnan Çelik and Namık Kemal Dinç, *Yüz yıllık ah! Toplumsal hafızanın izinde 1915 Diyarbekir* [Century-old curse: 1915 Diyarbekir in search of social memory] [Istanbul: İsmail Beşikçi Vakfı, 2015]). Still, even official numbers capture something of the decimation that the genocide caused: the number of Armenians recorded in the Amed of 1914 alone (65,850) was about twenty-five times what the first republican census of 1927 documented (2,490). In republican Turkey, the number of non-Muslims living in the city continued to fall, with the Wealth Tax of 1942 targeting non-Muslims inflicting such financial ruin that by the early twenty-first century, Amed's non-Muslim population numbered virtually a dozen (Uğur Ümit Üngör, *The Making of Modern Turkey: Nation and State in Eastern Anatolia, 1913–1950* [Oxford: Oxford University Press, 2011]).

51. Ronald Grigor Suny, "The Hamidian Massacres, 1894–1897: Disinterring a Buried History," *Études arméniennes contemporaines*, no. 11 (2018): 125–134. For statistical figures detailing the "massive destruction of human lives and property" that the Hamidian massacres caused, see Üngör and Polatel, *Confiscation and Destruction*, 136.

52. Üngör, *Making of Modern Turkey*, 133–164.

53. Talin Suciyan, "Armenian Genocide and Its Denial: A Comprehensive Tool of Supremacism?," in *Denial of Genocides in the Twenty-First Century*, ed. Bedross Der Matossian (Lincoln: University of Nebraska Press, 2023), 65–96.

54. Dirik, *Kurdish Women's Movement*, 20.

55. Jongerden, *Settlement Issue*, 305.

56. Zeynep Kezer, "Spatializing Difference: The Making of an Internal Border in Early Republican Elazığ, Turkey," *Journal of the Society of Architectural Historians* 73, no. 4 (2014): 507–527.

57. Kezer, "Spatializing Difference," 509.

58. Welat Zeydanlioglu, "Torture and Turkification in the Diyarbakır Military Prison," in *Rights, Citizenship and Torture: Perspectives on Evil, Law and the State*, ed. John Parry and Welat Zeydanlioglu (Oxford: Inter-Disciplinary Press, 2009), 73–92.

59. Leila Harris, "Water and Conflict Geographies of the Southeastern Anatolia Project," *Society and Natural Resources* 15, no. 8 (2002): 743–759.

60. Jongerden, *Settlement Issue*, 85–86, 138–146. On the village evacuations, which the state carried out as part of its scorched-earth offensive against the PKK, see Joost Jongerden, "Under (Re)Construction: The State, the Production of Identity, and the Countryside in the Kurdistan Region in Turkey," in *After Civil War: Division, Reconstruction, and Reconciliation in Contemporary Europe*, ed. Bill Kissane (Philadelphia: University of Pennsylvania Press, 2014), 166–167.

61. Joost Jongerden, "Village Evacuation and Reconstruction in Kurdistan (1993–2002)," *Études rurales*, no. 186 (2010): 77–100; Joost Jongerden, "Dams and Politics in Turkey: Utilizing Water, Developing Conflict," *Middle East Policy* 17, no. 1 (2010): 137–143.

62. On the halted peace talks, officially called "the resolution process," see Bahar Başer, *Diasporas and Homeland Conflicts: A Comparative Perspective* (Surrey: Ashgate, 2014), 64–70. On the new dams being commissioned during this period, see Zeynep S. Akıncı, Arda Bilgen, Antònia Casellas, and Joost Jongerden, "Development Through Design: Knowledge, Power, and Absences in the Making of Southeastern Turkey," *Geoforum*, no. 114 (2020): 181–188.

63. Sayak Valencia, *Gore Capitalism*, trans. John Pluecker (Los Angeles: Semiotext[e], 2018).

64. On "decolonization" and "anticolonization," see, respectively, Zeynep Gambetti, "Decolonizing Diyarbakır: Culture, Identity, and the Struggle to Appropriate Urban Space," in *Comparing Cities: The Middle East and South Asia*, ed. Kamran Asdar Ali and Martina Rieker (Karachi: Oxford University Press, 2009), 95–127; Joost Jongerden, "Crafting Space, Making People: The Spatial Design of Nation in Modern Turkey," *European Journal of Turkish Studies*, no. 10 (2009): 13–18. On "de-Turkification" and "Kurdification," see Muna Güvenç, "Constructing Narratives of Kurdish Nationalism in the Urban Space of Diyarbakır, Turkey," *Traditional Dwellings and Settlements Review* 23, no. 1 (2009): 25–40. On "activists in office," see Nicole Watts, *Activists in Office: Kurdish Politics and Protest in Turkey* (Seattle: University of Washington Press, 2010).

65. Gambetti, "Decolonizing Diyarbakır," 95–127; Güvenç, "Constructing Narratives," 25–40. On the "spectacle" value, see Muna Güvenç, "Propositions for the Emancipatory Potential of Urban Spectacle," *City* 23, no. 3 (2019): 342–365.

66. Ayşe Seda Yüksel, "Rescaled Localities and Redefined Class Relations: Neoliberal Experience in South-East Turkey," *Journal of Balkan and Near Eastern Studies* 13, no. 4 (2011): 433–455; Zeynep Gambetti and Joost Jongerden, "The Spatial (Re)Production of the Kurdish Issue," *Journal of Balkan and Near Eastern Studies* 13, no. 4 (2011): 375–388; Fırat Genç, "Suriçi in Destruction-Regeneration Dialectic," *Heinrich Böll Stiftung*, April 15, 2016, https://tr.boell.org/en/2016/04/15/surici-destruction-regeneration-dialectic; Özgür Güven, "'Our City Is Our Identity!': A Field Study on Kurdish Local Government Experiences in Diyarbakır," *GeoJournal*, no. 86 (2021): 1029–1041.

67. Hişyar Özsoy, "Between Gift and Taboo: Death and the Negotiation of National Identity and Sovereignty in the Kurdish Conflict in Turkey" (PhD diss., University of Texas at Austin, 2010).

68. Umut Yıldırım, "Space, Loss, and Resistance: A Haunted Pool-Map in South-Eastern Turkey," *Anthropological Theory* 19, no. 4 (2019): 459.

69. Yıldırım, "Space, Loss, and Resistance," 452–453, 465.

70. Specifically, the existing analyses Yıldırım references are Gambetti, "Decolonizing Diyarbakır," 95–127; Özsoy, "Between Gift and Taboo"; Yüksel, "Rescaled Localities," 433–455.

71. Yıldırım, "Space, Loss, and Resistance," 461.

72. On landscapes of extraction, see Martín Arboleda, "In the Nature of the Non-City: Expanded Infrastructural Networks and the Political Ecology of Planetary Urbanisation," *Antipode* 48, no. 2 (2016): 234. On large-scale infrastructures, see Alex Loftus and Hug March, "Financializing Desalination: Rethinking the Returns of Big Infrastructure," *International Journal of Urban and Regional Research* 40, no. 1 (2016): 46–61. On networked infrastructures, see Maria Kaika, *City of Flows: Modernity, Nature, and the City* (Abingdon: Routledge, 2005); Creighton Connolly, "Urban

Political Ecology Beyond Methodological Cityism," *International Journal of Urban and Regional Research* 43, no. 1 (2019): 71–72; Hillary Angelo and David Wachsmuth, "Urbanizing Urban Political Ecology: A Critique of Methodological Cityism," *International Journal of Urban and Regional Research* 39, no. 1 (2015): 24.

73. The direct quote comes from Heynen and Ybarra, "On Abolition Ecologies," 21. For the literature on anti-Kurdish racism in contemporary Turkey, see Mücahit Bilici, *Hamal Kürt* (Istanbul: Avesa, 2017); Murat Ergin, "The Racialization of Kurdish Identity in Turkey," *Ethnic and Racial Studies* 37, no. 2 (2014): 322–341; Barış Ünlü, *Türklük sözleşmesi: Oluşumu, işleyişi ve krizi* [Turkishness contract: Its formation, its operation and its crisis] (Ankara: Dipnot, 2018); Cenk Saraçoğlu, "The Changing Image of the Kurds in Turkish Cities: Middle-Class Perceptions of Kurdish Migrants in İzmir," *Patterns of Prejudice* 44, no. 3 (2010): 239–260; Gullistan Yarkın, "Fighting Racism in Turkey: Kurdish Homeownership as an Anti-Racist Practice," *Ethnic and Racial Studies* 43, no. 15 (2020): 2705–2723. The last two articles are particularly relevant to my work, as they constitute rare instances where critical analysis of anti-Kurdish racism has adopted a materially and spatially relevant focus on the urban, albeit through cases in the west of Turkey and through an approach that focuses on the city proper, an approach that my tracing of materialities and images traversing spaces of various kinds and scales aims to rethink.

74. On international conflict over riparian resources, see Jongerden, "Dams and Politics in Turkey," 137–143. On militarization of the countryside and dispossession of villagers, see Zeynep S. Akıncı and Pelin Tan, "Waterdams as Dispossession: Ecology, Security, Colonization," in *Climates: Architecture and the Planetary Imaginary*, ed. James Graham, Caitlin Blanchfield, Alissa Anderson, Jordan Carver, and Jacob Moore (Zurich: Lars Müller, 2016), 142–148.

75. See, for example, Jonathan Peyton and Aaron Franks, "The New Nature of Things? Canada's Conservative Government and the Design of the New Environmental Subject," *Antipode* 48, no. 2 (2016): 459.

76. In interweaving colonialist and nation-statist histories here, I build on political historian and theorist Mahmoud Mamdani's recent book *Neither Settler nor Native: The Making and Unmaking of Permanent Minorities* (Cambridge, MA: Harvard University Press, 2020). He argues that "modern colonialism was not something that states started doing in the eighteenth century. Modern colonialism and the modern state were born together with the creation of the nation-state. Nationalism did not precede colonialism. Nor was colonialism the highest or the final stage in the making of a nation. The two were co-constituted" (1–2). Mamdani's insight is particularly relevant to Kurdistan, as it is now divided between nation-states that originated concomitantly with European imperial powers' direct intervention into the region during World War I and that then inherited many of the latter's colonial methods (Mehmet Gurses, *Anatomy of a Civil War: Sociopolitical Impacts of the Kurdish Conflict in Turkey* [Ann Arbor: University of Michigan Press, 2018], 164–166).

77. Johan Andersson, "Landscape and Gentrification: The Picturesque and Pastoral in 1980s New York Cinema," *Antipode* 49, no. 3 (2017): 539–556; Andrew Harris, "Art and Gentrification: Pursuing the Urban Pastoral in Hoxton, London," *Transactions of the Institute of British Geographers* 37, no. 2 (2012): 226–241; Alex Vasudevan, "'The Photographer of Modern Life': Jeff Wall's Photographic Materialism," *Cultural Geographies* 14, no. 4 (2007): 563–588; Harriet Hawkins, "Turn Your Trash

into. . . Rubbish, Art and Politics: Richard Wentworth's Geographical Imagination," *Social and Cultural Geography* 11, no. 8 (2010): 805–827; Barry, *Material Politics*, 86–92; Ashley Dawkins and Alex Loftus, "The Senses as Direct Theoreticians in Practice," *Transactions of the Institute of British Geographers* 38, no. 4 (2013): 665–677; Cecilie Sachs Olsen, "Collaborative Challenges: Negotiating the Complicities of Socially Engaged Art Within an Era of Neoliberal Urbanism," *Environment and Planning D: Society and Space* 36, no. 2 (2018): 273–293; Alan Ingram, "Making Geopolitics Otherwise: Artistic Interventions in Global Political Space," *Geographical Journal* 177, no. 3 (2011): 218–222; Alan Ingram, "Rethinking Art and Geopolitics Through Aesthetics: Artist Responses to the Iraq War," *Transactions of the Institute of British Geographers* 41, no. 1 (2016): 1–13; Cecilie Sachs Olsen, "Urban Space and the Politics of Socially Engaged Art," *Progress in Human Geography* 43, no. 6 (2019): 985–1000.

78. Nazan Üstündağ, "Pornographic State and Erotic Resistance," *South Atlantic Quarterly* 118, no. 1 (2019): 95–110; Beja Protner, "Reading and Feeling Gender in Perpetrator Graffiti and Photography in Turkey," *Kurdish Studies* 6, no. 1 (2018): 59–83; Adi Kuntsman and Rebecca L. Stein, *Digital Militarism: Israel's Occupation in the Social Media Age* (Stanford, CA: Stanford University Press, 2015).

79. James C. Scott, *Seeing Like a State: How Certain Schemes to Improve the Human Condition Have Failed* (New Haven, CT: Yale University Press, 1998).

80. See, for example, Keysar, "Spatial Testimony," 523–541; Kurgan, "Conflict Urbanism, Aleppo," 72–77; Staal, "Law of the State," 14–23; Weizman, "Introduction," 9–32; Meszaros Martin, "Defoliating the World," 230–253; Sheikh, "Future of the Witness," 145–162.

81. Marc Nichanian, *The Historiographic Perversion*, trans. Gil Anidjar (New York: Columbia University Press, 2008), 11, 94.

82. Nivi Manchanda and Sara Salem, "Empire's H(a)unting Grounds: Theorising Violence and Resistance in Egypt and Afghanistan," *Current Sociology Monograph* 68, no. 2 (2020): 241–262.

83. Mark S. Jackson, "Aesthetics, Politics, and Attunement: On Some Questions Brought by Alterity and Ontology," *GeoHumanities* 2, no. 1 (2016): 10; cf. Hawkins and Straughan, *Geographical Aesthetics*, 3. The caution here is against scholars' risk of overshadowing the agency of those engaged in politics proper—the political work of protest, mobilization, organization, and so on—that is essential to contending with violence and challenging rights violations. See also Malcolm Miles, "Representing Nature: Art and Climate Change," *Cultural Geographies* 17, no. 1 (2010): 32; Harriet Hawkins, "Geography and Art: An Expanding Field," *Progress in Human Geography* 37, no. 1 (2012): 53; Arun Saldanha, "Aestheticism and Post-Humanism," *Dialogues in Human Geography* 2, no. 3 (2012): 278; Alan Ingram, Isla Forsyth, and Nicola Gauld, "Beyond Geopower: Earthly and Anthropic Geopolitics in *The Great Game* by War Boutique," *Cultural Geographies* 23, no. 4 (2016): 646–647; Ingram, "Art, Geopolitics and Metapolitics," 725; Andersson, "Landscape and Gentrification," 552.

84. Saldanha, "Aestheticism and Post-Humanism," 278; Ingram, "Rethinking Art and Geopolitics," 4. In other words, what is theorizable through aesthetics may serve "geopower" as both a progressive and regressive phenomenon; it may facilitate not only struggles for justice but also governmentalities "that make territory and the biosphere accessible, legible, knowable, useable." Christian Parenti, "The Environment Making State: Territory, Nature, and Value," *Antipode* 47, no. 4 (2015): 835; see also Gearóid

Ó Tuathail, *Critical Geopolitics: The Politics of Writing Global Space* (Minneapolis: University of Minnesota Press, 1996). On a progressivist notion of "geopower," see Elizabeth Grosz, *Chaos, Territory, Art: Deleuze and the Framing of the Earth* (Irvington, NY: Columbia University Press, 2008); Yusoff, "Politics of the Anthropocene," 274.

85. Jackson, "Aesthetics, Politics, and Attunement," 8–23. From outside of geography, a similar point is made in Nicholas Mirzoeff, "Visualizing the Anthropocene," *Public Culture* 26, no. 2 (2014): 219–220. The evisceration mentioned here also involved the visual artistic realm (Yusoff et al., "Geopower," 971n1; Michele Lobo, "Encountering the City: Haptic Images of Suburban Darwin," *Area* 53, no. 2 [2019]: 201–210). On a broader level of scholarship, the critique discussed in this paragraph dovetails with recent decolonial and posthumanist turns in the humanities and social sciences in that it problematizes the role of racial and colonial humanism in the politics of ecology by focusing not only on visual practices but also on theorizations; see Ruth Panelli, "More-than-Human Social Geographies: Posthuman and Other Possibilities," *Progress in Human Geography* 34, no. 1 (2010): 79–87; Jamie Lorimer, "Aesthetics for Post-Human Worlds: Difference, Expertise and Ethics," *Dialogues in Human Geography* 2, no. 3 (2012): 284–287; Juanita Sundberg, "Decolonizing Posthumanist Geographies," *Cultural Geographies* 21, no. 1 (2014): 33–47; Mabel Denzin Gergan, "Animating the Sacred, Sentient and Spiritual in Post-Humanist and Material Geographies," *Geography Compass* 9, no. 5 (2015): 262–275; Mark Jackson, ed., *Coloniality, Ontology, and the Question of the Posthuman* (Abingdon: Routledge, 2018); Nina Williams, Merle Patchett, Andrew Lapworth, Tom Roberts, and Thomas Keating, "Practising Post-Humanism in Geographical Research," *Transactions of the Institute of British Geographers* 44, no. 4 (2019): 637–643; Adam J. Barker and Jenny Pickerill, "Doings with the Land and Sea: Decolonising Geographies, Indigeneity, and Enacting Place-Agency," *Progress in Human Geography* 44, no. 4 (2020): 640–662.

86. On humanity, see Kathryn Yusoff, "Geologic Subjects: Nonhuman Origins, Geomorphic Aesthetics and the Art of Becoming Inhuman," *Cultural Geographies* 22 (2015): 383–407; Jones, "Navigating Norman Creek," 497–504; Elizabeth R. Straughan, "A Touching Experiment: Tissue Culture, Tacit Knowledge, and the Making of Bioart," *Transactions of the Institute of British Geographers* 44, no. 2 (2019): 214–215; Harriet Hawkins, "Underground Imaginations, Environmental Crisis and Subterranean Cultural Geographies," *Cultural Geographies* 27, no. 1 (2020): 3–22.

On reason, or judgment, see Nina J. Morris and Sarah G. Cant, "Engaging with Place: Artists, Site-Specificity and the Hebden Bridge Sculpture Trail," *Social and Cultural Geography* 7, no. 6 (2006): 863–888; Danny McNally, "Comforting Others and the Ethical Aesthetics of Being-Together," in *Geographical Aesthetics: Imagining Space, Staging Encounters*, ed. Harriet Hawkins and Elizabeth Straughan (Basingstoke: Ashgate, 2015), 121–136; Yusoff, "Geologic Subjects," 383–407; Thomas Dekeyser, "The Gaps of Architectural Life: The Affective Politics of Gordon Matta-Clark's Conical Intersect," *Transactions of the Institute of British Geographers* 42, no. 2 (2017): 179–191; Jones, "Navigating Norman Creek," 497–504. On speech or text, see McNally, "Comforting Others," 121–136; Dekeyser, "Gaps of Architectural Life," 179–191; Straughan, "Touching Experiment," 214–225.

87. Dixon, Hawkins, and Straughan, "Of Human Birds," 249–270; Saldanha, "Aestheticism and Post-Humanism," 276–279; Hawkins and Straughan, *Geographical Aesthetics*.

88. Yusoff et al., "Geopower," 971; Hawkins and Straughan, *Geographical Aesthetics*, 284.

89. Judith Butler, *Senses of the Subject* (New York: Fordham University Press, 2015), 12 (as cited in Yusoff, *Billion Black Anthropocenes or None*, 62). My point about incorporating ethics into aesthetics echoes Thomas Jellis's observation that geographers might do well to learn from Guattari's "ethico-aesthetics," which "stresses that art does not have a monopoly on aesthetics . . . [and] urges us to think about aesthetics in conjunction with ethics," a thinking that remains underexplored in recent work on aesthetics in geography. See Thomas Jellis, "Geoaesthetics Redux," *Social and Cultural Geography* 17, no. 8 (2016): 1171; cf. Félix Guattari, *Chaosmosis: An Ethico-Aesthetic Paradigm*, trans. Paul Bains and Julian Pefanis (Sydney: Power Publications, 1995). Kurdish Women's Liberation Ideology, developed by members of the eponymous movement, has reconceptualized beauty in a way that resonates strongly with my approach to aesthetics here: as the stuff of organizing and relationality. Specifically, this ideology's notion of beauty is "a value created" through the struggle for "justice, autonomy, truth" and "liberation from patriarchal, capitalist, and colonial standards" (Dirik, *Kurdish Women's Movement*, 67).

90. I discuss this research in my first monograph (Eray Çaylı, *Victims of Commemoration: The Architecture and Violence of Confronting the Past in Turkey* [Syracuse, NY: Syracuse University Press, 2022]).

91. Eray Çaylı and Herdem Doğrul, "Emergency as Normalcy in Mid-2010s Amed/Diyarbakır," in *Architectures of Emergency in Turkey: Heritage, Displacement, and Catastrophe*, ed. Eray Çaylı, Pınar Aykaç, and Sevcan Ercan (London: Bloomsbury / I. B. Tauris, 2021), 69–88.

92. Timothy Neale and Eve Vincent, "Mining, Indigeneity, Alterity: Or, Mining Indigenous Alterity?," *Cultural Studies* 31, no. 2–3 (2017): 417–439; Lisa Tilley, "Resisting Piratic Method by Doing Research Otherwise," *Sociology* 51, no. 1 (2017): 27–42; Ranjan Datta, "Decolonizing Both Researcher and Research and Its Effectiveness in Indigenous Research," *Research Ethics* 14, no. 2 (2018): 1–24; Sam Halvorsen, "Cartographies of Epistemic Expropriation: Critical Reflections on Learning from the South," *Geoforum*, no. 95 (2018): 11–20; Ramón Grosfoguel, "Epistemic Extractivism: A Dialogue with Alberto Acosta, Leanne Betasamosake Simpson, and Silvia Rivera Cusicanqui," in *Knowledges Born in the Struggle: Constructing the Epistemologies of the Global South*, ed. Boaventura de Sousa Santos and Maria Paula Meneses (New York: Routledge, 2019), 203–218; Eleanor Knott, "Beyond the Field: Ethics After Fieldwork in Politically Dynamic Contexts," *Perspectives on Politics* 17, no. 1 (2019): 140–153; Melany Cruz and Darcy Luke, "Methodology and Academic Extractivism: The Neo-Colonialism of the British University," *Third World Thematics: A TWQ Journal* 5, no. 1–2 (2020): 154–170; Timothy Neale and Emma Kowal, "'Related' Histories: On Epistemic and Reparative Decolonization," *History and Theory* 59, no. 3 (2020): 403–412; Natalie Oswin, "An Other Geography," *Dialogues in Human Geography* 10, no. 1 (2020): 9–18.

93. See, for example, Knott, "Beyond the Field," 141–142; Oswin, "Other Geography," 13–14.

94. See, for example, Carrie Mott and Daniel Cockayne, "Citation Matters: Mobilizing the Politics of Citation Toward a Practice of 'Conscientious Engagement,'" *Gender, Place and Culture* 24, no. 7 (2017): 954–973; Leila C. Nadir, "More Life After

Ruins: Autotheory, the Politics of Citation, and the Limits of the Scholarly Gaze," *ASAP/Journal* 6, no. 3 (2021): 547–550.

95. Max Liboiron and Rui Li, "Citational Politics in Tight Places," *CLEAR*, March 2, 2022, https://civiclaboratory.nl/2022/03/02/citational-politics-in-tight-places. Also see Kerryn Drysdale and Karen-Anne Wong, "Sensory Ethnography," in *The SAGE Encyclopedia of Research Methods*, ed. Paul Atkinson, Sara Delamont, Alexandru Cernat, Joseph W. Sakshaug, and Richard A. Williams (London: Sage, 2019), https://www.doi.org/10.4135/9781526421036775965.

96. Charmaine Chua, "Abolition Is a Constant Struggle: Five Lessons from Minneapolis," *Theory and Event* 23, no. 5 (2020): 127–147. As a case in point, in the summer of 2019, when I shared an earlier version of chapter 1 in a reading group on political violence, nearly all of whose membership was composed of anthropologists of Turkey, the text was criticized for concluding with examples from activist work rather than first subjecting them to analysis as empirical data.

97. Ingram, "Making Geopolitics Otherwise," 222.

98. For the direct quote, see Ingram, "Making Geopolitics Otherwise," 222. For the broader point about the relevant necessity of political work, see Saldanha, "Aestheticism and Post-Humanism," 276–279; Anthony Gardner, "Aesthetics of Emptiness and Withdrawal: Contemporary European Art and Actually Existing Democratization," *Postcolonial Studies* 13, no. 2 (2010): 179–197; Ingram, "Art, Geopolitics and Metapolitics," 719–739.

99. Ingram, "Making Geopolitics Otherwise," 218.

100. Ingram, "Making Geopolitics Otherwise," 222; Stratford and Langridge, "Critical Artistic Interventions," 839; Dawkins and Loftus, "Senses as Direct Theoreticians," 666; Ingram, Forsyth, and Gauld, "Beyond Geopower," 636.

Chapter 1: Extractivist and Antiextractivist Aesthetics

1. Felat Bozarslan, "Ayda 100 bin TL zarara rağmen kuşların yuvasını bozmadılar" [They did not spoil birds' nests despite incurring a monthly cost of 100 thousand Turkish Lira], *Deutsche Welle*, July 11, 2019, http://www.dw.com/tr/ayda-100-bin-tl-zarara-rağmen-kuşların-yuvasını-bozmadılar/av-49539280.

2. AA, "Kırlangıçlar kum yığınına yuva yaptı" [Swallows nested in a sandpile], *Gazete Duvar*, June 29, 2019, http://www.gazeteduvar.com.tr/turkiye/2019/06/29/kirlangiclar-kum-yigina-yuva-yapti; Ahmet Kaplan, "Kırlangıç yuvaları için zarar etmeyi göze aldılar" [They risked money loss to keep swallow nests], *AA*, June 26, 2019, http://www.aa.com.tr/tr/turkiye/kirlangic-yuvalari-icin-zarar-etmeyi-goze-aldilar/1516189.

3. Hüseyin Kaçar, "İşte insanlık örneği" [Humanity in action], *Sabah*, July 14, 2019, https://sabah.com.tr/yasam/2019/07/14/iste-insanlik-ornegi.

4. See, for example, mahiramca, "100 bin tl zarara rağmen kuş yuvasını bozmamak" [To avoid spoiling birds' nests despite incurring a monthly cost of 100 thousand Turkish Lira], Ekşi Sözlük (Sour Dictionary), July 10, 2019, https://eksisozluk.com/entry/92425698). The Ekşi Sözlük (Sour Dictionary) website is the Turkish equivalent of Reddit.

5. bozacininsahidi, "100 bin tl zarara rağmen kuş yuvasını bozmamak" [To avoid spoiling birds' nests despite incurring a monthly cost of 100 thousand Turkish Lira], Ekşi Sözlük, July 10, 2019, https://eksisozluk.com/entry/92427113. This

comment seems to have been removed from the site. I preserved the Turkish-language original in a short essay (see http://www.mimarlikdergisi.com/index.cfm?sayfa=mimarlik&DergiSayi=426&RecID=4978): "Hep diyorum, kürtler kadar adam olabilseydiniz bu ülke bu durumda olmazdı gidin doğu illerine, sokakta kalmış olun, birinin evine gidin kapısını çalın sokakta kaldım deyin evinizi açar size. Bunu karadenizde yapın yemediğiniz dayak kalmaz, iç anadoluda yapın hayatınızı bile kaybedebilirsiniz. Pkk hariç, pkk gerektiğinde fetö, üst akıl, dhkpc vs hepsi bir olur ülkeyi yıkmak için emperyalist maşa olurlar, tecrübeyle sabittir. Pkk yok edilmesi gereken bir numaralı terör örgütlerindendir. Yok öyle canlı bombayı uçağa koyup suçu masum insanların üzerine atmaya çalışmak, bilmemne yaptığımın vatan haini pislikleri sizi, hak ettiğiniz muameleyi bir gün göreceksiniz. Başınızdan aşağı bombaları boşaltacağız."

6. For examples of geography scholarship that has engaged Rancièrian aesthetics, see Deborah Dixon, "Creating the Semi-Living: On Politics, Aesthetics, and the More-than-Human," *Transactions of the Institute of British Geographers* 34, no. 4 (2009): 411–425; Ingram, "Rethinking Art and Geopolitics," 1–13; Divya P. Tolia-Kelly, "Rancière and the Re-Distribution of the Sensible: The Artist Rosanna Raymond, Dissensus, and Postcolonial Sensibilities Within the Spaces of the Museum," *Progress in Human Geography* 43, no. 1 (2019): 123–140. For geography scholarship that has done so beyond the arts-based origins of Rancière's theory, see Mustafa Dikeç, "Immigrants, Banlieues," 23–42; Derek Ruez, "'Partitioning the Sensible' at Park 51: Rancière, Islamophobia, and Common Politics," *Antipode* 45, no. 5 (2013): 1128–1147.

7. For "nonhuman," see Hawkins and Straughan, *Geographical Aesthetics*; Rosa and Díaz, "Raciontologies," 122–123. For "inhuman," see Yusoff, "Politics of the Anthropocene," 255–276; Yusoff, *Billion Black Anthropocenes or None*; Yusoff et al., "Geopower," 971–988. For "insentient," see Matthew Hall, "Beyond the Human: Extending Ecological Anarchism," *Environmental Politics* 20, no. 3 (2011): 375.

8. Rancière, *Politics of Aesthetics*, 13.

9. Rancière, *Dissensus*, 36.

10. Rancière, *Dissensus*, 36–37.

11. Hawkins and Straughan, *Geographical Aesthetics*, 10, 287–289; Elizabeth Povinelli, *Economies of Abandonment: Social Belonging and Endurance in Late Liberalism* (Durham, NC: Duke University Press, 2011), 7; Rosa and Díaz, "Raciontologies," 128–129; Yusoff, *Billion Black Anthropocenes or None*, 65–85; Yusoff, "Politics of the Anthropocene," 260; Yusoff et al., "Geopower," 972–973.

12. Bruce Braun, "New Materialisms and Neoliberal Natures," *Antipode* 47, no. 1 (2015): 1–14; Mabel Denzin Gergan, "Animating the Sacred," 271–272; Susan W. S. Millar and Don Mitchell, "The Tight Dialectic: The Anthropocene and the Capitalist Production of Nature," *Antipode* 49, no. s1 (2017): 88; Junxi Qian and Lei Wei, "Development at the Edge of Difference: Rethinking Capital and Market Relations from Lugu Lake, Southwest China," *Antipode* 52, no. 1 (2020): 247; Saldanha, "Aestheticism and Post-Humanism," 276–279; Arun Saldanha, "A Date with Destiny: Racial Capitalism and the Beginnings of the Anthropocene," *Environment and Planning D: Society and Space* 38, no. 1 (2020): 12–34.

13. Baldwin and Erickson, "Introduction," 6–7.

14. Saldanha, "Date with Destiny," 25.

15. Parenti, "Environment Making State," 831.

16. Guyot, "Eco-Frontier Paradigm," 682; Vasudevan, "Intimate Inventory," 785. On "wilderness," see Richard A. Walker, "Editor's Introduction," *Antipode* 11, no. 2 (1979): 9. On "wetlands," see Morgan M. Robertson, "No Net Loss: Wetland Restoration and the Incomplete Capitalization of Nature," *Antipode* 32, no. 4 (2000): 463–493. On "Indigeneity," see Erickson, "Anthropocene Futures," 113.

17. On "danger," see Dikeç, "Immigrants, Banlieues," 23–42. On "endangerment," see Austin Zeiderman, "Danger Signs: The Aesthetics of Insecurity in Bogotá," in *Futureproof*, ed. D. Asher Ghertner, Hudson McFann, and Daniel M. Goldstein (Durham, NC: Duke University Press, 2020), 63–86.

18. On the negation of the subaltern, see Jonathan Paquette and Aurélie Lacassagne, "Subterranean Subalterns: Territorialisation, Deterritorialisation, and the Aesthetics of Mining," *Culture and Organization* 19, no. 3 (2013): 242–260. On the negation of the inhuman, see Vasudevan, "Intimate Inventory," 770–790.

19. Peyton and Franks, "New Nature of Things?," 459.

20. "Dicle ile Diyarbakır barışıyor" [The Tigris and Diyarbakır are making peace], *Evrensel*, April 17, 2007, https://www.evrensel.net/haber/246035/dicle-ile-diyarbakir-barisiyor.

21. The following history demonstrates how extractivism is a thread running through and interweaving actors and methods that may otherwise seem separately associated with imperialism, colonialism, and the nation-state. Following its failed attempts in the 1830s to carve out a "Euphrates Route" to India, Britain launched a commercial steamship navigation program along the Tigris in 1861 with the aim of "buffering" its colony "against Russian and French aggression" (Camille Lyans Cole, "Precarious Empires: A Social and Environmental History of Steam Navigation on the Tigris," *Journal of Social History* 50, no. 1 [2016]: 75). In 1935, the nascent Turkish Republic launched a "river flow monitoring" program, followed in 1946 by the construction of "research and observation stations" on the Tigris and Euphrates Rivers (Ünal Öziş, Türkay Baran, and Nurhan Demirci, "Türkiye'de Dicle havzasındaki başlıca akım gözlem istasyonlarının aylık akışları" [Monthly streamflow data from major stream gauging stations in Turkey's Tigris River basin], *Teknik Dergi* 10, no. 4 [1999]: 2030). Also in the 1930s, the Turkish state built a new railway line connecting Amed to Turkey's eastern Mediterranean cities of maritime and industrial significance and later to its capital, Ankara. If post–World War I borders had already impaired the Tigris's centuries-old function as a cross-Mesopotamian thoroughfare, this railway line went a step further by reorienting the upper Tigris valley to Anatolia (İhsan Seddar Kaynar, "Nehir taşımacılığından demiryoluna Diyarbakır'ın ulaşım ağı" [Diyarbakır's transportation network from river transport to railways], in *Tanzimat'tan günümüze Diyarbakır* [Diyarbakır from the Tanzimat to the present], ed. Oktay Bozan, Hakan Asan, Hatip Yıldız, and Mehmet Salih Erpolat [Elazığ: Manas, 2019], 269–270). The new railway was dubbed "the copper line" after the metal extracted from mines just north of Amed, which it would transport to central Turkey (Kaynar, "Diyarbakır'ın ulaşım ağı" [Diyarbakır's transportation network], 282). In line with this reorientation, Amed's official name was changed in 1937 from Diyar-ı Bekr ("Land of Bekr," after the Arab tribe that had settled there during the seventh-century Muslim conquests) to Diyarbakır: "Land of Copper" (Kaynar, "Diyarbakır'ın ulaşım ağı" [Diyarbakır's transportation network], 271). Not incidentally, this rebranding followed from the 1935 renaming of Dêrsim (situated in the northernmost tip of Kurdistan about two

hundred kilometers north of Amed) as Tunceli—"Land of Bronze"—in the run-up to the violent campaign the state conducted there in 1937–1938.

22. Jongerden, "Dams and Politics in Turkey," 137–143.

23. Dogan Altınbilek, "Development and Management of the Euphrates-Tigris Basin," *International Journal of Water Resources Development* 20, no. 1 (2004): 18.

24. Murat Biricik and Şemsettin Turğa, "Description of a Euphrates Softshell Turtle Nest from the Tigris River," *Salamandra* 47, no. 2 (2011): 99–102.

25. Mehmet Nazım Özer, "Diyarbakır Büyükşehir Belediyesi: Diyarbakır 'Dicle Vadisi Peyzaj Planlama Kentsel Tasarım ve Mimari Proje Yarışması' " [Diyarbakir Metropolitan Municipality: Diyarbakir 'Dicle Valley Landscape Planning Urban Design and Architectural Project Competition'], *Planlama* 41 (2007): 198–199.

26. Sertaç Erten and Devrim Çimen, "Türkiye'de kentsel tasarım yarışmalarının proje olarak uygulanma(ma) süreçleri" [The (in)application processes of urban design competition projects in Turkey], *Planlama*, no. 51 (2011): 42–43.

27. Mehmet Aslanoğlu, "Baydemir: Başbakan proje hırsızı" [Baydemir: Prime Minister is a project thief], *Evrensel*, June 3, 2011, https://www.evrensel.net/haber/7207/baydemir-basbakan-proje-hirsizi.

28. Halil Aydın, "Vadideki 'Big Chefs'!" ["Big Chefs" in the valley!], *Siyasi Haber*, July 4, 2014, https://siyasihaber.org/sectiklerimiz/vadideki-big-chefs-halil-aydin.

29. Prasad Daggupati, Raghavan Srinivasan, Yihun Taddele Dile Ahmadi, and Deepa Verma, "Spatial and Temporal Patterns of Precipitation and Stream Flow Variations in Tigris-Euphrates River Basin," *Environmental Monitoring and Assessment* 189, no. 50 (2017), https://doi.org/10.1007/s10661-016-5752-y.

30. Vecdi Erbay, "Dicle budur işte!" [This is the real Tigris!], *Gazete Duvar*, December 15, 2018, https://www.gazeteduvar.com.tr/gundem/2018/12/15/dicle-budur-iste; Özer Akdemir, "Kentleri ve nehirleri kederli ülke" [The country of sorrowful cities and rivers], *Evrensel*, December 23, 2018, https://www.evrensel.net/yazi/82921/kentleri-ve-nehirleri-kederli-ulke.

31. Burak Emek, "@burakemek10: Yıllar sonra su seviyesi eski görünümüne kavuştu" [Years later the water level regains its historical appearance], Twitter, December 15, 2018, accessed October 31, 2024, https://twitter.com/burakemek10/status/1073839724643651585.

32. Ömer Yasin Ergin, "Dicle Nehri son 30 yılın en berrak görünümünde" [The Tigris River has the clearest appearance of the past 30 years], *AA*, May 25, 2019, https://www.aa.com.tr/tr/turkiye/dicle-nehri-son-30-yilin-en-berrak-gorunumunde/1488977; Deniz İke, "Dicle Nehri berrak aksın" [Let the Tigris flow clearly], *ANF*, May 28, 2019, https://anfturkce.com/toplum-ekoloji/dicle-nehri-berrak-aksin-125728.

33. Sümeyra Kurt, "Historical Progress of Laws and Regulations on Coastal Use in Turkey," *Eastern Geographical Review* 20, no. 33 (2015): 96–99.

34. The two dams are named Kralkızı and Dicle. Kralkızı's construction was begun in 1985, and Dicle's in 1986; both were completed in 1997.

35. On "rivers," see Dilip da Cunha, *The Invention of Rivers: Alexander's Eye and Ganga's Descent* (Philadelphia: University of Pennsylvania Press, 2019). On "water," see Jeffrey M. Banister and Stacie G. Widdifield, "The Debut of 'Modern Water' in Early 20th Century Mexico City: The Xochimilco Potable Waterworks," *Journal of Historical Geography* 46 (2014): 36–52.

36. Yusoff, "Geologic Subjects," 399.

37. Yusoff, "Geologic Subjects," 399; cf. Yusoff et al, "Geopower," 972–973.

38. See, for example, Naomi Millner, "Activist Pedagogies Through Rancière's Aesthetic Lens," in *Geographical Aesthetics: Imagining Space, Staging Encounters*, ed. Harriet Hawkins and Elizabeth Straughan (Farnham: Ashgate, 2015), 76–78.

39. Yusoff, "Politics of the Anthropocene," 262.

40. DHA, "Balık avlamak için Dicle Nehri'ne giren genç boğuldu" [Youth drowns while guddling in the Tigris River], *Hürriyet*, May 26, 2019, http://www.hurriyet.com.tr/yerel-haberler/diyarbakir/bismil/balik-avlamak-icin-dicle-nehrine-giren-genc-bo-41226599.

41. Hasan Gündüz, "Köylülerden 'kum ocakları kapatılsın' eylemi" ["Close the sand quarries" protest by villagers], *Doğru Haber*, February 1, 2013, https://dogruhaber.com.tr/haber/68484-koylulerden-kum-ocaklari-kapatilsin-eylemi.

42. İdris Emen, "Sırrını sadece ölenler biliyor" [Only the dead know its secret], *Hürriyet*, May 14, 2016, https://www.hurriyet.com.tr/gundem/sirrini-sadece-olenler-biliyor-40104031.

43. Derek Gregory, "The Natures of War," *Antipode* 48, no. 1 (2016): 4–5.

44. On "indigenous" senses of and attachments to place, see, for example, Arturo Escobar, *Territories of Difference: Place, Movements, Life,* Redes (Durham, NC: Duke University Press, 2017), 5–7. On "local" ones, see, for example, Li, "Contesting Equivalences," 32.

45. Miraz Rûsipî, "Kırklar Dağı Konakları'ndan komün olur mu?" [Could the Mount Kırklar Villas become a commune?], *BirGün*, January 31, 2015, http://www.birgun.net/haber-detay/kirklar-dagi-konaklari-ndan-komun-olur-mu-74502.html.

46. Yusoff, *Billion Black Anthropocenes or None*, 51–62; Yusoff, "Politics of the Anthropocene," 266–268.

Chapter 2: The Art of Peace and Its Extractivisms

1. Robert A. Pois, "Nature Devours History: National Socialism and the Death of Romanticism," *History of European Ideas* 16, no. 1–3 (1993): 315–321. This is not to say that there was a straight line leading from Romanticism to violent nationalist ideology; the relationship between the two has been much more fluctuating and contested than what my limited space here allows me to expound (Max Blechman, "The Revolutionary Dream of Early German Romanticism," in *Revolutionary Romanticism*, ed. Max Blechman [San Francisco: City Lights Books, 1999], 1–34).

2. On these concepts developed in response to the Anthropocene, see Elizabeth M. DeLoughrey, *Allegories of the Anthropocene* (Durham, NC: Duke University Press, 2019), 22.

3. Yusoff, *Billion Black Anthropocenes or None*, 1–22.

4. See, for example, Heather Davis and Etienne Turpin, eds., *Art in the Anthropocene: Encounters Among Aesthetics, Politics, Environments and Epistemologies* (London: Open Humanities Press, 2015); Kerry Oliver-Smith, ed., *The World to Come: Art in the Age of the Anthropocene* (Gainesville, FL: Harn Museum of Art, 2018); Susan Ballard and Liz Linden, "Spiral Jetty, Geoaesthetics, and Art: Writing the Anthropocene," *Anthropocene Review* 6, no. 1–2 (2019): 142–161. For an approach that has altogether rejected the Anthropocene, see Demos, *Against the Anthropocene*.

5. Relevant here is the history of "imperial forestry and colonial land use" that has relied as much on imaginaries developed and circulated through "German

Romanticism" as they did on the "extractive logic of silviculture and agriculture in the globalized circuits of capital" (Iain A. Boal, "Marjorie Nicolson and the Aesthetics of Nature," *Antipode* 28, no. 3 [1996]: 304).

6. Andersson, "Landscape and Gentrification," 539–556; Harris, "Art and Gentrification," 226–241.

7. Vasudevan, "'Photographer of Modern Life,'" 563–588; Hawkins, "Turn Your Trash," 805–827.

8. Barry, *Material Politics*, 86–92; Dawkins and Loftus, "Senses as Direct Theoreticians," 665–677; Sachs Olsen, "Collaborative Challenges," 273–293.

9. Ingram, "Making Geopolitics Otherwise," 218–222; Ingram, "Rethinking Art and Geopolitics," 1–13; Sachs Olsen, "Urban Space and the Politics of Socially Engaged Art," 985–1000.

10. Jamie Doucette, "Political Will and Human Geography: Non-Representational, Post-Political, and Gramscian Geographies," *Progress in Human Geography* 44, no. 2 (2020): 315–332; Susan Roberts, Anna Secor, and Matthew Sparke, "Neoliberal Geopolitics," *Antipode* 35, no. 5 (2003): 886–897; Erik Swyngedouw, "The Antinomies of the Postpolitical City: In Search of a Democratic Politics of Environmental Production," *International Journal of Urban and Regional Research* 33, no. 3 (2009): 601–620; Japhy Wilson and Erik Swyngedouw, eds., *The Post-Political and Its Discontents* (Edinburgh: Edinburgh University Press, 2014); on aesthetics beyond art, see Goonewardena, "Urban Sensorium," 46–71; David Harvey, "Between Space and Time: Reflections on the Geographical Imagination," *Annals of the Association of American Geographers* 80, no. 3 (1990): 418–434.

11. Gómez-Barris, *Extractive Zone*.

12. Gómez-Barris, *Extractive Zone*, 6–8. Gómez-Barris has conceptualized this gaze elsewhere as "the extractive gaze" and "the extractivist viewpoint." See, respectively, Macarena Gómez-Barris, "Protecting Water and Forest Resources Against Colonization in the Indigenous Américas," in *The Oxford Handbook of Economic Imperialism*, ed. Zak Cope and Immanuel Ness (Oxford: Oxford University Press, 2022), 323–332; Macarena Gómez-Barris, "Inverted Visuality: Against the Flow of Extractivism," *Journal of Visual Culture* 15, no. 1 (2016): 29–31.

13. Gómez-Barris, *Extractive Zone*, 16. For a comparable argument that problematizes the "extractive eye" on Latin America, see Andermann, *Entranced Earth*, 12.

14. Sachs Olsen, "Collaborative Challenges," 273–293; Dixon, "Creating the Semi-Living," 411–425; Harriet Hawkins, "Dialogues and Doings: Sketching the Relationships Between Geography and Art," *Geography Compass* 5, no. 7 (2011): 464–478; Harriet Hawkins, "Geography's Creative (Re)Turn: Toward a Critical Framework," *Progress in Human Geography* 43, no. 6 (2019): 963–984; Divya Tolia-Kelly and Rosanna Raymond, "Decolonising Museum Cultures: An Artist and a Geographer in Collaboration," *Transactions of the Institute of British Geographers* 45, no. 1 (2020): 2–17; John Wylie and Catrin Webster, "Eye-Opener: Drawing Landscape Near and Far," *Transactions of the Institute of British Geographers* 44, no. 1 (2019): 32–47; Hawkins, "Underground Imaginations," 3–22.

15. Özlem Özyurt, "Diyar diyar güncel sanat" [Contemporary art from land to land], *Arkitera*, November 14, 2002, https://v3.arkitera.com/v1/sanat/2002/11/haberler/ozlemozyurt.htm.

16. Jean-François Polo, "Turkish Cultural Policy: In Search of a New Model?," *Turkish Cultural Policies in a Global World*, ed. Muriel Girard, Jean-François Polo, and Clémence Scalbert-Yücel (Basingstoke: Palgrave Macmillan, 2018), 96.

17. Rıdvan Kuday, "Neoliberalism's Impact on Contemporary Art" (master's thesis, Mardin Artuklu University, 2019), 57.

18. Indeed, it was with Tekin's solo exhibition in 2008 that the center began to organize original exhibitions showcasing contemporary art from Amed. The only near-precedent to this was a repeat event of the sort the center held in its first years, an exhibition originally curated by René Block as part of the 2004 Cetinje Biennial in Montenegro. The three Amed-based artists participating in this exhibition, including Tekin, used their artist fees to fund it being brought to their hometown and restaged at the center (Cengiz Tekin, personal communication, February 2021).

19. Stadt Münster, "Ein interkultureller Austausch mit Tradition" [An intercultural exchange with tradition], *Presse Service*, March 17, 2006, https://www.presse-service.de/data.aspx/static/630325F.html.

20. Serfiraz Ergun, "3 Michelin Yıldızlı Bir Şefimiz ve Bir Lokantamız Olacak" [We will have a Michelin 3-star chef and restaurant], *Milliyet*, September 11, 2008, https://www.milliyet.com.tr/cadde/serfiraz-ergun/3-michelin-yildizli-bir-sefimiz-ve-bir-lokantamiz-olacak-989410.

21. "Planet K," *Rebiennale*, May 1, 2009, http://rebiennale.org/it/planet-k; Diyarbakır Metropolitan Municipality, *Diyarbakır Büyükşehir Belediyesi 2013 Faaliyet Raporu* [Diyarbakır Metropolitan Municipality annual report for 2013] (Istanbul: Gün, 2014), 93.

22. Cengiz Tekin, personal communication, July 2020.

23. Jaś Elsner, "Style," in *Critical Terms for Art History*, ed. Robert S. Nelson and Richard Shiff (Chicago: University of Chicago Press, 2003), 98–109.

24. James C. Scott, *Against the Grain: A Deep History of the Earliest States* (London: Yale University Press, 2017), 55, 128.

25. Mehrdad Izady, *Kurds: A Concise Handbook* (London: Taylor & Francis, 1992), 24.

26. Andersson, "Landscape and Gentrification," 547.

27. Roger Célestin and Eliane Françoise DalMolin, *France from 1851 to the Present* (Basingstoke: Palgrave Macmillan, 2007), 135–137; Nellie Hermann, "Idle Bird," *Paris Review*, June 10, 2015, www.theparisreview.org/blog/2015/06/10/idle-bird.

28. Carl Woodring, "Nature and Art in the Nineteenth Century," *PMLA* 92, no. 2 (1977): 193–202.

29. Derya Erdem, "Representation of Democratic Society Party in Mainstream Turkish Media," in *The Kurdish Question in Turkey: New Perspectives on Violence, Representation and Reconciliation*, ed. Cengiz Gunes and Welat Zeydanlioğlu (Abingdon: Routledge, 2014), 55–56.

30. Frank F. Cunningham, "J. M. W. Turner and the Landscape Revolution" (discussion paper, *Simon Fraser University Department of Geography Discussion Paper* Series 12, Burnaby, 1981), http://summit.sfu.ca/item/15464.

31. Biner, *States of Dispossession*, 33–100.

32. Nicolas Bourriaud, *Relational Aesthetics* (Paris: Les Presses du Réel, 2002).

33. Tania Bruguera, "Introduction on Useful Art," *Tania Bruguera*, April 23, 2011, accessed October 31, 2024, https://taniabruguera.com/introduction-on-useful-art.

34. Larne Abse Gogarty, "'Usefulness' in Contemporary Art and Politics," *Third Text* 31, no. 1 (2017): 117–132.

35. On the point about "commodification," see Anthony Downey, "Towards a Politics of (Relational) Aesthetics," *Third Text* 21, no. 3 (2007): 267–275. On the point about "participation," see Claire Bishop, "Antagonism and Relational Aesthetics," *October*, no. 110 (2004): 51–79.

36. Cases in point include the Office for Useful Art established in 2017 at Turkey's foremost contemporary art institution, Salt, and the Anthropocene-themed 2019 Istanbul Biennial curated by relational aesthetics' founder Nicolas Bourriaud.

37. On the point about education and the young, see Beral Madra, "The Hot Spot of Global Art," *Third Text* 22, no. 1 (2008): 107. On the point about constituting a public forum for expression, see Cem Erciyes, "'Nefes alınabilecek bir vaha olduk" [We became an oasis where one can breathe], *Radikal*, October 26, 2008, accessed August 12, 2021, https://radikal.com.tr/kultur/nefes-alinabilecek-bir-vaha-olduk-905258.

38. In the late 2000s, several curators responded to the body of photographic work discussed here by encouraging Tekin to shift to videography instead, as they considered videos sensorially more engrossing and logistically more advantageous than photography (Cengiz Tekin, personal communication, July 2020). In May 2020, following a talk I gave on Tekin's work, an influential Istanbul-based art critic responded that he had "always criticized" it "for insisting that we remain in the realm of representation. But, having heard your take on it, I can see the rationale behind this insistence" (Poşe Art Space, *Açık Seminer: Eray Çaylı* [Open seminar: Eray Çaylı], moderated by Murat Alat on May 2, 2020, posted online on May 12, 2020, https://www.youtube.com/watch?v=1F3aaw3yIAo).

39. This is a dichotomy that has also been problematized by recent scholarship on art's aesthetics-as-geopolitics (Andersson, "Landscape and Gentrification," 552; Ingram, Forsyth, and Gauld, "Beyond Geopower," 646–647).

40. Muna Guvenc, "Propositions for the Emancipatory Potential of Urban Spectacle," *City* 23, no. 3 (2019): 342–365.

41. Abdulsamet Aydeniz, "Identity Formation and Politicization of Children Affected by Anti-Terror Law" (master's thesis, Istanbul Bilgi University, 2013), 94–95.

42. Veronica della Dora, "Putting the World into a Box: A Geography of Nineteenth-Century 'Travelling Landscapes,'" *Geografiska Annaler: Series B* 89, no. 4 (2007): 287–306.

43. Mücahit Bilici, "Kürt'e bakan Türklük" [The Turkishness that gazes at the Kurd], *Birikim*, no. 371 (2020): 54–58.

44. John Paul Catungal, "Imagining Between Possible and Realised: Creative World-Making as Politically Situated Knowledge Production," *Dialogues in Human Geography* 9, no. 2 (2019): 150–153.

45. Catungal, "Imagining Between Possible and Realised," 152–153.

46. Tolia-Kelly and Raymond, "Decolonising Museum Cultures," 2–17.

47. Janae Davis, Alex Moulton, Levi Van Sant, and Brian Williams, "Anthropocene, Capitalocene, . . . Plantationocene? A Manifesto for Ecological Justice in an Age of Global Crises," *Geography Compass* 13, no. 5 (2019): e12438.

48. Derek Gregory, *The Colonial Present: Afghanistan, Palestine, Iraq* (Oxford: Blackwell, 2004), 5–12.

Chapter 3: War's Hypervisibility and Humanitarian Extractivisms

1. The original Turkish monologue uses the word *doğru* to refer to what I have translated here as "truth." This is a word with multiple denotations, including straightness, rightness, and correctness as well as truth.

2. According to the Human Rights Foundation of Turkey, fifty-two curfews took place between mid-August and mid-December 2015 across seven of the region's provinces, amounting to an area inhabited by approximately 1.3 million people (Şeyhmus Çakan, "Clashes in Southeast Turkey Kill Seven, New Curfews Declared," Reuters, December 14, 2015, https://www.reuters.com/article/world/clashes-in-southeast-turkey-kill-seven-new-curfews-declared-idUSKBN0TX17K).

3. Episodes were weekly and around twenty-five minutes each. An archive is available at https://youtube.com/playlist?list=PL1NMKszIR_pQA5FJolFiNU4IQAy9_6Ows. When asked for the reasons behind his 2004 resignation from the army, the show's host, Mete Yarar, cited three: "the increasing distance" that separated the army from the people in the aftermath of the 1980 military coup; the so-called Hood Event, where the US military seized a number of Turkish soldiers situated in northern Iraq, put sacks over their heads, and kept them for sixty hours; and, simply, "wanting to live life" (Müjgan Halis, "Hayatımı yaşamak için orduyu bıraktım" [I quit the army to live my life], *Sabah*, April 22, 2012, http://www.sabah.com.tr/pazar/2012/04/22/hayatimi-yasamak-icin-orduyu-biraktim). Such statements implying adventurousness, unorthodoxy, and, most importantly, a part-insider/part-outsider position vis-à-vis the military are in concert with his show *Bear Witness*'s own characteristics unpacked in this chapter (e.g., its claims to impartiality and credibility and its prioritization of sensation and experience over discourse and interpretation).

4. The best-known precedents of state television series chronicling the army's operations against the PKK, produced between the 1990s and today, include (in nearly chronological order) *Panorama from Anatolia* (*Anadolu'dan Görünüm*), *The Armed Forces Hour* (*Silahlı Kuvvetler Saati*), and *The Turkish Army in War and Peace* (*Savaşta Barışta Türk Ordusu*).

5. Tahir Elçi, head of Diyarbakır Bar Association, was assassinated on November 28, 2015, in his hometown's historic center moments after reading a press statement that criticized all parties involved in the armed conflict for the damage they impinged upon the city's architectural heritage (Jared Malsin, "The Killing of a Kurdish Lawyer Means Dark Days for Turkey," *Time*, November 29, 2015, https://time.com/4128696/tahir-elci-kurdish-lawyer-assassination-turkey/). Military surveillance from both sides and footage filmed by anti-Assad forces in Syria played an important role in the debates around the downing of the Russian jet fighter on November 24, 2015 (Huizhong Wu, "Maps from Russia and Turkey Tell Very Different Stories About the Downed Jet," *Mashable*, November 24, 2015, http://www.mashable.com/2015/11/24/turkey-russia-plane-map/#lUIROoN7eOqN).

6. Eyal Weizman, *Hollow Land: Israel's Architecture of Occupation* (London: Verso, 2007), 185–210.

7. Paul Virilio, *The Original Accident* (Cambridge: Polity Press, 2007), 57–69, 83–101.

8. Susan Sontag, *Regarding the Pain of Others* (New York: Picador, 2003); Jean Baudrillard, *Simulacra and Simulation*, trans. Sheila Faria Glaser (Ann Arbor:

University of Michigan Press, 1994). For examples of scholarship that thinks beyond Sontag and Baudrillard, see, respectively, Azoulay, "Getting Rid of the Distinction," 239–262; Philip Hammond, "The Gulf War Revisited," in *Jean Baudrillard: Fatal Theories*, ed. David B. Clarke, Marcus Doel, William Merrin, and Richard G. Smith. (London: Routledge, 2008), 118–135.

9. M. Hakan Yavuz, *Secularism and Muslim Democracy in Turkey* (Cambridge: Cambridge University Press, 2009), 172.

10. Virilio, *Original Accident*, 62.

11. Amy Coplan, "Catching Characters' Emotions: Emotional Contagion Responses to Narrative Fiction Film," *Film Studies* 8, no. 1 (2006): 26–38.

12. Jennifer M. Barker, *The Tactile Eye: Touch and the Cinematic Experience* (Berkeley: University of California Press, 2009), 23.

13. Such forging of intimacy recalls the etymological link between the concepts of *intimate* and *inmost* found in a number of languages relevant to this chapter. The word *intimate* originates in the Latin concept of *intimus*, meaning "inmost." The connection exists also in both of the two Turkish-language words that correspond to "intimate": *içten*, which literally means "from inside," and the loanword *samimi*, which originates in the Arabic concept of "inmost" (*ṣamīm*; صميم).

14. Virilio, *Original Accident*, 83–101.

15. The theme of postconflict reconstruction has also figured much more sinisterly in mainstream media coverage of the operations. "Urban transformation" in areas like Suriçi has been proposed as a potential measure for preventing the recurrence of insurgency (Zübeyde Yalçın, "Sur sakinleri yeni evlerine taşınacak" [Sur residents will move into their new homes], *Sabah*, December 20, 2015, http://www.sabah.com.tr/gundem/2015/12/20/sur-sakinleri-yeni-evlerine-tasinacak). For a critique of "urban transformation" as a counterinsurgency measure, see Ronay Bakan, "Counterinsurgent Urbanism: Mastering Heritage in Post-Conflict Diyarbakır" (paper presented at the Middle East Studies Association Annual Meeting, Montreal, Canada, November 3, 2023).

16. The methods and tools associated with construction work also figure prominently in *Bear Witness*'s coverage of the counterinsurgency. For example, the series frequently features counterinsurgency units employing armored excavators to level the streetscape by filling in ditches and demolishing barricades in areas under curfew.

17. Richard Spencer, "What Does Turkey's Involvement in Air Strikes Mean for Kurds, Isil, Syria and Nato?," *The Telegraph*, July 29, 2015, www.telegraph.co.uk/news/worldnews/europe/turkey/11769463/What-does-Turkeys-involvement-in-air-strikes-mean-for-Kurds-Isil-Syria-and-Nato.html.

18. Such positioning of the state vis-à-vis the conflict was in many ways heralded by an AKP television commercial produced ahead of the 2014 local elections. Set in a district of Hakkâri Province (Colemêrg, in Kurdish) that has long been an epicenter of war, the commercial begins with an extremely close shot of visually illegible machinery accompanied by machine-gun-like sounds, to then zoom out and reveal that this is in fact the construction site of a newly built airport and that the machines are actually hydraulic bursters and crushers (Editor, "Türkiye AK Parti'nin Hakkari reklam filmini konuşuyor" [AK Party's Hakkari commercial is on Turkey's lips], *Yeni Şafak*, March 14, 2014, https://www.yenisafak.com/video-galeri/politika/turkiye-ak-partinin-hakkari-reklam-filmini-konusuyor-14458). More recently, in the aftermath

of Kobanê's liberation from ISIS, this positioning was also extended to the Turkish authorities' involvement in Syria when President Erdoğan said the following about those celebrating the liberation in Turkey: "Now, they (Kurds) are dancing. What happened? ISIS was ousted from there. Okay. But who will repair the places that were bombarded? Who will repair those demolished places?" (Yerevan Saeed, "US Congratulates Kurds over Kobane as Turkey Slams Celebrations," *Rudaw*, January 28, 2015, http://www.rudaw.net/english/middleeast/syria/28012015).

19. Eliana Dockterman, "Turkey Bans Twitter," *Time*, March 20, 2014, https://time.com/32864/turkey-bans-twitter.

20. See, for example, Nurcan Baysal, "Cizre'deki evlerin içinden: 'Kızlar biz geldik siz yoktunuz' yazıları, yerlerde sergilenen kadın çamaşırları!" [From inside homes in Cizre: 'Girls, we came but you were not here' writings, lingerie displayed on floors!], *T24*, March 7, 2016, 2024, https://t24.com.tr/yazarlar/nurcan-baysal/cizrenin-gorunmeyenleri,14049; "'Duvara Yazılanlar'" [Writings on the wall], *140journos*, April 8, 2016, https://140journos.com/duvara-yazilanlar-9fef4c991829.

21. Üstündağ, "Pornographic State and Erotic Resistance," 95.

22. Protner, "Reading and Feeling Gender," 59–83.

23. Protner, "Reading and Feeling Gender," 67.

24. Protner, "Reading and Feeling Gender," 68.

25. Aydın Hasan, "MHP'li vekilden Bahçeli'ye Gezi isyanı" [MHP parliament member's Gezi plea to Bahçeli], *Milliyet*, June 11, 2013, https://www.milliyet.com.tr/siyaset/mhpli-vekilden-bahceliye-gezi-isyani-1721489; DHA, "Devlet Bahçeli'den Gezi Parkı açıklaması" [Gezi Park statement from Devlet Bahçeli], *Habertürk*, June 7, 2013, https://www.haberturk.com/gundem/haber/850763-devlet-bahceliden-gezi-parki-aciklamasi.

26. İrfan Bozan, "Kararsızların üçte biri MHP-HDP arasında" [A third of floating voters are oscillating between MHP and HDP], *Al Jazeera Turk*, April 10, 2015, www.aljazeera.com.tr/al-jazeera-ozel/kararsizlarin-ucte-biri-mhp-hdp-arasinda.

27. Kuntsman and Stein, *Digital Militarism*, 8

28. Kuntsman and Stein, *Digital Militarism*, 9; italics mine.

29. Kuntsman and Stein, *Digital Militarism*, 9.

30. Kuntsman and Stein, *Digital Militarism*, xiii.

31. The original word these slogans use for "love" is *aşk*, which denotes "passionate love" and is therefore distinct from *sevda*, "a patriot's feeling for his country or mother," although the latter is often also rendered as "love" in English. For this distinction, see Protner, "Reading and Feeling Gender," 77; Nükhet Sirman, "The Making of Familial Citizenship in Turkey," in *Challenges to Citizenship in a Globalizing World: European Questions and Turkish Experiences*, ed. Fuat Keyman and Ahmet İçduygu (London: Routledge, 2005), 147–172.

32. Radikal, "Silvan'daki yazılamalarla ilgili soruşturma başlattı" [Investigation started regarding the writings in Silvan], *Hakkari Haber TV*, November 18, 2015, http://www.hakkarihabertv.com/silvandaki-yazilamalarla-ilgili-sorusturma-baslatti-25305h.htm.

33. Robert Mackey, "Turkey to Investigate Images of Dead Kurdish Man Being Dragged," *New York Times*, October 5, 2015, https://www.nytimes.com/2015/10/06/world/europe/turkey-to-investigate-images-of-dead-kurdish-man-being-dragged.html.

34. TMMOB Diyarbakir Provincial Coordination Board, *2015–2016: TMMOB Destroyed Cities Report*, 46.

35. In speaking of "*feelings* associated *publicly*" with the protests, I echo recent scholarship on affect while also nuancing it as indicated in my reference to their "*medium*-specificity" (emphasis mine). I especially echo the numerous scholars of affect who have understood it as indicative of a socially structured yet embodied economy of "public feelings." See Ann Cvetkovich, *Depression: A Public Feeling* (Durham, NC: Duke University Press, 2012); Kathleen Stewart, *Ordinary Affects* (Durham, NC: Duke University Press, 2007); Sara Ahmed, *The Cultural Politics of Emotion* (New York: Routledge, 2004); Lauren Berlant, *Cruel Optimism* (Durham, NC: Duke University Press, 2011); Sianne Ngai, *Ugly Feelings* (Cambridge, MA: Harvard University Press, 2005). But my usage differs from understandings of affect that have centered embodiment at the expense of structural and systemic dynamics. See Eve Kosofsky Sedgwick, *Touching Feeling: Affect, Pedagogy, Performativity* (Durham, NC: Duke University Press, 2002); Brian Massumi, *Parables of the Virtual* (Durham, NC: Duke University Press, 2002). I consider what this book features as the stuff of aesthetics a particular manifestation of such "public feelings"—one that is especially attuned to form, as well as experiences mediated by form. See Eugenie Brinkema, *The Forms of the Affects* (Durham, NC: Duke University Press, 2014), xvi; Mike Michael, Alex Wilkie and Liliana Ovalle, "Aesthetics and Affect: Engaging Energy Communities," *Science as Culture* 27, no. 4 (2018): 443. The nuance is that in the case of the social media images I discuss in this chapter, questions concerning form (e.g., graffiti, the selfie, the makeshift) are markedly inseparable from those pertaining to medium (e.g., two-dimensionality, instantaneousness, and brevity), just as the medium is inextricable from the socially structured character of the feelings the images turn on—hence these feelings' "medium-specificity" and "publicness" being co-constitutive of each other.

36. See, for example, *Takvim*, "Nusaybin temiz!" [Nusaybin is clean!], June 6, 2016, https://www.takvim.com.tr/guncel/2016/06/06/nusaybin-temiz.

37. *Susma 24*, "Resmi onlar yaptı, cezayı ben aldım" [They made the painting, I received the punishment], March 12, 2017, https://susma24.com/resmi-onlar-yapti-cezayi-ben-aldim.

38. Aladdin Sinayic, "Kobanê'nin duvarlarına direnişi çizeceğim" [I will draw resistance on Kobanê's walls], *Yeni Özgür Politika*, June 19, 2019, https://www.ozgurpolitika.com/haberi-kobanenin-duvarlarina-direnisi-cizecegim-128525.

39. The work is available at https://vimeo.com/720636136 using the password "cngz123" (accessed October 31, 2024).

40. The official trailer is available at https://www.youtube.com/watch?v=Zzi3R1oUZKk (accessed October 31, 2024).

41. Seran Vreskala, "'Gerçek anlamda Türk kimliğine sahip olanlar daha az milliyetçi'" [Those who truly possess the identity of a Turk are less nationalist], *Artı Gerçek*, November 15, 2019, https://artigercek.com/makale/gercek-anlamda-turk-kimligine-sahip-olanlar-daha-az-milliyetci-79008.

42. George Mürer and Argun Çakır, "Introduction: New Contours in Kurdish Music Research," *World of Music* 11, no. 2 (2022): 5–24.

43. The video is available in full at https://www.youtube.com/watch?v=Dd18UEzAgGU (accessed October 31, 2024).

44. The same applies to the reports and documentation Forensic Architecture has shared online about their investigation. This documentation (including the Turkish-language version of the video) is available in full at https://forensic-architecture.org/investigation/the-killing-of-tahir-elci (accessed October 31, 2024).

45. Examples include the group exhibitions *Fractured Spine: Making Resistance to Censorship Visible in Journalism and Art* (Photobastei in Zurich, 2021) and *Under the Radar* (Swiss Architecture Museum in Basel, 2018–2019), and the agency's solo exhibition *Counter Investigations* (Institute of Contemporary Arts in London, 2018).

46. The artistic process behind *Silence* gives further substance to its critical import regarding the question of hypervisibility. Tekin's initial response to the counterinsurgency campaign was to stop his artistic practice altogether. Then, in 2017, he began to sketch, as a slow and bodily way of registering the violence visually. His sketches exclusively portrayed domestic spaces—the kind violated by the counterinsurgents as explained in this chapter. They helped Tekin return to life in the city after months of living as a recluse of sorts, eventually enabling him to establish, together with fellow Amed-based artist Erkan Özgen, the independent artist-run space Loading so that the city's creatively minded residents could have a place of refuge and an opportunity to regroup. Upon returning to urban life, Tekin noticed that residents on the streets had been preoccupied with the sounds of weapons reaching their ears from the historic core of the city since the start of the fighting. They were talking profoundly knowledgeably about what weapons they were hearing—what their make, model, and country of origin were—hence the information presented in *Silence*.

47. In her article on these images, Protner refuses to include the images she analyzes, for fear of contributing to their circulation (Protner, "Reading and Feeling Gender," 60n1). I acknowledge the problem she raises but see it as one arising not simply from the dissemination of images but rather from their being disseminated in ways that obfuscate the violence that their production and dissemination facilitate. To be sure, this chapter in its entirety is dedicated to critiquing the violence in question and differs from the overwhelming majority of the discourse-light and visuality-heavy ways in which the images have circulated on social media and on the websites of various news outlets from across the political spectrum. Therefore I include here some but not all of the images I discuss, featuring especially those images whose content is significant in more than textual ways.

Chapter 4: Testifying to Survival Environmentally and Nonextractivist Aesthetics

1. Ferit Aslan and Burak Emek, "Dicle Nehri'ndeki ıslah çalışmasıyla Cizre farklı bir görünüme kavuştu" [Cizre has gained a different appearance thanks to Tigris River rehabilitation project], *Hürriyet*, August 12, 2018, https://www.hurriyet.com.tr/dicle-nehrindeki-islah-calismasiyla-cizre-fark-40926061.

2. See especially pp. 13, 32, and 36–37 of İnsan Hakları İnceleme Heyeti, İnsan Hakları Derneği (İHD), Türkiye İnsan Hakları Vakfı (TİHV), Sağlık ve Sosyal Hizmet Emekçileri Sendikası (SES), and Diyarbakır Barosu ve Gündem Çocuk Derneği, *14/12/2015-–02/03/2016: 79 günlük sokağa çıkma yasağı Cizre gözlem raporu*, [14/12/2015—02/03/2017: 79-day Cizre curfew survey report], March 31, 2016, accessed October 31, 2024, https://www.ihd.org.tr/wp-content/uploads/2016/04/Cizre-G%C3%B6zlem-Raporu_31-Mart2016.pdf. See also Burcu Karakaş, "Avukatlar

AYM'ye başvurdu: Cizre'de ceset parçaları Dicle'ye atılıyor" [Lawyers have applied to the Constitutional Court: Body parts are being dumped in the Tigris], *Diken*, February 27, 2016, https://www.diken.com.tr/avukatlar-aymye-basvurdu-cizrede-ceset-parcalari-dicleye-atiliyor.

3. ÇT, "Barış İçin Kadın Girişimi Cizre'de: Zılgıtları çoğaltmaya geldik" [Women For Peace Initiative is in Cizre: We are here to propagate the ululations], *Bianet*, September 20, 2015, https://bianet.org/haber/baris-icin-kadin-girisimi-cizre-de-zilgitlari-cogaltmaya-geldik-167777.

4. Baris icin Kadin Girisimi, "Women Talk About Cizîre and Silopi—Women's Initiative for Peace," *YouTube*, October 28, 2015, accessed October 31, 2024, https://www.youtube.com/watch?v=6qpCi3qEOm4.

5. sağ, personal communication, April 2019.

6. "Erdoğan: Bir gece ansızın gelebiliriz" [Erdoğan: One night we might suddenly show up], *Al Jazeera Turk*, April 29, 2017, https://www.aljazeera.com.tr/haber/erdogan-bir-gece-ansizin-gelebiliriz.

7. Protner, "Reading and Feeling Gender," 59–83.

8. The film is available at https://vimeo.com/143186689/1defee9262 (accessed October 31, 2024).

9. On the point about organized action, see Thomas Keenan, "Publicity and Indifference (Sarajevo on Television)," *PMLA* 117, no. 1 (2002): 104–116; Alisa Lebow, "Shooting with Intent: Framing Conflict," in *Killer Images: Documentary Film, Memory, and the Performance of Violence*, ed. Joram ten Brink and Joshua Oppenheimer (New York: Wallflower Press, 2012), 41–61. On the point about desensitization, see Allen Feldman, "On Cultural Anesthesia: From Desert Storm to Rodney King," *American Ethnologist* 21, no. 2 (1994): 404–418; Luc Boltanski, *Distant Suffering: Morality, Media, and Politics* (Cambridge: Cambridge University Press, 1999), 9.

10. On "rawness," see Anthony McCosker, "De-Framing Disaster: Affective Encounters with Raw and Autonomous Media," *Continuum* 27, no. 3 (2013): 382–396. On "banality," see Rebecca A. Adelman and Wendy Kozol, "Discordant Affects: Ambivalence, Banality, and the Ethics of Spectatorship," *Theory and Event* 17, no. 3 (2014), https://muse.jhu.edu/article/553380.

11. See, for example, Walter Benjamin, *Understanding Brecht*, trans. Anna Bostock (London: Verso, 1998), 85–103; John Berger, *About Looking* (New York: Vintage, 1980), 41–44; Allan Sekula, *Photography Against the Grain: Essays and Photo Works, 1973–1983* (Halifax: Press of the Nova Scotia College of Art and Design, 1984); Abigail Solomon-Godeau, "Lament of the Images: Alfredo Jaar and the Ethics of Representation," *Aperture*, no. 181 (2005): 36–47; Susan Sontag, *On Photography* (New York: Farrar, Straus and Giroux, 1977). Surely, there are important nuances between the ways each of these critics of the photography of suffering problematizes its limitations and seeks to overcome this problem as they see it. While I intend to frame the problem altogether differently and thus do not dwell on these nuances here, I must note that they have been discussed critically and thoroughly elsewhere. See Mark Reinhardt, "Picturing Violence: Aesthetics and the Anxiety of Critique," in *Beautiful Suffering: Photography and the Traffic in Pain*, ed. Mark Reinhardt, Holly Edwards, and Erina Duganne (Williamstown: Williams College Museum of Art; Chicago: University of Chicago Press, 2007), 13–36; Frank Möller, "The Looking / Not Looking Dilemma," *Review of International Studies* 35, no. 4 (2009): 781–794.

12. Azoulay, "Getting Rid of the Distinction," 240–241.

13. Ariella Azoulay, *Civil Imagination: A Political Ontology of Photography*, trans. Louise Bethlehem (London: Verso, 2015), 24.

14. Azoulay, *Civil Imagination*, 26–27.

15. Ariella Aïsha Azoulay, *Potential History: Unlearning Imperialism* (London: Verso, 2019), 240; emphasis mine.

16. The film is available at https://vimeo.com/143163812 (accessed October 31, 2024).

17. Judith Butler, *Frames of War: When Is Life Grievable?* (London: Verso, 2009), 67.

18. Butler, *Frames of War*, 71–72.

19. See also p. 10 of the report "Cizre olayları gözlem raporu" [Cizre incidents survey report], *MAZLUMDER*, September 12, 2015, accessed October 31, 2024, https://www.mazlumder.org/webimage/files/MAZLUMDER%20Cizre%20Olaylar%C4%B1%20Raporu%20-%2012.9.2015.pdf.

20. The film is available at https://vimeo.com/141734221 (accessed October 31, 2024).

21. The film is available at https://vimeo.com/153263803 (accessed October 31, 2024).

22. Allen Feldman, "Violence and Vision: The Prosthetics and Aesthetics of Terror," *Public Culture* 10, no. 1 (1997): 43.

23. Cf. Paul Virilio, *War and Cinema: The Logistics of Perception*, trans. Patrick Caimler (London: Verso, 1989).

24. Butler, *Frames of War*, 80.

25. Butler, *Frames of War*, 80.

26. Ruthie Ginsburg, "Gendered Visual Activism: Documenting Human Rights Abuse from the Private Sphere," *Current Sociology* 66, no. 1 (2018): 38–55.

27. Ginsburg, "Gendered Visual Activism," 39.

28. Ginsburg, "Gendered Visual Activism," 38–39.

29. Caitlin Frances Bruce, "*Episode III: Enjoy Poverty*: An Aesthetic Virus of Political Discomfort," *Communication, Culture and Critique* 9, no. 2 (2016): 299; Nicola Perugini and Francesco Zucconi, "Enjoy Poverty: Humanitarianism and the Testimonial Function of Images," *Visual Studies* 32, no. 1 (2017): 32.

30. Lebow, "Shooting with Intent," 57–58; T. J. Demos, "Gentrification After Institutional Critique: On Renzo Martens's Institute for Human Activities," *Afterall: A Journal of Art, Context and Enquiry*, no. 40 (2015): 88–89.

31. Feldman, "Violence and Vision," 30.

32. Kelly Oliver, *Witnessing: Beyond Recognition* (Minneapolis: University of Minnesota Press, 2001); Michael Rothberg, *The Implicated Subject: Beyond Victims and Perpetrators* (Stanford, CA: Stanford University Press, 2019).

33. On the point about environments, see Keysar, "Spatial Testimony," 523–541; Kurgan, "Conflict Urbanism, Aleppo," 72–77; Staal, "Law of the State," 14–23; Weizman, "Introduction," 9–32. On the point about the earth, see Meszaros Martin, "Defoliating the World," 230–253; Sheikh, "Future of the Witness," 145–162.

34. See, for example, Sheikh, "Future of the Witness," 145–162.

35. Nichanian, *Historiographic Perversion*, 11, 94.

36. Raymond Kévorkian, *The Armenian Genocide: A Complete History* (London: I. B. Tauris, 2011), 378.

37. Üngör, *Making of Modern Turkey*, 98.
38. Üngör, *Making of Modern Turkey*, 98.
39. Çelik and Dinç, *Yüz yıllık ah!* [Century-old curse!], 190–206.
40. Kévorkian, *Armenian Genocide*, 378.
41. Vartan Estukyan, "Yine Ermeni'siz yapamadılar" [Once again they could not do without the Armenian], *Agos*, September 17, 2015, www.agos.com.tr/tr/yazi/12772/yine-ermeni-siz-yapamadilar; Karin Karakaşlı, "Cizre halkından güç almaya gidiyorum" [I am coming to gain strength from Cizre's people], *Agos*, September 26, 2015, http://www.agos.com.tr/tr/yazi/12849/cizre-halkindan-guc-almaya-gidiyorum.
42. William J. T. Mitchell, ed., *Landscape and Power* (Chicago: University of Chicago Press, 1994); Simon Schama, *Landscape and Memory* (Toronto: Random House, 1995); Martin Warnke, *Political Landscape: The Art History of Nature* (London: Reaktion, 1994).
43. On the inextricable link between visuality and coloniality, see Mirzoeff, *Right to Look*.
44. Feldman, "Violence and Vision," 24–60.
45. Selahattin Demirtaş, "Kobanê üzerinden HDP'ye kumpas" [Using Kobanê to plot against HDP], *Gazete Duvar*, October 19, 2020, https://www.gazeteduvar.com.tr/kobane-uzerinden-hdpye-kumpas-haber-1502010.

Chapter 5: Haunting as Ecology and Counterextractivist Aesthetics

1. On "structural violence," see Paul Farmer, "An Anthropology of Structural Violence," *Current Anthropology* 45, no. 3 (2004): 305–325. On "slow violence," see Nixon, *Slow Violence*.
2. Çaylı, *Victims of Commemoration*.
3. Emre Tansu Keten, "Haziran seçimleri, Haziran Hareketi ve HDP" [June elections, the June Movement and HDP], *Yeniyol* 14 (2015), https://yeniyol1.org/haziran-secimleri-haziran-hareketi-ve-hdp.
4. Exactly one year before, in 2014, Prime Minister Erdoğan wrote a letter expressing his "wish that the Armenians who lost their lives in the context of the early twentieth century rest in peace" and his "condolences to their grandchildren" (Constanze Letsch, "Turkish PM Offers Condolences over 1915 Armenian Massacre," *Guardian*, April 23, 2014, https://www.theguardian.com/world/2014/apr/23/turkey-erdogan-condolences-armenian-massacre).
5. Carolyn Christov-Bakargiev, "Preface" in *SALTWATER: A Theory of Thought Forms*, ed. Süreyya Evren (Istanbul: Istanbul Foundation for Culture and Arts, 2015), l–lviii. Relatedly, the Pavilion of Turkey at the 56th Venice Biennale, which opened in May 2015 and featured a solo exhibition by Istanbul-born, Paris-based Armenian artist Sarkis, made ample references in its curatorial texts to "1915," "healing," and "wounds" (Defne Ayas, "Sarkis: Staging Simultaneity," in *Respiro: Sarkis*, ed. Defne Ayas [Istanbul: Istanbul Foundation for Culture and Arts, 2014], 22–31).
6. Personal communication, September 18, 2018. Periscope was Twitter's live-streaming app, discontinued in March 2021.
7. Anadolu Agency, "US Couple Hunt, Kill Mountain Goat in Turkey's Adıyaman," *Hürriyet Daily News*, February 26, 2020, https://www.hurriyetdailynews.com/us-couple-hunt-kill-mountain-goat-in-turkeys-adiyaman-152465.
8. Nico Marzano, *Landscape* (London: Institute of Contemporary Art, 2018), 3.

9. Ozan Unsalan et al., "The Sariçiçek Howardite Fall in Turkey: Source Crater of HED Meteorites on Vesta and Impact Risk of Vestoids," *Meteoritics and Planetary Science* 54, no. 5 (2019): 953–1008.

10. Çelik and Dinç, *Yüz yıllık ah!* [Century-old curse!].

11. Çelik and Dinç, *Yüz yıllık ah!* [Century-old curse!], 180–181, 201, 205–206. Such attribution of the cause of adverse events to "the Armenians' curse" is not just a contemporary phenomenon in the region; its history stretches as far back as the immediate aftermath of the genocide (Yves Ternon, *Mardin 1915: Anatomie pathologique d'une destruction* [Paris: Geuthner, 2007], 341–346).

12. Biner, *States of Dispossession*, 82–100.

13. Alice von Bieberstein, "Treasure/Fetish/Gift: Hunting for 'Armenian Gold' in Post-Genocide Turkish Kurdistan," *Subjectivity*, no. 10 (2017): 175.

14. On Darbasan, see Index Anatolicus, "Sarıçiçek," *Nişanyan Yeradları: Türkiye ve çevre ülkeler yerleşim birimleri envanteri* [Nişanyan place-names: Inventory of settlements in Turkey and surrounding countries], August 1, 2018, https://www.nisanyanyeradlari.com/?y=Darbasan&ul=All&o=c&s=1&n=1. For an example of the treasure hunters' forums mentioned here, see Osman Naci Kanat, "Uzaydan gelen meteor taşları" [Meteorites coming from outer space], *Nacibaba*, December 22, 2015, http://nacibaba.com/forum_posts.asp?TID=149&PN=11

15. Jacques Derrida, *Specters of Marx: The State of the Debt, the Work of Mourning and the New International* (New York: Routledge, 1994); Avery F. Gordon, *Ghostly Matters: Haunting and the Sociological Imagination* (Minneapolis: University of Minnesota Press, 1997).

16. Manchanda and Salem, "Empire's H(a)unting Grounds," 245–251.

17. Manchanda and Salem, "Empire's H(a)unting Grounds," 246.

18. Manchanda and Salem, "Empire's H(a)unting Grounds," 246.

19. For a notable Turkish-language example of such scholarship, see Nermin Saybaşılı, *Sınırlar ve hayaletler: Görsel kültürde göç hareketleri* [Borders and ghosts: Migration movements in visual culture] (Istanbul: Metis, 2011), 30–41.

20. Martha Lincoln and Bruce Lincoln, "Toward a Critical Hauntology: Bare Afterlife and the Ghosts of Ba Chúc," *Comparative Studies in Society and History* 57, no. 1 (2015): 191–220.

21. Lincoln and Lincoln, "Toward a Critical Hauntology," 200–202.

22. Lincoln and Lincoln, "Toward a Critical Hauntology," 196.

23. Douglas Hollan, "Who Is Haunted by Whom? Steps to an Ecology of Haunting," *Ethos* 47, no. 4 (2020): 460–461.

24. Hollan, "Who Is Haunted by Whom?," 461 (emphasis mine). See also Bateson, *Steps to an Ecology*.

25. The commercial processes at work here included not only the villagers and the scientists who directly engaged with one another in transaction, but also the international market involving meteorite hunters. The Sarıçiçek meteorites (more than ten of them at the time of writing) went up for sale at a rate of US$110 per gram on a website set up by a French meteorite hunter (Pierre-Marie Pelé, "Sarıçiçek," *Meteor-Center*, November 15, 2016, accessed November 7, 2021, https://meteor-center.com/blog/project/saricicek/). The webpage states that Sarıçiçek "specimens have been on the market from the end of October 2015 at the Munich Mineral Fair." A news report on this commercial aspect of the Sarıçiçek meteorite shower suggested that "the

villagers have reportedly fetched some 1 million Turkish lira (about US$350,000) so far, and some are still holding onto pieces as big as 4–5 kilograms (9–11 pounds) in weight" and that "foreign dealers are said to have offered the villagers US$30 to US$60 per gram" (Zülfikar Doğan, "You Won't Believe How This Turkish Village Became Rich Overnight," *Al-Monitor*, December 3, 2015, https://www.al-monitor.com/originals/2015/12/turkey-godsend-treasure-comes-with-tax-jitters-for-poor.html).

26. Personal communication, September 18, 2018. This is not to say that the filmmaker has altogether avoided activism. In the lead-up to and the first months of the state's violent counterinsurgency campaign in northern Kurdistan, he did participate in two important interventions categorizable as activist. The first was during the 34th Istanbul Film Festival (held just a few months before the outbreak of full-blown war) and in response to its censorship of *Bakur*, a film that explores the lives of the guerrillas in the mountains of northern Kurdistan. Keltek pulled his film *Colony* (2015) from the festival together with twenty-three other filmmakers (Mehmet Keskin, " 'Bakur' belgeseline bakanlık sansürü geldi" [The Ministry censors the documentary 'Bakur'], *Cumhuriyet*, April 13, 2015, https://www.cumhuriyet.com.tr/haber/bakur-belgeseline-bakanlik-sansuru-geldi-252941). And afterward, during the first months of the counterinsurgency campaign, when some two thousand academics signed a stop-the-war petition, to then become the target of government-led prosecution, Keltek was among the 433 filmmakers who signed their own petition in support of the academics (BIA News Desk, "Support for Academics from Film-Makers," *English Bianet*, January 15, 2016, https://bianet.org/english/human-rights/171125-support-for-academics-from-film-makers).

27. Gómez-Barris, *Extractive Zone*.

28. This point resonates partially with Alisa Lebow's discussion of visual realist films on violence that use footage filmed by non-filmmaker civilians but attribute it to individuals or organizations different from those who have done the filming even if they are credited as sources. She considers the political economy of such films symptomatic of "the classic colonial model of the raw materials extracted at low cost" (Lebow, "Shooting with Intent," 57). The footage they use, notes Lebow, is sourced inexpensively and at no risk to the professional individuals or organizations who stand to gain from the final product, whether financially, symbolically, or both. For Lebow, even crediting footage to its amateur videographers serves to exacerbate extractivism by both "indemnifying" the professionals "from legal claims" and "instilling doubt in the viewer as to the veracity of the footage itself" (Lebow, "Shooting with Intent," 51). While I take my cue from Lebow's materialist approach to found-footage-based filmic portrayal of violence, I hesitate to categorize *Meteors*' use of footage by others as extractivist in the sense that emerges from her discussion. A certain production and accumulation of profit is doubtless at work in this film, too, as it is in any work of professional cultural production. But *Meteors* is distinguished by refusing to bet its filmic value on the footage's capacity to document violence—perhaps with the exception of just one of its six sections (the one titled "Disintegration")—and by mobilizing the footage's material possibilities instead. It is through this refusal and this mobilization that the film invites (if not always intentionally) precisely the kind of extractivism-wary materialist approach that Lebow and I share.

29. Eray Çaylı, "Inheriting Dispossession, Mobilizing Vulnerability: Heritage amid Protest in Contemporary Turkey," *International Journal of Islamic Architecture* 5, no. 2 (2016): 361.

30. Vryonis Speros Jr., *The Mechanism of Catastrophe: The Turkish Pogrom of September 6–7, 1955, and the Destruction of the Greek Community of Istanbul* (New York: Greekworks, 2005), 154.

31. Koca Mehmet Kentel, "Assembling 'Cosmopolitan' Pera: An Infrastructural History of Late Ottoman Istanbul" (PhD diss., University of Washington, 2018), 137–141.

32. Sami Kısaoğlu, "İz Öztat ile suluboyaları üzerine" [With İz Öztat on her watercolors], *Unlimited*, March 26, 2021, https://www.unlimitedrag.com/post/i-z-öztat-ile-suluboyaları-üzerine.

33. The way this folk belief was recently recounted by a young Armenian American woman is instructive and evocative here: "Since I was young, my mom told me that if I ever had a nightmare at night, to wake up the following morning and go to the bathroom, turn on the sink, let the water run, and tell my bad dreams to the water . . . as a way of letting them be washed away and not come true. And I did this for a very long time and often, if my dreams are bad enough, I still follow through with it just to give myself the reassurance" (Nicole Vartanyan, "Nightmares to the Water," *USC Digital Folklore Archives*, April 18, 2013, folklore.usc.edu/nightmares-to-the-water/).

34. The quote is taken from English subtitles provided in the video.

35. In fact, ghostliness figures prominently not only in the specific body of work I discuss here but also across much of Öztat's oeuvre, and does so in ways pertinent to the Armenian genocide. She often produces work in "untimely" and "future-facing collaboration" with a fictional persona: a queer Ottoman woman named Zişan (1894–1970), whose estranged father was an Armenian photographer. Zişan, who learned photography from her father, fled her hometown during the Armenian genocide, and went on to produce texts and images of artistic merit but never identified as an artist, "appears to" Öztat "as a historical figure, a ghost and an alter ego." See Zeynep Günsür Yüceil, "Umut eden beden tekinsiz mekânlara kayıyor ya da boşluğa övgü" [The hoping body veers towards uncanny spaces or ode to emptiness], *Hafıza ve sanat konuşmaları* [Conversations on memory and art], ed. Eylem Ertürk and Sevim Sancaktar (Istanbul: Hafıza Merkezi, 2020), 100; cf. Nora Tataryan, "Şiddetin temsili ve yüzleşmenin imkânı üzerine bir deneme" [An essay on the representation of violence and the possibility of reckoning], *Hafıza ve sanat konuşmaları* [Conversations on memory and art], ed. Eylem Ertürk and Sevim Sancaktar (Istanbul: Hafıza Merkezi, 2020), 71.

36. Macarena Gómez-Barris, "How to Block the Extractive View," *GLQ: A Journal of Lesbian and Gay Studies* 24, no. 4 (2018): 527–532; Lisa Blackmore, "Turbulent River Times: Art and Hydropower in Latin America's Extractive Zones," *Liquid Ecologies in Latin American and Caribbean Art*, ed. Lisa Blackmore and Liliana Gómez (New York: Routledge), 13–34; T. J. Demos, *Beyond the World's End: Arts of Living at the Crossing* (Durham, NC: Duke University Press, 2020), 41, 48, 101, 177–179; Macarena Gómez-Barris, "Submerged Perspectives: The Arts of Land and Water Defense," *Globalizations* 18, no. 6 (2021): 854–863.

37. Michael Taussig, *What Color Is the Sacred?* (Chicago: University of Chicago Press, 2009), 159. See also Natasha Eaton, *Colour, Art and Empire: Visual Culture and the Nomadism of Representation* (London: I. B. Tauris, 2013).

38. See, for example, Donna Carstens, "Fibre Art and Fashion: Contemporary Approaches to Indigenous Art," *Signals*, no. 117 (2016): 68–71; Sigrid Holmwood, "Cultivating Colour: Making Mayan Blue from Woad," *Third Text* 32, no. 2–3 (2018): 330–349.

39. Da Cunha, *Invention of Rivers*.

40. Eren Barış, "Talin Suciyan'la modern Türkiye'de Ermeniler ve inkâr habitusu: Kendi evinde diasporada olmak" [With Talin Suciyan on Armenians and the denial habitus in modern Turkey: Being diasporic in one's own home], *1+1 Express*, April 23, 2020, accessed October 31, 2024, https://birartibir.org/kendi-evinde-diasporada-olmak.

41. Yetvart Danzikyan, "'Ermeni idaresinin akamete uğratılmasında 103 yıl sonra en dip noktadayız'" ["'After 103 years we are at the lowest point in the disruption of Armenian administration'"], *Agos*, December 24, 2018, www.agos.com.tr/tr/yazi/21776/ermeni-idaresinin-akamete-ugratilmasinda-103-yil-sonra-en-dip-noktadayiz.

42. Barış, "Talin Suciyan'la" [With Talin Suciyan]; Danzikyan, "'Ermeni idaresinin akamete uğratılmasında 103 yıl sonra en dip noktadayız'" ["'After 103 years'"].

43. Christina Sharpe, *In the Wake: On Blackness and Being* (Durham, NC: Duke University Press, 2016), 21 and 112, respectively.

44. Sharpe, *In the Wake*, 106.

45. Personal communication, February 6, 2021.

46. Vicken Cheterian provides further detail on the connection between 1915–1916 and 1937–1938 in Dêrsim: "During the genocide, some 20,000 Armenians who had been deported from Erzincan (Yerzenga, in Armenian) were kept by the Dersim Kurdish population and thus saved from destruction" by "assimilating with" them. But just a couple of decades later, they became yet again "subject to mass slaughter, this time at the hands of the Turkish republican armies" (Vicken Cheterian, *Open Wounds: Armenians, Turks and a Century of Genocide* [Oxford: Oxford University Press, 2015], 208).

47. Ayşe Gül Altınay and Fethiye Çetin, *The Grandchildren: The Hidden Legacy of "Lost" Armenians in Turkey* (London: Routledge, 2014).

48. Aylin Demir, "Oral Poetry and Weeping in the Case of Dersimli Women" (master's thesis, Middle East Technical University, 2010), 34.

49. Fatma Belkıs and İz Öztat, "Who Carries the Water: Feminist Reflections on Anatolian Hydroelectric Power Plants, Rivers, and Resistance," *Journal of Middle East Women's Studies* 14, no. 3 (2018): 371.

50. In addition to those already mentioned, the full list of agents is as follows: Chorus of Goats, Peasant, Oak, State Company, Pipe, Concrete, Citizens, Comrade, Friend, Police, Witch, Prosecutor, Lawyer, Translator, Master, Student, Feminist, Parliamentarian, Philosopher, Poet, Traveler, Psychologist, Writer, and Pepug Bird. The leaflets are openly accessible at https://archive.org/details/WhoCarriesTheWater (accessed October 31, 2024).

51. İz Öztat, "Duyuyorum" [I hear], *5 Harfliler*, January 21, 2016, https://www.5harfliler.com/duyuyorum. See also Zabel Yesayan, *In the Ruins: The 1909 Massacres of Armenians in Adana, Turkey*, trans. Geoffrey Michael Goshgarian (Boston: Armenian International Women's Association Press, 2016 [1911]).

52. Personal communication, February 6, 2021.

53. Derrida, *Specters of Marx*, 63. Geographer Elisabeth Roberts has also discussed being photographed as spectralization—a mode of becoming ghostly that is constituted in photography's "non-signifying" elements imbricating with "language, representation, universality" (Elisabeth Roberts, "Geography and the Visual Image: A Hauntological Approach," *Progress in Human Geography* 37, no. 3 [2013]: 398).

54. My emphasis here on how ghostliness figures in Öztat's work both as a legacy of genocide and as the stuff of survival and defiance resonates with a point Deniz Yonucu has made in her ethnography of policing in Istanbul's racialized neighborhoods. Yonucu has called on anthropologists of state violence to consider "hauntings of resistance" alongside "hauntings of oppression," conceptualizing the former as "inspirational hauntings" (Deniz Yonucu, "Inspirational Hauntings and a Fearless Spirit of Resistance: Negotiating the Undercover Police Surveillance of Racialized Spaces in Istanbul," *Current Anthropology* 64, no. 4 [2023]: 359–379; Deniz Yonucu, *Police, Provocation, Politics: Counterinsurgency in Istanbul* [Ithaca, NY: Cornell University Press, 2022], 116–137). Noteworthily, much of what sparks Yonucu's ethnographic attention to specters of survival and defiance is visual (e.g., urban walls covered in revolutionary graffiti and posters, photographs of deceased militants, and landscapes such as parks commemorating victims of state violence through the way they are named or the monuments they host) even as she does not further explore what this medium-specificity might mean for the politics of inspirational hauntings. My point here complements hers by showing that the markedly visual character of specters of survival and defiance is integral to their capacity to regain social and political currency, including through artistic practice.

55. Mark Fisher, *Ghosts of My Life: Writings on Depression, Hauntology and Lost Futures* (Winchester: Zero Books, 2014), 27.

56. Sharpe, *In the Wake*, 106.

Movement in and with Ashen Country, or Toward Nonextractivist Scholarship

1. Melissa Bilal, "Lullabies and the Memory of Pain: Armenian Women's Remembrance of the Past in Turkey," *Dialectical Anthropology*, no. 43 (2019): 185–206.

2. Tilley, "Resisting Piratic Method," 27. Tilley's article relies on Indigenous thinkers such as Silvia Rivera Cusicanqui and Linda Tuhiwai Smith. See Silvia Rivera Cusicanqui, "Ch'ixinakax utxiwa: A Reflection on the Practices and Discourses of Decolonization," *South Atlantic Quarterly* 111, no. 1 (2012): 95–109; Linda Tuhiwai Smith, *Decolonising Methodologies: Research and Indigenous Peoples* (London: Zed Books, 1999).

3. Cruz and Luke, "Methodology and Academic Extractivism," 159. Cruz and Luke's article draws on Black feminist and Indigenous scholars such as Linda Tuhiwai Smith, Patricia Hill Collins, and Azeezat Johson. See Linda Tuhiwai Smith, *Decolonising Methodologies*; Patricia Hill Collins, *Black Feminist Thought: Knowledge, Consciousness, and the Politics of Empowerment* (New York: Routledge, 2000); Azeezat Johnson, "Throwing Our Bodies Against the White Background of Academia," *Area* 52, no. 1 (2020): 89–96. What Cruz and Luke call "academic extractivism" has been conceptualized as "epistemic extractivism" by Ramón Grosfoguel, "cognitive extractivism" by Leanne Betasamosake Simpson, and "epistemic expropriation" by Sam Halvorsen. See Grosfoguel, "Epistemic Extractivism," 209; Naomi Klein, "Dancing the World into Being: A Conversation with Idle No More's Leanne Simpson," *Yes!*, March 6, 2013, https://www.yesmagazine.org/social-justice/2013/03/06/dancing-the-world-into-being-a-conversation-with-idle-no-more-leanne-simpson; Halvorsen, "Cartographies of Epistemic Expropriation," 11.

4. Tilley, "Resisting Piratic Method," 28; Cruz and Luke, "Methodology and Academic Extractivism," 166; Halvorsen, "Cartographies of Epistemic Expropriation," 18.

5. Çaylı and Doğrul, "Emergency as Normalcy."

6. Walter Benjamin, "The Translator's Task," trans. Steven Rendall, *TTR: traduction, terminologie, rédaction* 10, no. 2 (1997): 151–165.

7. Tuhiwai Smith, *Decolonizing Methodologies*, xiii; Audra Simpson, *Mohawk Interruptus: Political Life Across the Borders of Settler States* (Durham, NC: Duke University Press, 2014), 101–102.

8. Grosfoguel, "Epistemic Extractivism," 207–208, 210–211; Halvorsen, "Cartographies of Epistemic Expropriation," 14–15.

9. The sovereignty-related significance of arts and culture institutions in northern Kurdistan became salient during the fallout from the recent episode of war. Arts and culture were chief among the areas where the central government confiscated whatever resources and infrastructures Kurdish-run municipalities had been able to develop since their mid-2000s rise to power, including archives of artistic and cultural events and initiatives. As a result, "Archive" is one of the few headings under which Loading defines its work. See Zehra Doğan and Refik Tekin's three-part report "Ohal'de sanat" [Art under emergency rule], *Bianet*, May 1, 2017, https://bianet.org/bianet/sanat/185444-kayyum-kiskacinda-kalan-sanat; https://bianet.org/bianet/sanat/185453-sanatcilar-ve-seyirciler-sahnesiz-ogrenciler-konservatuvarsiz-kaldi; https://bianet.org/bianet/siyaset/185825-kayyum-kiskacinda-sanatin-veri-haritasi.

10. This point echoes recent critics of the contemporary scholarly fascination with decolonization as a methodological question. They have warned that in an inextricably interconnected world where methodologies, forms, and languages circulate and hybridize ever more rapidly, there can be no recipes for what an ideal decolonial method, form, and language entail except those developed collectively by communities contending daily with colonialism on their own terms and in their own areas of practice. See, for example, Adom Getachew, *Worldmaking After Empire: The Rise and Fall of Self-Determination* (Princeton, NJ: Princeton University Press, 2019); Olúfẹ́mi O. Táíwò, *Against Decolonisation: Taking African Agency Seriously* (London: Hurst, 2022). My emphasis on instituting sovereignty resonates with recent decolonial scholarship that has advocated centering the work of building or rebuilding noncolonial worlds rather than simply negating colonial ones. See David Scott, *Conscripts of Modernity: The Tragedy of Colonial Enlightenment* (Durham, NC: Duke University Press, 2004); Michelle Murphy, "Alterlife and Decolonial Chemical Relations," *Cultural Anthropology* 32, no. 4 (2017): 494–503; Kim TallBear, "Caretaking Relations, Not American Dreaming," *Kalfou: A Journal of Comparative and Relational Ethnic Studies* 6, no. 1 (2019): 24–41; for a synthesis, see Neale and Kowal, " 'Related' Histories," 411–412. My more specific point in this paragraph about visual culture being a realm unto itself for the work of instituting sovereignty nuances T. J. Demos, Emily Eliza Scott, and Subhankar Banerjee's call for placing "the creative instituting of new knowledges, organizations, and networks at the forefront of the visual culture of climate justice" ("Introduction," *The Routledge Companion to Contemporary Art, Visual Culture, and Climate Change*, ed. T. J. Demos, Emily Eliza Scott, and Subhankar Banerjee [Abingdon: Routledge, 2021], 9). The nuance is that such institutions do already exist in relevant contexts and thus the priority must be strengthening them rather than founding new ones.

11. The quotations in this paragraph are from the project proposal for the workshop series "Photography's Violent Ecology."

12. Lisel Hintz, *Identity Politics Inside Out: National Identity Contestation and Foreign Policy in Turkey* (New York: Oxford University Press, 2018), 25.

13. DHA, "Diyarbakır'da zırhlı polis aracıyla define aradılar" [They hunted for treasure in Diyarbakır using an armored police vehicle], *Duvar*, February 4, 2019, https://www.gazeteduvar.com.tr/turkiye/2019/02/04/diyarbakirda-zirhli-polis-araciyla-define-aradilar; MA, "AKP'li belediye başkanının oğlu belediyenin kepçesiyle define aradı" [AKP member mayor's son hunted for treasure using the municipality's excavator], *Yeni Yaşam*, November 15, 2019, https://yeniyasamgazetesi3.com/akpli-belediye-baskaninin-oglu-belediyenin-kepcesiyle-define-aradi; Ferit Aslan, "Diyarbakır'daki 500 yıllık Surp Sarkis Kilisesi yok olmanın eşiğinde" [Diyarbakır's 500-year-old Surp Sarkis Church is on the brink of extinction], *Medyascope*, November 20, 2019, https://medyascope.tv/2019/11/20/diyarbakirdaki-500-yillik-surp-sarkis-kilisesi-yok-olmanin-esiginde.

14. Sinan Uçar and Selay Saykal, "Sır kazının nedeni ortaya çıktı! Dipsiz Göl'de 15'inci Apollinaris lejyonunun altın küpü aranmış" [The reason for the secret excavation has been revealed! The search in the Bottomless Tarn was for the 15th Apollinarian legion's golden jar], *Hürriyet*, November 14, 2019, https://www.hurriyet.com.tr/gundem/sir-kazinin-nedeni-ortaya-cikti-dipsiz-golde-15inci-apollinaris-lejyonunun-altin-kupu-aranmis-41373938.

15. On treasure hunting in the region around this tarn, see Erol Sağlam, "Presumed Dead but Lived On: Treasures and Discreet Afterlives of Greek Heritage in Contemporary Turkey," *Allegra Lab*, May 15, 2020, accessed October 31, 2024, https://allegralaboratory.net/afterlives-presumed-dead-but-lived-on. The plateau hosting the tarn is still called İstavroma—from the Greek Orthodox ritual of the same name—and the village, while now named Dumanlı, was previously called Sanda, a Greek name meaning "defender of humanity" (İHA, "Çevre ve Şehircilik Bakanlığı 'Dipsiz Göl' için 4 maddelik eylem planını açıkladı" [Environment and Urbanism Ministry has announced its 4-part plan for the "Bottomless Tarn"], *Sabah*, November 19, 2019, https://www.sabah.com.tr/galeri/turkiye/cevre-ve-sehircilik-bakanligi-dipsiz-gol-icin-4-maddelik-eylem-planini-acikladi).

16. For a laudatory review of the exhibition published in a pro-government newspaper, see Deniz Renkveren, "A Pomegranate for Turks and Armenians: It Is Time to Remember, Not Forget," *Daily Sabah*, April 29, 2016, https://www.dailysabah.com/arts-culture/2016/04/29/a-pomegranate-for-turks-and-armenians-it-is-time-to-remember-not-forget. For a critique published in Turkey's only Armenian newspaper, see Yektan Türkyılmaz, "Tarih vertigosu, hafıza hipnozu: Nar Niyetiyle Hatırlamak" [History vertigo, memory hypnosis: Remembering with the Intention of Pomegranate], *Agos*, April 21, 2016, https://www.agos.com.tr/tr/yazi/15089/tarih-vertigosu-hafiza-hipnozu-nar-niyetiyle-hatirlamak. Precedents to this official acknowledgment of Armenian loss—albeit never as genocide—stretch back to the Republic of Turkey's first years. The republican regime's lawmakers were heard acknowledging this loss, but only when they spoke of industries previously reliant on Armenian labor and expertise that now suffered from a massive lack thereof. Among such industries were indeed the copper mines located just north of Amed. Some even requested the wealth confiscated from the Armenians to be used for reinvesting in the mines and reviving mineralogical know-how. This process got underway in the mid-to-late 1930s under state monopoly and German supervision (thus building on the same martial alliance

that had been at work during the genocide itself), "generating up to US$17 million" (Üngör and Polatel, *Confiscation and Destruction*, 159–160).

17. Imre Szeman and Jennifer Wenzel, "What Do We Talk About When We Talk About Extractivism?," *Textual Practice* 35, no. 3 (2021): 505–523 (the direct quote is from 514–515). Szeman and Wenzel's text is the afterword to a special issue on "extractivism's role as a formal, structural principle of literary texts, located beyond (or below) the level of the 'merely' thematic" (Justin Parks, "The Poetics of Extractivism and the Politics of Visibility," *Textual Practice* 35, no. 3 [2021]: 357).

18. Szeman and Wenzel, "What Do We Talk About," 515.

19. Szeman and Wenzel, "What Do We Talk About," 516–517. For an expansive conceptualization of the sort that Szeman and Wenzel caution against, see Laura Junka-Aikio and Catalina Cortes-Severino's introduction to the special double issue they co-edited, "Cultural Studies of Extraction," *Cultural Studies* 31, no. 2–3 (2017), with an introduction by the same title on pp. 175–184. There, the co-editors suggest that "no longer necessarily defined by certain types of industries and activities, or tied to questions of land and natural resources as given objects that are disconnected from others, 'extractivism' is increasingly understood also as an analytical and also political concept that enables the examination and articulation of deeper underlying logics of exploitation and subjectification that are central to the present conjuncture of capitalist globalization and neoliberalism" (177).

20. For criticism of such developments in the UK, see Marian Mayer and Sue Eccles, "Reclaiming Our Universities: A Manifesto to Dismantle the UK HE Sector Neoliberal Agenda," *Angles* 8 (2019), http://journals.openedition.org/angles/653; Sarah Burton, "Writing Yourself In? The Price of Playing the (Feminist) Game in the Neoliberal University," in *Feeling Academic in the Neoliberal University: Feminist Flights, Fights and Failures*, ed. Yvette Taylor and Kinneret Lahad (Basingstoke: Palgrave Macmillan, 2018), 115–136.

21. Jules Marchal, *Lord Leverhulme's Ghosts: Colonial Exploitation in the Congo* (London: Verso, 2008); Brian Lewis, *So Clean: Lord Leverhulme, Soap and Civilisation* (Manchester: Manchester University Press, 2012), 154–198; Reuben Loffman and Benoît Henriet, " 'We Are Left with Barely Anything': Colonial Rule, Dependency, and the Lever Brothers in the Belgian Congo, 1911–1960," *Journal of Imperial and Commonwealth History* 48, no. 1 (2020): 71–100.

22. Alice Udale-Smith, Bethany Elsey, and Aisha Zahid, "Eight Out of 10 Councils Considering Future of Contentious Statues After Black Lives Matter Protests," *Sky News*, June 11, 2020, https://news.sky.com/story/eight-out-of-10-councils-considering-action-on-statues-after-black-lives-matter-protests-12004923. A crowdsourced map of relevant campaigns is available at https://www.toppletheracists.org.

23. See https://www.leverhulme.ac.uk/history-trust and https://www.leverhulme.ac.uk/Equality-diversity-inclusion (accessed October 31, 2024).

INDEX

Page numbers in *italics* refer to illustrations.